The Complete Beginner's Guide to

Genealogy, the Internet, and Your Genealogy Computer Program

By Karen Clifford

Published by Genealogical Publishing Company
3600 Clipper Mill Rd., Suite 260
Baltimore, MD 21211-1953

Library of Congress Catalogue Card Number 2010940792
ISBN: 978-0-8063-1875-2

Made in the United States of America

Table of Contents

Chapter 5 Printing Your Records

Chapter 6 Your Family History Notebook

Chapter 7 Developing a Sense of Our Ancestors' Environment

Chapter 8 Resolving Conflict

Chapter 9 State Vital Record Offices, Public Libraries, Courthouses and Local Repositories

Chapter 10 Resources of the Family History Library

Chapter 11 Major Databases of the Family History Library

Chapter 12 Using Local Family History Centers

Chapter 13 National Archives and Regional Records Services Facilities

Chapter 14 Census Records Between 1850 and 1930

Chapter 15 Analysis and Goal Setting

Chapter 16 Sharing Your Family History Research

Appendix A

The Internet and Genealogy

Appendix B

Genealogical Forms

Index

ACKNOWLEDGMENTS

Gratitude is extended to Maureen Girard for reading every word of the first edition and offering wonderful counsel and support in the years that followed. Thanks to Michael Clifford for the professional advice on the graphics and many supportive documents for this second edition.

Everyone at GenealogicalPublishing Company has been both patient and pleasant to work with as I did three re-writes due to changing technology.

Gratitude is expressed to hundreds of beginning on-line students who have given suggestions and ideas for this latest edition as well as book reviewers who have helped me understand the needs of others. If this wasn't a season of economic instability, I would start over from scratch, but too many people are waiting for this update. Besides, I want to see what happens in the continuing saga of New FamilySearch updates.

Which leaves me expressing appreciation to the many people who have helped me research *New FamilySearch* in the past three years and the fine workers at the Family History Library who continue to answer my questions with a smile (which I always took as encouragement). They deserve the very best in their pioneering endeavors to make the records of the world available in an easy-to-use and free-to-the-public format.

Introduction

The purpose of this book is to demystify genealogy and its supportive tools—genealogy computer programs and the Internet. It is a guide for the beginning family historian. It contains the research methodology you need to start your family history research using both traditional and Internet sources. It shows you how to organize your family papers and how to enter information into a genealogy computer program of your choice so that you can easily manage, store, and retrieve your electronic data. It also shows you how to put together a Family History Archival Notebook that supports the research, archives personal papers, and protects the evidence that supports the research hypotheses.

HOW THIS BOOK IS ARRANGED

Each chapter in this book has several components—each of which serves a complementary purpose.

- The main body of the text provides instruction supported by illustrations, charts, and examples.
- "Your Turn" activities serve as application modules asking the reader to apply the instruction to his or her own research needs.
- Assignments serve as a review and comprehension check.
- Computer checklists give the reader hands-on experience with his or her personal genealogy computer program.
- Web site addresses are listed at the end of each chapter to guide the reader to valuable Internet resources related to the topics.
- Entries in the chapter bibliographies serve as resources for further study of the topics covered.

Taking advantage of these resources before beginning each new chapter will provide the knowledge-base and experience needed to do well in subsequent chapters.

THE ROLE OF THE TEACHER

The value of this book multiplies when a good instructor provides experiences, case studies, and first-hand knowledge. If that instructor can "hold your hand" for that first visit into the deep recesses of a "strange and awesome library" haunted by family historians, or who can explain the ins and outs of various genealogy computer programs and Internet sites, you will be doubly rewarded.

SUPPLEMENTAL MATERIALS

Whether you are working with an instructor or on your own, be sure to take advantage of the supplemental materials to this textbook. Web page supplements are located at *http://www.genealogylessons.com*. These supplements are constantly updated to provide the users of this books with:

■ Current information about various genealogy computer programs including links to data that explains individual features of each program. This information allows you to compare and decide which program or programs best meet the needs of your family, different branches of your family, or other current reasons for using the program.

■ New or updated information on genealogy Internet sites including options for free trials.

■ New resources of various record repositories such as libraries, archives, and courthouses used by beginners.

This book continues with guidelines for using public libraries, courthouses, and archives to their greatest advantage. The value of Family History Centers and Regional Records Services Facilities of the National Archives, as well as other repositories, is explained, and a step-by-step guide for using the records in each facility is provided, including general background information on how to obtain vital, probate, military, and census records. This book will help you master the foundation skills of this most fascinating pursuit as you confidently probe further into your family's history. And now let us begin this great adventure.

Karen Clifford, Accredited Genealogist®
Instructor-Curriculum Developer for
    Online Genealogy, Internet, and Computer Courses
President, Genealogy Research Associates, Inc.
Co-Chair, ICAPGen Testing Committee

CHAPTER 1

Principles of Success for the Family Historian

Some have been denied families of example, but somewhere on every family tree there is a hero. There are also explanations for feelings, for traditions, for understanding ourselves. There are examples of histories we don't want to see repeated, lessons learned, and visions of what we may become.

—Karen Clifford

So much has been located, organized, inventoried, cataloged, shared on computer programs or online systems, microfilmed, photocopied, and alphabetized, that genealogy "research" is much more reliable, fulfilling, and easier to do today than ever before.

There was a time when the pursuit of family genealogy was left to the lone aunt or widower uncle who had plenty of time and nothing else to do. Times have changed!

Today this fascinating pursuit is being accomplished by rising executives, young mothers with growing children, teachers, construction workers, retired couples, high school and college students and many others. In fact anyone who enjoys putting together a puzzle, reading mystery stories or historical novels, or solving problems will find genealogy utterly absorbing.

Even with our many other family, educational, civic, and professional pursuits, there are formulas, techniques, flow charts, computer programs, and the Internet to help the would-be "family historian" be successful in limited time. Even the amateur can produce a praiseworthy family history on a limited budget in a short period of time.

". . .produce a praiseworthy family history on a limited budget in a short period of time."

FAMILY HISTORY

Genealogy is a branch of history--Family History. At its best, it also involves scientific study to determine family relationships. "Only when systematic knowledge is derived from observation, study, and experimentation to arrive at a hypotheses, does genealogy become a true science. When sloppy methods are used, it is lowered to the level of a mere pastime built upon false premises. It really is unworthy of all your fine efforts." (See Chapter 1, "Understanding Genealogical Research," in *The Researcher's Guide to American Genealogy* by Val Greenwood.)

📖	**Terms to Understand**

ge·ne·al·o·gy - A record or table of the descent of a person, family, or group from an ancestor or ancestors.

Terms to Understand

vi·tal rec·ord - An account made in an enduring form, especially in writing, that preserves the knowledge or memory of data pertinent to the birth, marriage or death of an individual.

In the past, genealogy was limited in scope to one or more ancestral lines. It concentrated on **vital records**. Its concern was primarily kinship and matters of descent. It did not engage in reasoned argument as to why certain events occurred.

Family History, on the other hand, is an extension of genealogy but with more depth. Meat is put on the bones of genealogy by including historical information in a narrative form. As someone once stated, "What is the use of digging up the skeletons in your closet, if you're not going to put flesh upon their bones." Genealogy in its expanded view, termed Family History, is what we will study. It includes an examination of individuals against the background, location and circumstances of their lives, because people and places are really inseparable.

This book will attempt to set forth the principles of success for the family historian using a variety of methods, sources, and repositories.

Bring your skeletons to life!

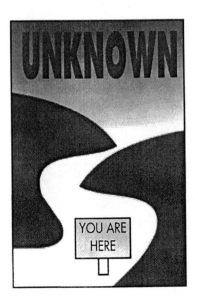

Sometimes, in the past, less effective techniques were followed, and these need to be corrected as they are discovered. For example, looking up everyone in the entire country with the last name you are seeking has been replaced with looking up your surname in the time period, locality, and among associates, starting from where your ancestor was last positively known to have been. In other words, always go from the *known to the unknown*.

Some research principles have never before been recorded. Some have yet to be discovered. Our success, however, depends upon our effectiveness as discoverers and followers of all those principles that will influence our success. Principles have great value. They outline what we must actually do to be successful. They are the ideas that we are willing to put into practice to accomplish our goals.

This book will cover the Sixteen Steps shown in Illustration 1-1. It will demonstrate how to organize, document, print, analyze, and locate the best places and types of records for answering your family history questions. This first chapter will cover the principles of genealogy research and formulas for the successful investigation of your family.

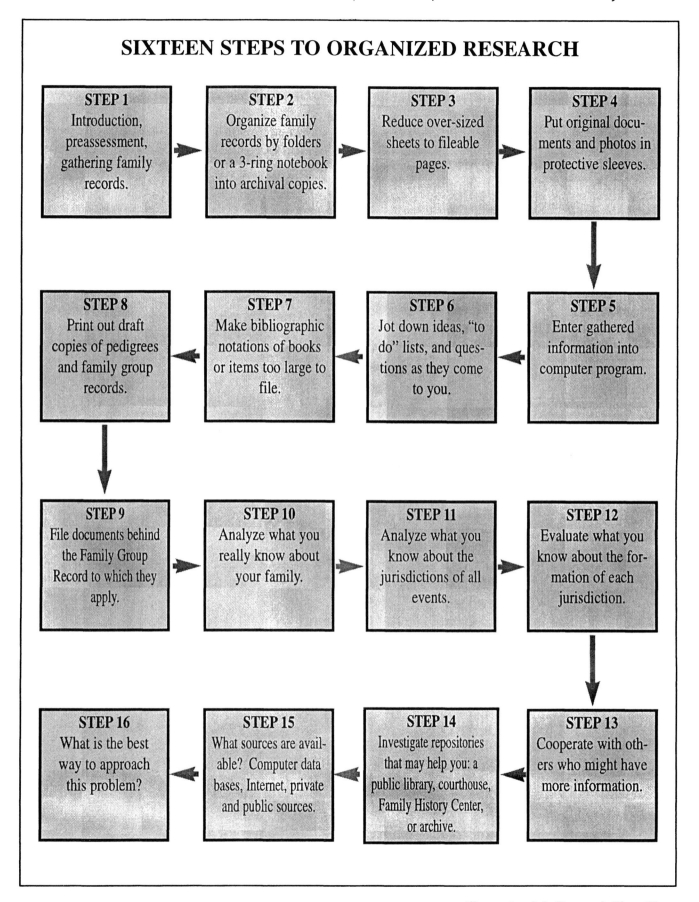

SIXTEEN STEPS TO ORGANIZED RESEARCH

STEP 1
Introduction, preassessment, gathering family records.

STEP 2
Organize family records by folders or a 3-ring notebook into archival copies.

STEP 3
Reduce over-sized sheets to fileable pages.

STEP 4
Put original documents and photos in protective sleeves.

STEP 8
Print out draft copies of pedigrees and family group records.

STEP 7
Make bibliographic notations of books or items too large to file.

STEP 6
Jot down ideas, "to do" lists, and questions as they come to you.

STEP 5
Enter gathered information into computer program.

STEP 9
File documents behind the Family Group Record to which they apply.

STEP 10
Analyze what you really know about your family.

STEP 11
Analyze what you know about the jurisdictions of all events.

STEP 12
Evaluate what you know about the formation of each jurisdiction.

STEP 16
What is the best way to approach this problem?

STEP 15
What sources are available? Computer data bases, Internet, private and public sources.

STEP 14
Investigate repositories that may help you: a public library, courthouse, Family History Center, or archive.

STEP 13
Cooperate with others who might have more information.

Illustration 1-1 Research Flow Chart

Terms to Understand

ju·ris·dic·tion - The territorial range of authority or control.

Terms to Understand

e·val·u·a·tion - To determine the value, worth, or quality of what you have found in light of the customs, events, time period, locality, and goal upon which you are working.

Terms to Understand

fact - Something that is real or actual determined by evidence; an event.

Terms to Understand

tra·di·tion - The passing down of unwritten family stories from generation to generation, especially by means of oral communication.

Terms to Understand

hy·poth·e·sis - A tentative explanation of an event that can be tested by further investigation; a theory.

THE RESEARCH CYCLE

Certain principles of success operate in the field of family history research. These principles involve customs, geography, and governmental **jurisdictions**, to name but a few. One of these principles is the process which will be used over and over in your research: we call it the *Research Cycle*. It naturally produces success again and again. Successful genealogists use this cycle because it stresses:

1. The critical step of reorganization of data in light of new findings; and

2. **Evaluation** of the new information in context with all of the information you have available.

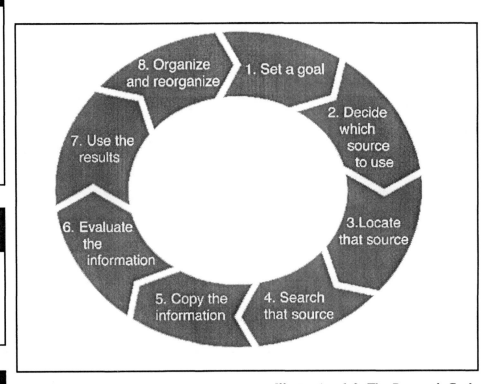

Illustration 1-2 The Research Cycle

Successful genealogists use this cycle, and you will find similar models in other books. However, the advantage of this formulation of the process is that it makes explicit the critical step of the *reorganization of data* in light of new findings and the *evaluation of the new information* in context with all the information you have available. Now that you have the general concept of the cycle, here are some specifics.

Fact vs Tradition

You cannot set a goal if you have not separated *fact* from **tradition, hypothesis** from actuality. You cannot comprehend what you *know* about an individual until you have organized your facts in a systematic manner.

What is a tradition? Simply stated, genealogists consider anything not proven by facts to be traditions. If the information is eventually proven, it is moved to the fact category.

It is in this preliminary separation of information that a computer serves the genealogist in a superior way. It records the facts and presents the facts.

WRONG WAY: If you record traditions in the same manner as facts, your computer program will not only *repeat*, but in the minds of readers, *transform*

FACT **vs** **TRADITION**

traditions into facts. This could launch your research into a totally erroneous direction. There is a proper way to record both facts and traditions, actuality and hypothesis. These methods will be explained in depth later, but basically:

* If information based on primary documentation is fact, then documentation must be listed.

* If information based on hearsay is tradition, it must be kept separated with a note to that effect, such as "TRADITION" in capital letters.

* There must also be a place for the researcher's evaluation of the documentation gathered, because *all evidence is not equal.*

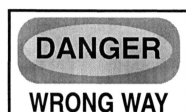

DANGER

WRONG WAY

If you record traditions in the same manner as facts, your computer program will not only *repeat*, but in the minds of readers, *transform traditions into facts*. This could launch your research into a totally erroneous direction.

YOUR TURN

Look at the example on the next page ("From Your Computer Screen"). Watch for differences between the actual records and what was said in the traditions. Then answer the question below.

What discrepancies do you see between what was found in the records and what was stated by the tradition?

1.

2.

3.

(Compare your answers with those provided at the end of the chapter.)

YOUR TURN

Facts

_____

_____

_____

_____

_____

_____

_____

Tradition

_____

_____

_____

_____

_____

_____

_____

_____

_____

_____

_____

_____

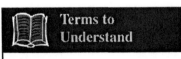

Terms to Understand

an·ces·tor - Any person from whom one is descended.

From Your Computer Screen

```
FACTS - - - - - - - - - - - - - - - - - - - - - - - - - - - - - -

1893 CHURCH:  Alexsis Nicholi Lehtonen entry, Rymattala,
Turku-Pori, Finland Christening Records, microfilm no.
0098764, item 4, Family History Library (FHL), Salt Lake
City, Utah.

[Translation] Alexsis Nicholi, the son of Johan Mattss.
Lehtonen, a tenant farmer, and Maria Henriksdr, was born 23
Mar 1893, in Rymattala.

1906 CHURCH:  Alexsis Nicholi Lehtonen entry, Rymattala,
Turku-Pori, Finland Christening Records, microfilm no.
0098764, item 6, Family History Library (FHL), Salt Lake
City, Utah.

Alexsis Nicholi Lehtonen attended communion classes, 25 Aug
1906.

1915 MARRIAGE:  Alex Lehtonen entry, Rymattala, Turku-Pori,
Finland Marriage Records, microfilm no. 0098765, item 2,
Family History Library (FHL), Salt Lake City, Utah.

Alex Lehtonen married Sophia Johansdr, May 15, 1915,
Rymattala.

TRADITION - - - - - - - - - - - - - - - - - - - - - - - - - - -

TRADITION:  From Lempi Lehtonen, daughter of Alex Lehtonen,
my mother, on Sept 5, 1985:

"Alex was the son of a wealthy carriage driver who owned
several carriages near the coast of Finland and transported
tourists.  He ran away from home because of a mean older
sister.  He was a cabin boy and came to America about age 12
and never returned.  By running away he lost his inheritance.
There is probably money in Finland waiting to be collected."
```

After more research was conducted on this family, it was discovered that part of the tradition was true. Alex had worked on a ship, not as a cabin boy, but as a regular worker. He ran away, not from his inheritance, but from the Russian draft. He did have money waiting for him due to his wages from working on the ship, not due to an inheritance.

Had the tradition not been separated from the facts, later information about Alex Lehtonen would have been disregarded in the search.

Your Turn

List some facts and traditions in the spaces provided at the left about an **ancestor** you are interested in locating.

Summary

The first step in setting a goal is to separate all facts from traditions. This will necessitate documenting all of the dates, localities, and relationships you have located.

STEP 1: SET A GOAL

Once you have separated facts from traditions, you can select a goal. Limit your goal to a single, clearly-defined objective. Include in that goal the full name, a time period, a location, and what you hope to find.

YOUR TURN

Here are three goals. Which meets the criteria for being a single, clearly-defined objective?

1. Find the birth date of Grandpa John Thornton Hansen, born about 1890/1895 in Ohio.   Yes   No

2. Track the ancestry of my Hansen line.   Yes   No

3. Write a book on my family.   Yes   No

(Compare your answers with those at the end of this chapter.)

YOUR TURN

Now, try writing a clearly-defined goal of your own.

My Goal:

Summary

Setting clearly-defined goals is very important if you wish to find clearly-defined results. Remember to record each goal separately as you set about to trace your family.

STEP 2: DECIDE WHICH SOURCE TO USE

Once a goal has been selected, you must learn what **sources** are available to reach that goal. Each goal you select requires specialized sources to prove a fact, but you will have a difficult time determining which to select if you are unaware of the many sources available to solve problems within each locality and time period. In addition, sources are being discovered constantly to aid the family historian. Although you may never learn about all of the sources available to genealogists, you should know those which are most successful and which pertain to your problem. Get the latest edition of Val Greenwood's *The Researcher's Guide to American Genealogy* for supplemental reading. Other excellent books that can aid in your source selections will be introduced in this text and in the chapter bibliographies as well.

The most basic genealogical sources include vital records such as the **civil registration** of birth, marriage, and death records; federal and state **census** records; and obituaries.

Terms to Understand

source - A book, document, or other record supplying primary or firsthand information.

Terms to Understand

ci·vil reg·is·tra·tion- Of, or pertaining to, citizens and their relations with one another or with the state.

YOUR TURN

List three sources you have used.

1. _____

2. _____

3. _____

Summary

There are innumerable sources which aid genealogists in answering their questions, but some sources are better than others for solving family puzzles during different time periods and localities. We will cover sources in several chapters starting with Chapter 7.

STEP 3: LOCATE THE SOURCE (REPOSITORIES)

Next, you must know what **repositories** contain which records, the addresses of the repositories, their availability, and how to use them. Step-by-step guides will be given in this book to aid you in the selection of the repositories that fit your needs. Examples of typical repositories containing genealogical information include:

1. Public Libraries

2. Courthouses

3. Family History Centers

Terms to Understand

cen·sus - An official, usually periodic, enumeration of a population.

Terms to Understand

re·pos·i·to·ry - A place, such as a library or an archive, where things may be put for safe-keeping.

4. State and Federal Archives

5. State Libraries.

RECORD REPOSITORY

YOUR TURN

List three repositories you have used.

1.

2.

3.

Summary

Records are stored in different facilities throughout the world. In order to do research effectively, it is necessary to locate the correct repository for the type of record desired. We will cover repositories in depth in Chapters 9 through 13.

Illustration 1-3 Researchers at a Record Repository

STEP 4: SEARCH THE SOURCE

4. Search that source

There are numerous ways to search a source, and there are shortcuts you can learn to use. For example, even in an unindexed source, it is not necessary to read from cover to cover. There are methods to shorten the process, thus helping you to use your time more wisely. The "Your Turn" assignment which follows provides typical situations you'll encounter in your research.

There are numerous ways to search a source.

Make accurate copies of
your sources!

 Terms to Understand

tran·scribe - To write or type a copy of a given text.

 Terms to Understand

ab·stract - To summarize the important points of a given text.

 Terms to Understand

ex·tract - To remove (a written passage, for example) for separate consideration or publication.

YOUR TURN

Can you do the following?

1. Explain how to search a 1910 census which has not been indexed? Yes   No

2. Explain how to search for a particular individual in an unindexed county history written about 1898? Yes   No

3. Locate an individual in an unindexed British census for 1881? Yes No   (Compare your answers with those at the end of this chapter.)

STEP 5: COPY THE INFORMATION

5. Copy the information

It's common for beginning researchers to neglect to make an accurate copy of a source the first time they find it.

YOUR TURN

Ask yourself if you have ever done the following:

1. Have you forgotten to photocopy the author/title page when you've photocopied other information from a book? Yes   No

2. Have you neglected to copy the complete source rather than just the date and name of the parties on an 1900 census, or copied only the Soundex (index) card, not the actual record? Yes   No

3. Have you ignored the names of the witnesses to an event for clues of possible kinship?   Yes   No

Summary

Even though copying information appears to be an easy thing to do, it is very wise for the beginning genealogist to make a photocopy of the entire document until they learn what is important to **transcribe, abstract** or **extract** from it.

STEP 6: EVALUATE THE INFORMATION

The next step is often the most neglected in the process: *evaluating the information.* When we locate a record, our excitement over the obvious might prevent a meticulous evaluation of the less obvious clues. Questions we should always ask ourselves are:

- What else is this record telling me?

- Can more information be obtained if I search this same source using **collateral** lines?

- Am I reading the old handwriting correctly?

- Should I ask someone for help?

- Have I looked at the front of the book for clues the author discovered when he or she compiled the source?

Terms to Understand

col·lat·er·al - Having an ancestor in common, but descended from a different line.

YOUR TURN

In the example below, you have located the birth of an ancestor in the International Genealogical Index (IGI).

In addition to the birth date on this *IGI* sample, list three more pieces of information this record gives.

1.

2.

3.

```
International Genealogical Index (R) - Main File - Version 4.01                British Isles
                                  INDIVIDUAL RECORD

16 FEB 1999                                                                    Page 1
============================================================================
NAME: YEARLEY, James Chalmers
----------------------------------------------------------------------------
SEX:  M

EVENT: Christening
       3 Feb 1836
       Perth, Perth, Scotland
FATHER: John YEARLEY
MOTHER: Jane DEIGHTON

============================================================================
SOURCE INFORMATION
============================================================================

Extracted birth and/or christening record for:
    Perth, Perth County, Scotland
Usually arranged chronologically by the birth/christening date.

Batch          | Dates         Source Call No.  Type | Printout Call No. Type
---------------|-------------------------------------|------------------------
C119485        | 1834-1840  1040162          Film    | NONE

============================================================================
Copyright © 1980, 1998 by Intellectual Reserve, Inc.  All rights reserved.
```

Illustration 1-4 Individual Record Printout from the IGI

Perhaps you remarked, "What is the *International Genealogical Index?*" You will learn all about it in Chapter 11.

Summary

Take as much time as is necessary to ask yourself many questions about each source that you locate. As you answer your own questions, you will be guided to more clues for solving your ultimate problem.

STEP 7: USE THE RESULTS

Once you have searched a source and found your ancestor, you usually discover more clues. For example, finding John Wilkinson in the Arkansas 1880 federal census as an 80-year-old, born in Georgia, with his parents born in North Carolina and a younger brother living with him, age 59, born in South Carolina provides these new clues:

- Birth year of John Wilkinson is 1800.
- Birthplace of John Wilkinson is Georgia.
- Birthplace of John Wilkinson's father is North Carolina.
- Birthplace of John Wilkinson's mother is North Carolina.
- Birthplace of John Wilkinson's brother is South Carolina.
- The family will probably be found in the 1820 federal census of South Carolina, since the brother was born there. This could lead to new county records to search.
- The published surname collections for Arkansas, South Carolina, and North Carolina should be searched for the surname "Wilkinson."

YOUR TURN

Your great-aunt Milly wrote a letter (above left) to your mother long ago, describing information she found in a marriage record of her parents. You are excited because you know nothing more about Aunt Milly's parents other than their names. List the new information you discovered from reading Aunt Milly's letter:

1.
2.
3.
4.
5.
6.
7.
8.
9.
10.
11.
12.

Summary

Using the results of one search will guide you to more searches. Once you have determined just what new information you have, you can set about considering new sources for extending your family lines further.

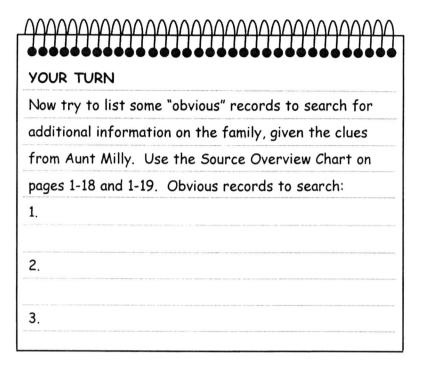

YOUR TURN

Now try to list some "obvious" records to search for additional information on the family, given the clues from Aunt Milly. Use the Source Overview Chart on pages 1-18 and 1-19. Obvious records to search:

1.

2.

3.

Terms to Understand

con·text - The circumstances in which a particular event occurs.

Terms to Understand

chro·nol·o·gy - The arrangement of items in the order of occurrence.

Terms to Understand

doc·u·men·ta·tion - The supplying of documents or supporting references or records.

STEP 8: ORGANIZE AND REORGANIZE

Finally, to benefit from this new information, you must place it in **context** with all the other facts. This is most simply accomplished by using a computer, because you can insert new information at the appropriate point in the **chronology** without retyping **documentation** and research notes. Then you can "reorganize the information" based on new information.

For example, **data fields** can also be quickly updated to allow for such things as corrected dates, places and family connections from your family letters or cen-

Terms to Understand

da·ta fields - a computer term for places to "type in" birth, marriage, and death dates and places.

". . .and here is a picture of Dad asking Grandpa for Mom's hand in marriage; then he belted the old dinosaur and gave Mom the ring. . ."

". . .use a computer. . . [to] insert new information at the appropriate point. . ."

Organizing family information

sus findings. A good genealogy computer program also aids in your analysis because it can search all notes for elusive clues such as, "Was the man listed as a witness also listed as a neighbor in a previous state, or later as a spouse of a direct, or collateral line person?"

Your "great ancestral hunt" should begin in your own home.

YOUR TURN

Use the new clues in the 1880 census example on page 1-12 to indicate what information you would put into your computer database about the John Wilkinson family.

1.

2.

3.

4.

5.

6.

7.

8.

9.

Summary

Setting a new goal will require another cycle of knowing what sources are available to obtain a goal, which sources to use due to availability and usability, and how to go about obtaining the sources.

PREASSESSMENT

The "Your Turn" self tests you have completed thus far in this chapter will help to preassess your previous genealogical experience. Circle one point for each correct answer given to the questions in the "Your Turn" self test (next page). On the six "Your Turn" assignments given previously, how did you rate?

You could also be at one level of expertise in genealogy and another in computer usage. Use the chart (Illustration 1-5) as well as the level statements (on the next page) to place yourself in one level as far as genealogy research is concerned, and another level as far as computer usage is concerned. Now you have an idea of where you stand in relation to others doing genealogy research.

To those of you who are Level Five in both categories, thanks for reading this book but you really should move on to the next level. If you are enjoying this book for little tidbits you might find herein, may you find what you are seeking.

GATHER FAMILY RECORDS

If you are working on your family history for the first time, you might find yourself with materials all over the house. There could be pictures in a drawer, certificates in a file, family albums on a bookshelf, counted-cross stitched pictures in the attic, a Civil War sword in a trunk in the basement, and obituaries in a

YOUR TURN Self Test   *(Circle one point for each correct answer.)*

Fact versus Tradition, p. 1-5 . . . . 1 2 3	
Goal Setting, p. 1-7. . . . . 1 2 3	
Sources to Use, p. 1-8 . . . . 1 2 3	
Repositories Used, p. 1-9 . . . . 1 2 3	
Search the Source (subtract 1 point), p. 1-10 . . . . . 1 2 3	
Copy the Information, p. 1-10 . . . . 1 2 3	
Evaluate the Information, p. 1-11. . . . . 1 2 3	
Organize and Reorganize, p.1-12 (1/3 pt for each) . 1 2 3	
Use the Results, p. 1-13, 1-14 (1 pt for each) 1 2 3	

GENEALOGICAL		Correct
LEVEL		Answers
LEVEL ONE	L-1	0-1
LEVEL TWO	L-2	2-6
LEVEL THREE	L-3	7-16
LEVEL FOUR	L-4	17-20
LEVEL FIVE	L-5	21-24

desk drawer somewhere. Use the charts entitled Source Overview (Illustrations 1-8a and 1-8b) to help you find other sources in your home.

Then, place a large box at the entrance of your most frequently used family bathroom. Don't use that room unless you have something pertaining to your family history to deposit in the box. Somehow, either the urgency of using that room requires the collection to mount quickly, or your innate neatness persuades you to spend a whole day gathering everything together.

If, on the other hand, you have been dabbling in family history for years and you have determined to go about it more systematically than in the past, you might have oodles of wonderful odds and ends. I have a friend whose husband's job takes him away for several months at a time. She had always used his side of the bed to store her family history "hobby" while he was away. One time he returned early and she nearly broke her back finding a place for everything. Things fell over, and got out of order, so she joined my classes in order to get organized and stay that way before her husband decided never to return.

Whether you have one box or thirty, they must be organized, analyzed, and filed in order to discover what you already know. If you believe others in your family have submitted information to the LDS Church's *Ancestral File*™ or put information onto the Internet, you could save yourself hours of data entry by locating that information and copying it to your own family records at this point. You could then locate the sources of that information by contacting the submitters and supplementing their sources with your own personal research. If corrections need to be made, you should set goals to do so (this will be covered in Chapter 11).

Preserve original documents by placing them in separate vertical files or into clear, acrylic, archival-quality protectors. Make copies of originals for data input if they are not filed with other records. Notes on small pieces of paper are easily lost, so copy them to full-size sheets. Oversized documents are usually reduced to a standard size to make filing and retrieval more efficient. Oversized copies may be torn, so use the special way to fold legal documents shown in Illustration 1-6.

If the documentation you need to preserve is an entire bound book, make a **bibliographic notation** and place it on a full-size (8 1/2 x 11 inch) sheet in the surname file portion of your notebook (this will be covered in Chapter 6).

 Terms to Understand

An·ces·tral File - A lineage-linked, surname-indexed data base of Pedigrees and Family Group Records submitted to the LDS Church since 1980 by researchers all over the world.

 Terms to Understand

bib·li·o·graph·ic no·ta·tion - Refers to the written description and identification of the editions, dates of issue, authorship, and typography of books or other written material.

GENEALOGY LEVEL	COMPUTER LEVEL
Level One I've never done genealogy.	**Level One** I've never used a computer.
Level Two I've put together Pedigree Charts and Family Group Records using information provided by others.	**Level Two** I've used a computer, but never a computer genealogy program.
Level Three I have used census records, can calculate a Soundex code, have used the IGI, FHLC, the FamilySearch™ Ancestral File™, Military Index, and Social Security files, as well as the items above. (All must be marked for credit.)	**Level Three** I've used a computer program to enter families from family records, and to organize the information, but I have not used the computer program as a research tool.
Level Four I've visited and used a Family History Center or major genealogy library for at least 250 hours, compiled Family Group Records and Pedigree Charts from original research, filled out at least 25 Research Planners or Logs recording both positive and negative searches and successfully taken a family back one generation through personal research, as well as the items above.	**Level Four** I have used the PAF program to enter original research materials; cited all documentation, including searches which were negative on the lines yet to be completed; made GEDCOM transfers from my Family Records Data to send to others; successfully produced a variety of alphabetical and numerical indexes to aid in the organization of family data; and put together a notebook of materials on my family's history.
Level Five I've visited at least 10 different repositories; used a Family History Center, FHL or other major genealogy library for at least 1000 hours; searched original probate, land and property, military service, pension, and bounty land records; attended at least two workshops or classes taught by professional researchers; and produced a family history, as well as all items above.	**Level Five** I've done all the above and made GEDCOM transfers from the FamilySearch program into the Family Records program, and I have developed research strategies using advanced research tools in the computer program I am using (i.e., in PAF, the Focus and Design Features, as well as Match/Merge features). I have helped others on their research and put together a book on someone else's line.

Illustration 1-5 Genealogy Level/Computer Level Chart

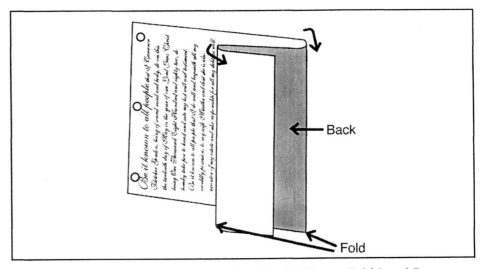

Illustration 1-6 A Special Way to Fold Legal Documents

CONCLUSION: A PROVEN FORMULA

There is a proven formula for success in family history studies: Combine a willingness to try new things (such as basic sources, techniques, and new repositories) with an ability to organize information. Then take that new information and use it wisely with the guidance of knowledgeable and experienced researchers as shown in Illustration 1-7.

Let us now apply this formula. First, it's obvious that you have a willingness to learn new things: we call this "a curious mind" (because you've read this far and haven't run away screaming)—this is a vital ingredient!

Second, you have a copy of this book, in which the bibliographies and assignments will guide you to good source books. You'll need to discover your own nearby public library, research repository, or Family History Center. There are good genealogy computer programs available via the Internet or your local book store. Now you have all of the ingredients to begin your own great adventure.

Start with the assignments on the next page so you can be prepared to learn the "tools of the trade" for organizing and demonstrating your facts—the Pedigree Chart and the Family Group Record, which will be explained in Chapter 2.

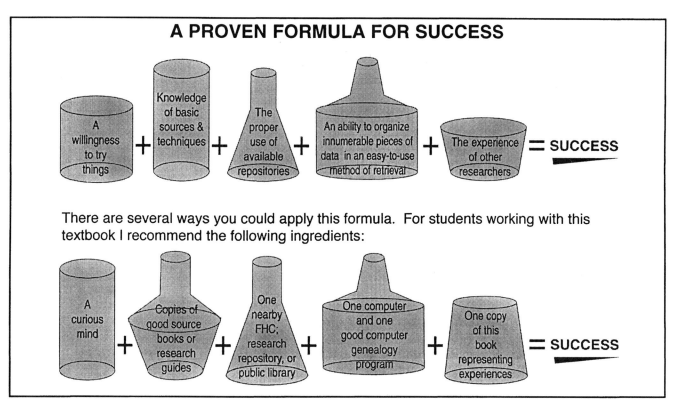

Illustration 1-7 "A Proven Success Formula"

GENEALOGY RESEARCH ASSOCIATES, INC.
Genealogical Source Overview & Checklist

This checklist has been designed to prompt genealogists for information from a wide variety of sources. Check the sources you have acquired or have investigated. Every clue you can uncover will speed up your research and save you time and money.

Family or individual _____   Identification numbers _____

HOME AND FAMILY SOURCES

Personal Records
- ❏ Scrapbooks
- ❏ Heirlooms
- ❏ Journals/Diaries
- ❏ Oral Histories
- ❏ Personal Histories
- ❏ Family Histories
- ❏ Diaries
- ❏ Personal Correspondence
- ❏ Photographs
- ❏ Funeral Cards
- ❏ Obituaries
- ❏ Medical Records
- ❏ Military Records
- ❏ Employment Records
- ❏ Social Security
- ❏ Social Security Application Forms
- ❏ Social Security Recipient Forms
- ❏ Social Security Cards
- ❏ Labels or Tags on Trunks or Baggage
- ❏ Films, Slides and Videos
- ❏ Tombstone Photos
- ❏ Autograph Books

Certificates
- ❏ Birth
- ❏ Military Discharge
- ❏ School Achievement
- ❏ Marriage
- ❏ Death
- ❏ Adoption
- ❏ Graduation
- ❏ Divorce
- ❏ Citizenship
- ❏ Manumission (Liberation/ Emancipation)

School Records
- ❏ Elementary
- ❏ Secondary
- ❏ Vocational, Trade
- ❏ College
- ❏ University
- ❏ Arts
- ❏ Private
- ❏ Ladies Finishing
- ❏ Correspondence Schools
- ❏ Yearbooks

Insurance
- ❏ Life
- ❏ Fire
- ❏ Accident
- ❏ Health
- ❏ Other

Business/Legal Records
- ❏ Accounting Books
- ❏ Bills
- ❏ Receipts
- ❏ Correspondence
- ❏ Credit Applications
- ❏ Citizenship Papers
- ❏ Passports and Visas
- ❏ Mortgage Records
- ❏ Deeds
- ❏ Property Titles
- ❏ Rental Agreements
- ❏ Bank Applications/Forms
- ❏ Bank Statements
- ❏ Wills
- ❏ Probate Papers
- ❏ Intestate Court Papers
- ❏ Legal Briefs
- ❏ Adoption Papers
- ❏ Court Orders

Religious Records
- ❏ Family Bibles
- ❏ Marriage
- ❏ Baptism
- ❏ Confirmation
- ❏ Christening
- ❏ Religious Office
- ❏ Religious Achievement

- ❏ Missionary Activity
- ❏ Ministerial Papers

Non-Document Record Sources
- ❏ Military Uniforms (insignias of organization, rank, service, awards, etc.)
- ❏ Dish and Glassware (manufacturers location and production insignia/dates)
- ❏ Furniture (manufacturers location and production insignia/dates)
- ❏ Photographs/Portraits (photographer's/artist's location, names and dates)
- ❏ Clothing (hand tailored items showing tailor and location)
- ❏ Quilts and stitchery with names
- ❏ Jewelry (watches, trophies, and hand made items with inscriptions and manufacturers)
- ❏ Luggage (inclusing tags and labels)
- ❏ Objects- such as flags, swords, guns, etc.

SOURCES OF RESEARCH DONE BY OTHERS

Personal Research
- ❏ Pedigree Charts
- ❏ Family Group Records
- ❏ Descendancy Charts
- ❏ Book of Remembrance
- ❏ Research Notes

Family History Library
- ❏ Temple Index Bureau
- ❏ Family Registry

- ❏ Family History Library Catalog (Surname Section for Family Histories Collection)
- ❏ International Genealogical Index (IGI)
- ❏ Family Group Record Archive
- ❏ Ancestral File

Printed Sources
- ❏ Family Histories
- ❏ Biographies
- ❏ Genealogies
- ❏ Pedigrees
- ❏ County/Local Histories
- ❏ State and Territorial Histories
- ❏ City Directories
- ❏ Indexes

Periodicals
- ❏ Genealogies
- ❏ Historical Items
- ❏ Queries
- ❏ Source Extracts
- ❏ Directories
- ❏ Genealogical and Historical Society Publications

CHURCH SOURCES (for Original Research)

Events
(Below, a type of event is listed rather than a specific record. Some events may have more than one type of record.)
- ❏ Birth
- ❏ Christening
- ❏ Circumcision
- ❏ Baptism
- ❏ Confirmation

- ❏ Communion
- ❏ Coming of Age (i.e. Bar Mitzvah)
- ❏ Ordination
- ❏ Primary or Sunday School
- ❏ Seminary
- ❏ Marriage
- ❏ Banns
- ❏ Divorce
- ❏ Annulment

- ❏ Death
- ❏ Burial
- ❏ Admissions
- ❏ Removals
- ❏ Disciplinary Proceedings
- ❏ Subscriptions
- ❏ Membership & Transfers

Records
- ❏ Ministers' Records

- ❏ Mission Reports
- ❏ Church Minutes
- ❏ Contribution Records
- ❏ Bishops' Transcripts (of records of original events)
- ❏ Church/Congregational Histories
- ❏ Historical Event and Anniversary Celebration Records

1999 **Genealogy Research Associates, Inc.** 189 East South Temple, Suite 300, Salt Lake City, UT 84111 *(www.graonline.com)*   7/99

Illustration 1-8a   Genealogical Source Overview & Checklist (page 1)

PRIVATE SOURCES (for Original Research)

Newspapers
- ❏ Indexes
- ❏ Births
- ❏ Marriages
- ❏ Deaths
- ❏ Anniversaries
- ❏ Obituaries
- ❏ Advertisements
- ❏ Local News
- ❏ Unclaimed Mail

Legal Notices
- ❏ Probate
- ❏ Auctions
- ❏ Forced Sales
- ❏ Divorces
- ❏ Elopement
- ❏ Bankruptcies

- ❏ Court Claims
- ❏ Convictions
- ❏ Lawyer Briefs
- ❏ Slavery Records

Employment
- ❏ Indentures
- ❏ Apprenticeships
- ❏ Licenses
- ❏ Pensions
- ❏ Service Awards
- ❏ Personal Files
- ❏ Account Books
- ❏ Retirement Records

Institutional
- ❏ Charities
- ❏ Hospitals
- ❏ Convents

- ❏ Seminaries
- ❏ Libraries
- ❏ Historical Societies
- ❏ Mission Societies
- ❏ Orphan Agencies
- ❏ Reunion Registers
- ❏ Schools
- ❏ Colleges and Universities

Mortuary Records
- ❏ Burial Records
- ❏ Funeral Cards
- ❏ Funeral Books

Collections of Historical Data
- ❏ DAR
- ❏ Oral Histories
- ❏ Personal papers
- ❏ Indexes

- ❏ Correspondence
- ❏ Surname Files
- ❏ Inscriptions
- ❏ Biographies
- ❏ Corporate Histories
- ❏ Histories of Charitable
  Institutions and
  Organizations

Organizations
- ❏ Clubs
- ❏ Societies
- ❏ Boy Scouts
- ❏ Girls Scouts
- ❏ Upper Class Society
  Organizations

PUBLIC SOURCES (for Original Research)

U.S. Federal/State Censuses
- ❏ Federal Census Index 1790
- ❏ Federal Census Index 1800
- ❏ Federal Census Index 1810
- ❏ Federal Census Index 1820
- ❏ Federal Census Index 1830
- ❏ Federal Census Index 1840
- ❏ Federal Census Index 1850
- ❏ Federal Census Index 1860
- ❏ Federal Census Index 1870
- ❏ Federal Census Soundex 1880
- ❏ Federal Census Soundex 1890
- ❏ Federal Census Soundex 1900
- ❏ Federal Census Soundex 1910
- ❏ Federal Census Soundex 1920
- ❏ Federal Census 1790
- ❏ Federal Census 1800
- ❏ Federal Census 1810
- ❏ Federal Census 1820
- ❏ Federal Census 1830
- ❏ Federal Census 1840
- ❏ Federal Census 1850
- ❏ Federal Census 1860
- ❏ Federal Census 1870
- ❏ Federal Census 1880
- ❏ Federal Census 1890
- ❏ Federal Census 1900
- ❏ Federal Census 1910
- ❏ Federal Census 1920
- ❏ Mortality Schedules
- ❏ Revolutionary War Veterans
- ❏ Union Army Veterans
- ❏ Agricultural
- ❏ State Censuses (years vary
  by state)

Land Records
- ❏ Grantor Index
- ❏ Grantee Index
- ❏ Bounty Warrants
- ❏ Deeds
- ❏ Tract Books

- ❏ Plat Maps
- ❏ Mortgages
- ❏ Grants, patents
- ❏ Homestead papers
- ❏ Surveys
- ❏ Indian Treaties

Court and Legal Records
- ❏ Dockets
- ❏ Minutes
- ❏ Judgements
- ❏ Orders, Decrees
- ❏ Case Files
- ❏ Indexes
- ❏ Sheriff/Police
- ❏ Justice of the Peace
- ❏ Lawyer Briefs
- ❏ Jail Records
- ❏ Poor House Records
- ❏ Jury Records
- ❏ Guardian and Ward
- ❏ Orphan Court Records
- ❏ Bankruptcy Records
- ❏ Certificates
- ❏ Licenses
- ❏ Chancery Court Records
- ❏ Civil/Criminal Court
  Records
- ❏ Correctional Records

Probate Records
- ❏ Indexes
- ❏ Wills
- ❏ Administrations
- ❏ Estate Records
- ❏ Inventories
- ❏ Bonds
- ❏ Settlements
- ❏ Packets
- ❏ Petitions

Tax Records
- ❏ Personal/Property
- ❏ Real Estate

- ❏ School
- ❏ Poor Rate
- ❏ Tax Exemptions
- ❏ Poll Tax (Voting)
- ❏ Householder's Index

Other Governmental Records
- ❏ Birth Records
- ❏ Marriage Records
- ❏ Death Certification
- ❏ Centennial Celebrations
- ❏ Native American Records
- ❏ Social Security Records

Military Records
- ❏ Service Record Index
- ❏ Pension Index
- ❏ Service Records
- ❏ Unit Correspondence
- ❏ Pension Files
- ❏ Bounty Awards
- ❏ Discharges
- ❏ Muster Rolls
- ❏ Regimental Histories
- ❏ Military Campaign and War
  History
- ❏ Desertion Records
- ❏ Burials
- ❏ Dependents of Personnel
  Born Abroad
- ❏ Admiralty Court Records

Immigrant Records
- ❏ Emigration (leaving)
  Records
- ❏ Passenger Lists
- ❏ Passports
- ❏ Vaccination Certificates
- ❏ Alien Registration
- ❏ Change of Name
- ❏ Oaths of Allegiance
- ❏ Register of Voters
- ❏ Citizenship Papers
- ❏ Naturalization Records

- ❏ Immigrant Aid Societies
- ❏ Custom Records
- ❏ Ship's Logbooks
- ❏ Border Crossings

Cemetery Records
- ❏ Sexton Records
- ❏ Cemetery Indexes
- ❏ Monuments
- ❏ Plat Books
- ❏ Tombstones
- ❏ Memorials
- ❏ Gifts
- ❏ Deeds
- ❏ Perpetual Care Funds

Newspapers
- ❏ Obituaries
- ❏ Biographical Articles
- ❏ News Articles

Histories
- ❏ State
- ❏ County
- ❏ Local
- ❏ Business
- ❏ Biographies
- ❏ Church
- ❏ Occupational/Guild
- ❏ Organizational
- ❏ Society
- ❏ Almanacs

Periodicals
- ❏ Genealogical Societies
- ❏ Historical Societies
- ❏ Military Organizations
- ❏ Military History Societies
- ❏ State/Locality News
- ❏ Family Organizations
- ❏ Surname Societies
- ❏ Local Heritage
- ❏ Heraldic Societies

Illustration 1-8b   Genealogical Source Overview & Checklist (page 2)

ASSIGNMENT 1: SORTING YOUR FAMILY MATERIALS

1. Sort your family records by surname and then by individual families; then opt for #2 or #3 below.
    A. Use shallow, empty boxes.
    B. Place a label on the side of each box for every surname.
    C. Place materials relating to a family in its box.

2. The *File Method*: Sort those surname boxes by individual families.
    A. Place individual families in file folders, keeping all documents flat.
    B. Unfold old letters; creases will later tear.
    C. Keep copies of originals in protective sleeves.
    This method sometimes results in the loss of records when things are removed or put out of order, but it does allow for great expansion.

3. The *Binder Method*: Place documents in a binder with index tabs dividing various surnames.
    A. Place individual families behind individual tabs, keeping all documents flat.
    B. Unfold old letters; creases will later tear.
    C. Keep copies of originals in protective sleeves.
    D. Reduce over-sized pages by photocopying to a smaller standard size, and store originals in large flat boxes or drawers, or place them in frames for display.

    This method keeps records in order and prepares the records for later placement in the family notebook by hole punching or placing in protective sleeves.

    Preserve original documents by placing them in separate vertical files or into clear, acrylic, archival-quality protectors. Make copies of originals for data input, if they are not filed with other records. Oversized documents are usually reduced to a standard size to make filing and retrieval more efficient.

    Notes on small pieces of paper are easily lost, so copy them to full-size sheets. Oversized copies may be torn, so use the special way to fold legal sized documents that is shown in Illustration 1-6.

YOUR TURN ANSWERS

Fact versus Tradition

1. Did you notice that the Alex listed under "Facts" was the son of a tenant farmer? He would not be of the same social status as a wealthy carriage owner.

2. Did you notice he was still living in Finland at the age of 16 and also at age 22 at the time of his marriage?

3. Did you observe that he either returned to Finland, left later than the tradition stated, or was a different person?

Decide Which Source to Use

Did you include any of those sources listed on the Source Checklist (Illustrations 1-8a and 1-8b)? As you can tell, sources are available in many varieties and locations.

Locate the Source (Repository)

Did you record any of the repositories listed on pages 1-8 and 1-9? Perhaps you have learned about others you would like to visit.

Search the Source

Although you'll discover more complete answers as you read this book, here are some common strategies you could have indicated for #1. The address could be found from a city directory, vital record, or other census, and the Enumeration District (E.D.) could be found from the address of the individual sought. Then, with the E.D. number, you could look through the actual census. Considering the number of rolls on a major city census, this is a much easier alternative.

For #2, you could locate the individual on a 1900 census, which is very well indexed. On that census, the township and county are listed. Going then to the table of contents in the county history, you could look for the township. With that information, you could locate the individual within the few pages devoted to that township without having to read the entire source.

For #3, you could use the quarterly vital records indexes for Great Britain and find at least one individual in the family born around the time period you are searching. With the address on the vital record, you can search an index by street addresses which will guide you to the proper census roll.

Evaluate the Information

Did you list some of these items:

1. The source of the entry.
2. Whether there is additional information in the original source.
3. Whether there are other family members in the same parish.

Use the Results

1. Moses Masterson and Mary Morrison were married 23 Mar 1860.
2. Moses and Mary Masterson were married in Clermont County, Ohio.
3. Mary Morrison was probably married before, because her surname was different than that of her father or her mother.
4. Mary was born in New York
5. Mary was born in 1839.
6. Mary's maiden name was Smithwick.
7. Mary's father was Joseph Smithwick.
8. Mary's mother was Susan Chambers.
9. Moses Masterson was born in 1835.
10. Moses Masterson was born in Ohio.
11. Moses Masterson's father was J. M. Masterson of Massachusetts.
12. Moses Masterson's mother was Martha Weems of Massachusetts.
13. Moses Masterson's occupation was a canal worker.

Organize and Reorganize

1. Add John Wilkinson's birth year of 1800.
2. Add John Wilkinson's birth state as Georgia.
3. Add John Wilkinson's father's birth state as North Carolina.
4. Add John Wilkinson's father's birth year as about 1765/1775.
5. Add John Wilkinson's mother's birth state as North Carolina.
6. Add John Wilkinson's mother's birth year as about 1765/1775.
7. Add John Wilkinson's brother's name.
8. Add John Wilkinson's brother's birth year as about 1821.
9. Add John Wilkinson's brother's birthplace as South Carolina.

COMPUTER CHECKLIST #1

1. Which of the following statements apply to you?

    a. I don't know how to use a typewriter or computer keyboard.

    b. I have never used a personal computer to locate record information.

    c. I don't have access to a computer and can't afford one.

    d. I don't know where to get help to learn how to use the computer.

    e. I get hives just thinking about computers.

    f. I am familiar with computers.

2. What kind of computer operating system do you have? Some genealogy programs only work in one operating system.

    a. Windows 7

    b. Windows XP

    c. Vista

    d. Mac

    f. Other

WEB SITE

http://www.GRAonline.com

The Genealogy Research Associates site contains supplemental materials which complement this book by allowing information to be included which requires frequent updating. For instance, comparisons of various genealogy computer programs can be found in these supplemental Web materials. Individual features of each program are taught and personal applications suggested which allow you to evaluate which program(s) best meet your needs. Free genealogy classes expand upon topics covered in this book and guide you to other Web sites on the Internet. Record look-up services are offered for a fee if you are unable to obtain copies of original documents (such as census records, vital records or military records), book pages (from books not currently microfilmed or microfiched), or manuscripts you seek.

BIBLIOGRAPHY

Greenwood, Val D. *The Researcher's Guide to American Genealogy.* 3rd ed. Baltimore: Genealogical Publishing Co., 2000.

Meyerink, Kory L. *Printed Sources: A Guide to Published Genealogical Records.* Salt Lake City: Ancestry Inc., 1998.

Szucs, Loretto Dennis and Sandra Hargreaves Luebking, Editors. *The Source: A Guidebook of American Genealogy.* Revised ed. Salt Lake City: Ancestry Inc., 1997.

CHAPTER 2

Organizing Family Information

> *"All things began in order, so shall they end, and so shall they begin again; according to the ordainer of order and mystical mathematics of the city of heaven."*
>
> —*Sir Thomas Browne*

BEFORE THE BEGINNING... there is usually chaos

When you began to look for your family data, you may have discovered that you had genealogical clues all over your home. Or perhaps the information was at someone else's home or in someone else's head. And now that you have gathered up the scattered facts, photos, letters, scribbled notes and documents, you may feel somewhat overwhelmed. In fact, you might even have laughed when you saw the heading for this chapter, "Organizing Family Information."

But don't despair! The purpose of this chapter is to help in that organizing process by showing you the charts and forms which are the foundation for building your family's tree, and which will make continued success easier both for you and for those who want to help you. Once information has been placed onto correct charts and forms, others can assimilate the data, assess the problems and offer suggestions more quickly. These charts and forms are the standard "tools of the trade."

THE PEDIGREE CHART

The **Pedigree** Chart gives the basic, **direct-line** "skeleton" of one's family tree. It gives only basic, necessary information because *its job is to show the direct line only.* It is the "map" or "table of contents" to your family tree. To see a filled-out sample Pedigree Chart, turn to page 2-7.

A Pedigree Chart usually begins with the person on whom you want to focus your attention; usually, family researchers begin with themselves and then include their direct ancestors for as many **generations** as they have information. However, you may want to have a Pedigree Chart which starts with your father or mother, if you decide that you want to separate the two sides of your family. From that first person, the chart continues up the direct line, showing only the

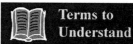

Terms to Understand

ped·i·gree - A line of ancestors.

Terms to Understand

di·rect line - The ancestral line of an individual.

Terms to Understand

gen·er·a·tion - A body of people constituting a single step in the line of descent from an ancestor.

Terms to Understand

sib·lings - One of two or more persons having one or especially both parents in common, e.g., a brother and a sister.

Terms to Understand

char·ac·ter - A symbol or mark used in a writing system, such as a letter of the alphabet.

Terms to Understand

field - A delineated area in a computer database in which a narrowly defined type of information may be entered.

Terms to Understand

da·ta en·try - The typing of information into a computer data-base.

Terms to Understand

trun·cate - To shorten by cutting off.

parents of each individual. Other family members, such as **siblings,** aunts, uncles and cousins, do not appear on a Pedigree Chart.

As you can probably guess from looking at the sample in Illustration 2-3, Pedigree Charts have room only for limited information. They are not the place for all the whys and wherefores of a family's history; those come later. Throughout this text, too, you'll notice that I refer to four-generation Pedigree Charts in the visuals. I prefer these charts over the five, six, or seven-generation charts, which are also available via computer printout, because there is more room for the complete locality to be printed. Your computer genealogy program is limited to a designated number of **characters** per **field** in the Pedigree Chart's spaces for the places of birth, death and marriage. Other charts, such as Family Group Records, allow for the entire locality entry.

The above reasoning is also why I choose to use two-letter state abbreviations over typing out the full state name as I do **data entry.** I want to be able to read

> **YOUR TURN**
>
> Imagine you were data entering the locality Cincinnati, Hamilton County, Ohio. Use only one letter per box, use one box for each comma, and leave a box blank for spaces.
>
> [grid of empty boxes]
>
> Now assume your piece of paper was not large enough and you had to put the same information in half as many boxes. That is what happens when words are truncated.
>
> [grid of empty boxes]
>
> You want to be able to read the complete town and county.

the complete town and county when space is limited, and I have learned the hard way that it is extremely time consuming to make changes. You see, the place of birth, death or marriage is limited to a designated number of characters per field. If you try to print seven generations on a chart, the locality names, of necessity, will be **truncated** by your program in order for the type font to remain the same size and still keep everything on the page. While Family Group Records allow for the entire locality entry to be printed, Pedigree Charts may only give abbreviated information. What is important is that you are consistent in your own data-

The Rule: Be consistent in your data entry.

entry work. It's easy to make changes in **databases** which are consistent if you later change your mind.

Pedigree Charts list, in order, the parents, grandparents, great-grandparents, etc., as far back as is known for the person listed as #1 on Pedigree Chart #1. Many researchers prefer genealogy computer programs where every person on the chart is given a chart number to the left of the person's name. So person #1's maternal grandfather would be #6. Person #1's father would be #2. The chart, pre-numbered, would look like Illustration 2-1.

Terms to Understand

da·ta·base - Information that is collected, usually on a computer, which fits into a narrowly defined set of parameters; once collected, this information can be sorted and analyzed to reach one or more conclusions.

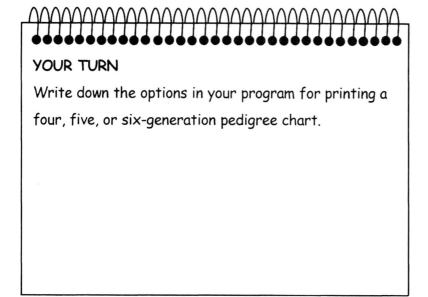

YOUR TURN

Write down the options in your program for printing a

four, five, or six-generation pedigree chart.

THE FAMILY GROUP RECORD

For each set of parents on a Pedigree Chart, there needs to be a Family Group Record. All of the information and documentation about the family is recorded on this form. It seems much less intimidating if you refer to it as the "fill in the blanks" form. A good Family Group Record will have a place to record each piece of vital information needed for each person. By filling in the blanks (or fields, in computer terminology), information is recorded in a standard format. Working from a standard form is much easier than a sheet of paper (or several sheets) covered with miscellaneous notes.

There are just three basic style rules for entering information on these two forms:

1. NAMES: Put the surname in capital letters: John TODD.

In order to prevent confusion between surnames and given names, the surname, when handwritten, should be written all in capital letters. In the *Personal*

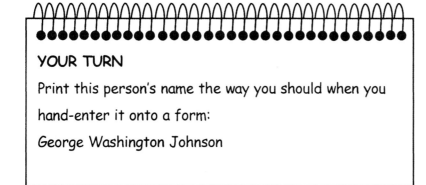

YOUR TURN

Print this person's name the way you should when you

hand-enter it onto a form:

George Washington Johnson

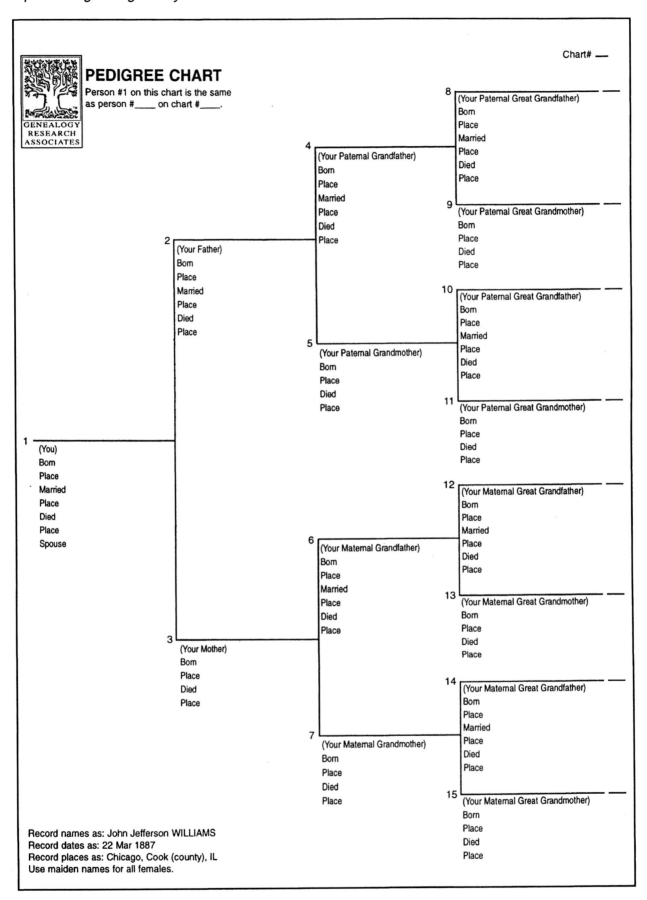

PEDIGREE CHART

Person #1 on this chart is the same
as person #____ on chart #____.

GENEALOGY
RESEARCH
ASSOCIATES

Chart# —

8 (Your Paternal Great Grandfather)
Born
Place
Married
Place
Died
Place

4 (Your Paternal Grandfather)
Born
Place
Married
Place
Died
Place

9 (Your Paternal Great Grandmother)
Born
Place
Died
Place

2 (Your Father)
Born
Place
Married
Place
Died
Place

10 (Your Paternal Great Grandfather)
Born
Place
Married
Place
Died
Place

5 (Your Paternal Grandmother)
Born
Place
Died
Place

11 (Your Paternal Great Grandmother)
Born
Place
Died
Place

1 (You)
Born
Place
Married
Place
Died
Place
Spouse

12 (Your Maternal Great Grandfather)
Born
Place
Married
Place
Died
Place

6 (Your Maternal Grandfather)
Born
Place
Married
Place
Died
Place

13 (Your Maternal Great Grandmother)
Born
Place
Died
Place

3 (Your Mother)
Born
Place
Died
Place

14 (Your Maternal Great Grandfather)
Born
Place
Married
Place
Died
Place

7 (Your Maternal Grandmother)
Born
Place
Died
Place

15 (Your Maternal Great Grandmother)
Born
Place
Died
Place

Record names as: John Jefferson WILLIAMS
Record dates as: 22 Mar 1887
Record places as: Chicago, Cook (county), IL
Use maiden names for all females.

Illustration 2-1 A Blank Pedigree Chart

Ancestral File (PAF) program, it is not necessary to remember to do this as you enter data, since the program automatically knows to convert the surname to all capital letters if you told it to do so during installation of the program, when you set your preferences. When entering other data into the computer, it is best that you not type in all caps, except for state abbreviations, such as OH, IL, MO, etc.

2. DATES: Enter the day, month and year.

In most countries, the month is written after the day, such as 6 February 1946. But in the U.S., the month is written before the day, as in February 6, 1946. In addition, we have become accustomed to dropping the first two digits of the year, as in 2-6-46, since few of the dates we customarily deal with occur in any century but the twentieth. Yet when you think about it, you can see that a date such as 2-6-46 could mean February 6, 1946, June 2, 1946, or even June 2, 1846. Therefore, the rule is to put the day, then the month (it is perfectly fine to use the three-letter abbreviation for the month: 23 Apr 1823), then the year. If you type, April 23, 1823 the computer will probably automatically convert it to 23 Apr 1823.

Illustration 2-2 Learning How to Write Names and Dates

3. PLACES: Town, county, state or country.

While your particular computer genealogy program may not be limited to a designated number of characters per field when you enter the names, printing the information is another matter. Once again, space is limited for localities. In addition, many newer computer genealogy programs do not designate a particular area for various locality **levels**. Places are entered with the smallest jurisdiction or level first (usually town, **township**, or **parish**), followed by the next largest level (county), followed by the next largest (state), and if a foreign country, by the country's name. Snowville Twp, Jackson, MO is a sample of such an entry (see the state abbreviation chart in Illustration 2-6). The word "county" or "Co." is not usually needed if the county is placed consistently in level two, but, if you think that a place name might be misunderstood, then go ahead and put in the designation "Co." for "County." Do not type USA or U.S.A. It is assumed that everything is in the U.S.A., unless otherwise stated.

There are times when all four location levels could change, thus causing a shifting of the levels and destroying the consistency of your data entry, such as when placing a cemetery name in as the burial place. If you were to enter the

Terms to Understand

lev·el - A position in the ranking of a locality that is entered into a genealogy database.

Terms to Understand

town·ship - 1. A subdivision of a county in most northeastern and midwestern states, having the status of a unit of local government with varying governmental powers. 2. A public land surveying unit of 36 sections or 36 square miles. 3. An ancient administrative division of a large parish in England.

Terms to Understand

par·ish - In Great Britain, a political division of a county for local civil government, usually corresponding to an ecclesiastical parish. In Louisana, counties are known as parishes.

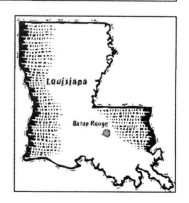

YOUR TURN

1. Write these locations as they should be written on Pedigree Charts and Family Group Records:

   A. Born in Mother of Charity Hospital, New York City, New York County, New York State

   B. Died in Monterey Community Hospital, Salinas, Monterey County, California

   C. Buried at Holy Cross Cemetery, Monterey County, California.

2. Can you find instructions in your genealogy computer program for printing Family Group Records? What are they?

3. Is a definition provided for each of the numbers indicated? What are they?

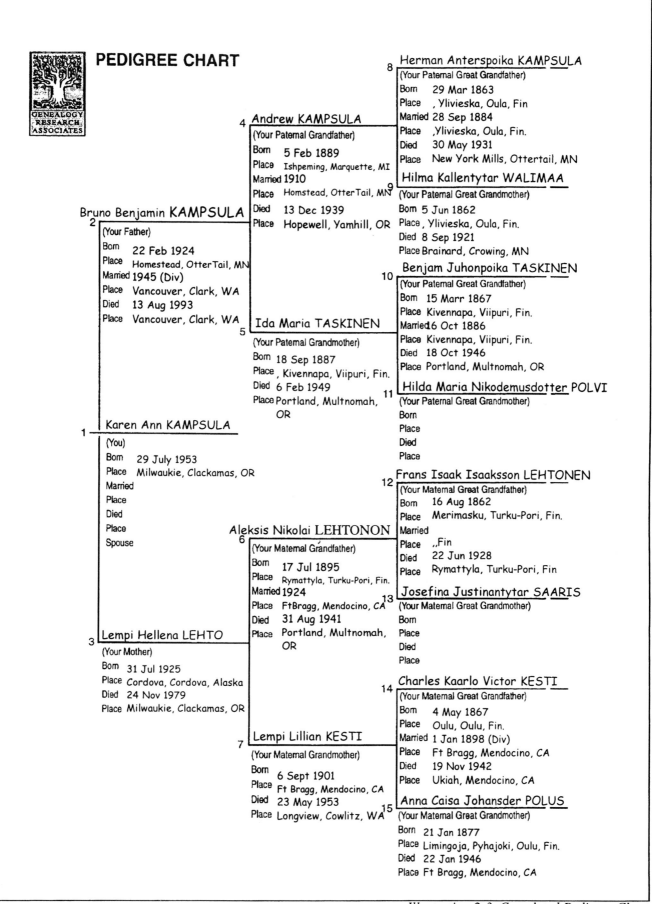

PEDIGREE CHART

8 Herman Anterspoika KAMPSULA
(Your Paternal Great Grandfather)
Born   29 Mar 1863
Place   , Ylivieska, Oula, Fin
Married 28 Sep 1884
Place   ,Ylivieska, Oula, Fin.
Died   30 May 1931
Place   New York Mills, Ottertail, MN

4 Andrew KAMPSULA
(Your Paternal Grandfather)
Born   5 Feb 1889
Place   Ishpeming, Marquette, MI
Married 1910
Place   Homstead, OtterTail, MN
Died   13 Dec 1939
Place   Hopewell, Yamhill, OR

9 Hilma Kallentytar WALIMAA
(Your Paternal Great Grandmother)
Born 5 Jun 1862
Place , Ylivieska, Oula, Fin.
Died 8 Sep 1921
Place Brainard, Crowing, MN

2 Bruno Benjamin KAMPSULA
(Your Father)
Born   22 Feb 1924
Place   Homestead, OtterTail, MN
Married 1945 (Div)
Place   Vancouver, Clark, WA
Died   13 Aug 1993
Place   Vancouver, Clark, WA

10 Benjam Juhonpoika TASKINEN
(Your Paternal Great Grandfather)
Born   15 Marr 1867
Place Kivennapa, Viipuri, Fin.
Married16 Oct 1886
Place Kivennapa, Viipuri, Fin.
Died   18 Oct 1946
Place Portland, Multnomah, OR

5 Ida Maria TASKINEN
(Your Paternal Grandmother)
Born   18 Sep 1887
Place   , Kivennapa, Viipuri, Fin.
Died   6 Feb 1949
Place   Portland, Multnomah, OR

11 Hilda Maria Nikodemusdotter POLVI
(Your Paternal Great Grandmother)
Born
Place
Died
Place

1 Karen Ann KAMPSULA
(You)
Born   29 July 1953
Place   Milwaukie, Clackamas, OR
Married
Place
Died
Place
Spouse

12 Frans Isaak Isaaksson LEHTONEN
(Your Maternal Great Grandfather)
Born   16 Aug 1862
Place   Merimasku, Turku-Pori, Fin.
Married
Place   ,,Fin
Died   22 Jun 1928
Place   Rymattyla, Turku-Pori, Fin

6 Aleksis Nikolai LEHTONON
(Your Maternal Grandfather)
Born   17 Jul 1895
Place   Rymattyla, Turku-Pori, Fin.
Married 1924
Place   FtBragg, Mendocino, CA
Died   31 Aug 1941
Place   Portland, Multnomah, OR

13 Josefina Justinantytar SAARIS
(Your Maternal Great Grandmother)
Born
Place
Died
Place

3 Lempi Hellena LEHTO
(Your Mother)
Born   31 Jul 1925
Place   Cordova, Cordova, Alaska
Died   24 Nov 1979
Place   Milwaukie, Clackamas, OR

14 Charles Kaarlo Victor KESTI
(Your Maternal Great Grandfather)
Born   4 May 1867
Place   Oulu, Oulu, Fin.
Married 1 Jan 1898 (Div)
Place   Ft Bragg, Mendocino, CA
Died   19 Nov 1942
Place   Ukiah, Mendocino, CA

7 Lempi Lillian KESTI
(Your Maternal Grandmother)
Born   6 Sept 1901
Place   Ft Bragg, Mendocino, CA
Died   23 May 1953
Place   Longview, Cowlitz, WA

15 Anna Caisa Johansder POLUS
(Your Maternal Great Grandmother)
Born 21 Jan 1877
Place Limingoja, Pyhajoki, Oulu, Fin.
Died 22 Jan 1946
Place Ft Bragg, Mendocino, CA

Illustration 2-3 Completed Pedigree Chart

HUSBAND Andrew KAMPSULA

		Place		Source
Born	5 Feb 1889	Place	Ishpeming, Marquette, MI	Source
Christened	————	Place		Source
Married	1910	Place	Homestead Twp, Otter Tail, MI	Source
Died	13 Dec 1939	Place	Hopewell, Yamhill, OR	Source
Buried		Place	Portland, Multnomah, OR	Source

Father Herman Anterapoika KAMSULA   Mother Hilma Kallentyter, Walitalo WALIMAA

WIFE   Ida Maria TASKINEN

		Place		Source
Born	18 Sep 1887	Place	, Kivennapa, Viipuri, Fin	Source
Christened	————	Place		Source
Died	6 Feb 1949	Place	Portland, Multnomah, OR	Source
Buried	9 Feb 1949	Place	Portland, Multnomah, OR	Source

Father Benjamin Juhnopoika TASKINEN   Mother Hilda Maria Nikodemusdotter POLVI

GENEALOGY RESEARCH ASSOCIATES

FAMILY GROUP RECORD

Husband is same as #___ on pedigree chart #___. Wife is same as #___ on pedigree chart #___.

CHILDREN (Write under number at left if male [m] or female [f]. List all children in birth order. Mark "X" under number of direct-line child.)

1 Name	Andrew Raymond KAMPSULA	Spouse		Source
Born	14 Jun 1913	Place	Homestead Twp, Otter Tail, MN	Source
Christened		Place		Source
Married		Place		Source
Died	5 May 1957	Place	Tieton, , WA	Source
Buried		Place		Source

2 Name	Alfred Filmore KAMPSULA	Spouse		Source
Born	13 Mar 1917	Place	New York Mills, Otter Tail, MN	Source
Christened		Place		Source
Married		Place		Source
Died	28 Nov 1985	Place	Vancover, Clark, WA	Source
Buried		Place		Source

3 Name	Lilian Victoria KAMPSULA	Spouse	Harold Jacob PERALA	Source
Born	2 Mar 1919	Place	Newton, Otter Tail, MN	Source
Christened		Place		Source
Married	Abt 1937 (div)	Place		Source
Died	28 Dec 1963	Place	, , Idaho	Source
Buried		Place		Source

4 Name		Spouse		Source
Born		Place		Source
Christened		Place		Source
Married		Place		Source
Died		Place		Source
Buried		Place		Source

Key for source abbreviations
PK=Personal knowledge   IF=Information from (name of person or document from which information came)   SE=See enclosed papers

Illustration 2-4 Completed Family Group Record

HUSBAND

Born	Place	Source
Christened	Place	Source
Married	Place	Source
Died	Place	Source
Buried	Place	Source
Father	Mother	Source

WIFE

Born	Place	Source
Christened	Place	Source
Died	Place	Source
Buried	Place	Source
Father	Mother	Source

FAMILY GROUP RECORD

Husband is same as #____ on pedigree chart #____. **Wife** is same as #____ on pedigree chart #____.

CHILDREN (Write under number at left if male [m] or female [f]. List all children in birth order. Mark "X" under number of direct-line child.)

1 | Name | Spouse | Source

Born	Place	Source
Christened	Place	Source
Married	Place	Source
Died	Place	Source
Buried	Place	Source

2 | Name | Spouse | Source

Born	Place	Source
Christened	Place	Source
Married	Place	Source
Died	Place	Source
Buried	Place	Source

3 | Name | Spouse | Source

Born	Place	Source
Christened	Place	Source
Married	Place	Source
Died	Place	Source
Buried	Place	Source

4 | Name | Spouse | Source

Born	Place	Source
Christened	Place	Source
Married	Place	Source
Died	Place	Source
Buried	Place	Source

Key for source abbreviations
PK=Personal knowledge   IF=Information from (name of person or document from which information came)   SE=See enclosed papers

Illustration 2-5 Blank Family Group Record Using PAF 4.0

STATE AND PROVINCE ABBREVIATIONS

United States

Alabama	AL	Montana	MT
Alaska	AK	Nebraska	NE
Arizona	AZ	Nevada	NV
Arkansas	AR	New Hampshire	NH
California	CA	New Jersey	NJ
Canal Zone	CZ	New Mexico	NM
Colorado	CO	New York	NY
Connecticut	CT	North Carolina	NC
Delaware	DE	North Dakota	ND
District of Columbia	DC	Ohio	OH
Florida	FL	Oklahoma	OK
Georgia	GA	Oregon	OR
Guam	GU	Pennsylvania	PA
Hawaii	HI	Puerto Rico	PR
Idaho	ID	Rhode Island	RI
Illinois	IL	South Carolina	SC
Indiana	IN	South Dakota	SD
Iowa	IA	Tennessee	TN
Kansas	KS	Texas	TX
Kentucky	KY	Utah	UT
Louisiana	LA	Vermont	VT
Maine	ME	Virginia	VA
Maryland	MD	Virgin Islands	VI
Massachusetts	MA	Washington	WA
Michigan	MI	West Virginia	WV
Minnesota	MN	Wisconsin	WI
Mississippi	MS	Wyoming	WY
Missouri	MO		

Canada

Alberta	AB	Northwest Territories	NT
British Columbia	BC	Ontario	ON
Manitoba	MB	Prince Edward Island	PE
New Brunswick	NB	Quebec	QC
Newfoundland	NF	Saskatchewan	SK
Nova Scotia	NS	Yukon	YN

Illustration 2-6 State and Province Abbreviations

The Complete Beginner's Guide

cemetery name, then town or township, county, and state, the state would end up in the country level. If you asked your computer program to search by a particular state by entering "TX," it would not find the Texas entries which had been moved to country level. MORAL: Put cemetery names and jurisdictions smaller than the town or parish into your notes, not into your locality levels.

As you can see in the sample PAF-generated Family Group Record in Illustration 5-2, many numbers are provided. These numbers allow for easy cross-referencing to any other record in the collection and make the research phase, the data entry, and the location of materials much easier to handle.

CONCLUSION

Now that you know the basic steps necessary to fill out the principal forms used by genealogists, the next chapter will begin the more detailed process of explaining how to record all facts and how to link each one to the individual to whom it pertains. Chapter 3 will cover some of the details of style, as well as an explanation of using the computer to store your notes. It is also time to begin working on the genealogy computer program you have selected. You will want to learn about how to set the **default preferences** to fit your specific needs. That will be covered under this chapter's Computer Checklist.

Terms to Understand

de·fault pref·er·ences - The manner in which your genealogy computer program is set up in advance to react under certain circumstances as you enter and report your genealogical data.

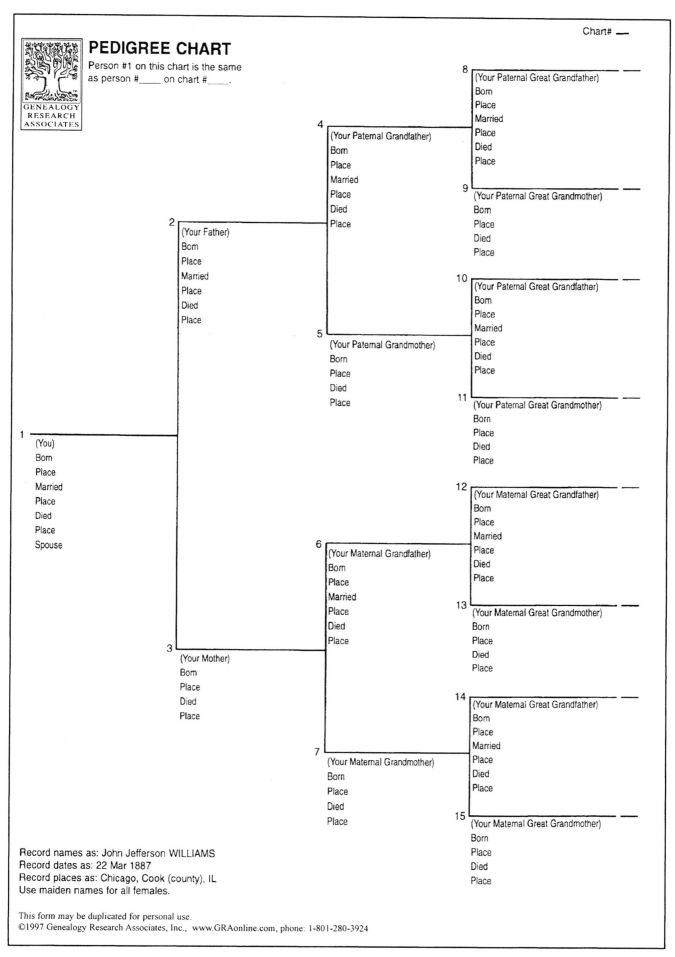

Chart# __

PEDIGREE CHART

Person #1 on this chart is the same as person #____ on chart #____.

8 (Your Paternal Great Grandfather)
Born
Place
Married
Place
Died
Place

9 (Your Paternal Great Grandmother)
Born
Place
Died
Place

4 (Your Paternal Grandfather)
Born
Place
Married
Place
Died
Place

10 (Your Paternal Great Grandfather)
Born
Place
Married
Place
Died
Place

11 (Your Paternal Great Grandmother)
Born
Place
Died
Place

2 (Your Father)
Born
Place
Married
Place
Died
Place

5 (Your Paternal Grandmother)
Born
Place
Died
Place

1 (You)
Born
Place
Married
Place
Died
Place
Spouse

12 (Your Maternal Great Grandfather)
Born
Place
Married
Place
Died
Place

6 (Your Maternal Grandfather)
Born
Place
Married
Place
Died
Place

13 (Your Maternal Great Grandmother)
Born
Place
Died
Place

3 (Your Mother)
Born
Place
Died
Place

14 (Your Maternal Great Grandfather)
Born
Place
Married
Place
Died
Place

7 (Your Maternal Grandmother)
Born
Place
Died
Place

15 (Your Maternal Great Grandmother)
Born
Place
Died
Place

Record names as: John Jefferson WILLIAMS
Record dates as: 22 Mar 1887
Record places as: Chicago, Cook (county), IL
Use maiden names for all females.

This form may be duplicated for personal use.
©1997 Genealogy Research Associates, Inc., www.GRAonline.com, phone: 1-801-280-3924

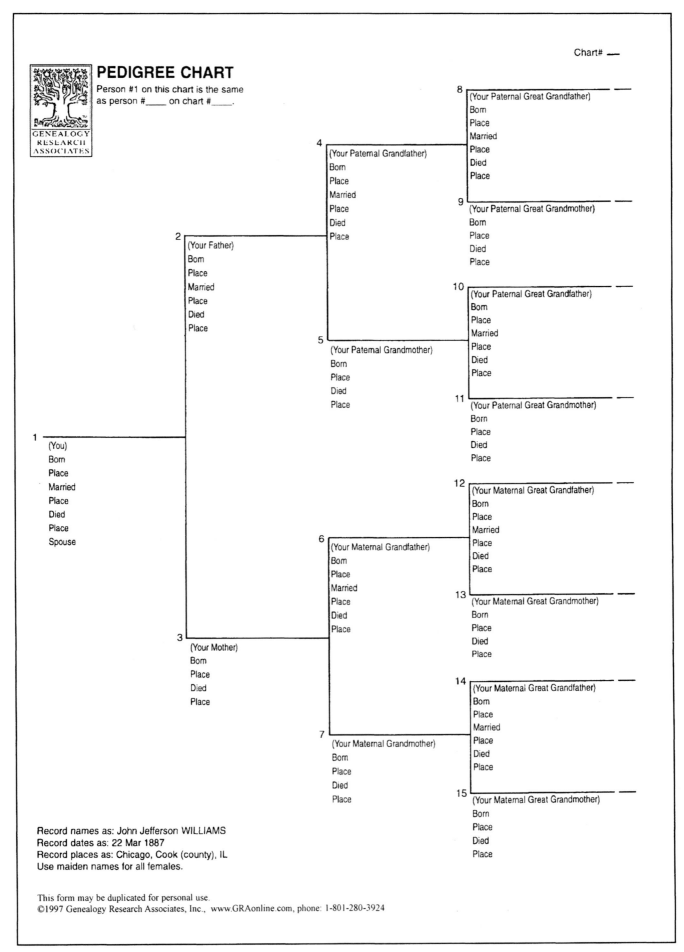

PEDIGREE CHART

Person #1 on this chart is the same
as person #____ on chart #____.

**GENEALOGY
RESEARCH
ASSOCIATES**

1 (You)
Born
Place
Married
Place
Died
Place
Spouse

2 (Your Father)
Born
Place
Married
Place
Died
Place

3 (Your Mother)
Born
Place
Died
Place

4 (Your Paternal Grandfather)
Born
Place
Married
Place
Died
Place

5 (Your Paternal Grandmother)
Born
Place
Died
Place

6 (Your Maternal Grandfather)
Born
Place
Married
Place
Died
Place

7 (Your Maternal Grandmother)
Born
Place
Died
Place

8 (Your Paternal Great Grandfather)
Born
Place
Married
Place
Died
Place

9 (Your Paternal Great Grandmother)
Born
Place
Died
Place

10 (Your Paternal Great Grandfather)
Born
Place
Married
Place
Died
Place

11 (Your Paternal Great Grandmother)
Born
Place
Died
Place

12 (Your Maternal Great Grandfather)
Born
Place
Married
Place
Died
Place

13 (Your Maternal Great Grandmother)
Born
Place
Died
Place

14 (Your Maternal Great Grandfather)
Born
Place
Married
Place
Died
Place

15 (Your Maternal Great Grandmother)
Born
Place
Died
Place

Record names as: John Jefferson WILLIAMS
Record dates as: 22 Mar 1887
Record places as: Chicago, Cook (county), IL
Use maiden names for all females.

HUSBAND

Born	Place	Source
Christened	Place	Source
Married	Place	Source
Died	Place	Source
Buried	Place	Source
Father	Mother	

WIFE

Born	Place	Source
Christened	Place	Source
Died	Place	Source
Buried	Place	Source
Father	Mother	Source

GENEALOGY
RESEARCH
ASSOCIATES

FAMILY GROUP RECORD

Husband is same as #___ on pedigree chart #___

Wife is same as #___ on pedigree chart #___.

CHILDREN (Write under number at left if male [m] or female [f]. List all children in birth order. Mark "X" under number of direct-line child)

1	Name	Spouse	Source
	Born	Place	Source
	Christened	Place	Source
	Married	Place	Source
	Died	Place	Source
	Buried	Place	Source
2	Name	Spouse	Source
	Born	Place	Source
	Christened	Place	Source
	Married	Place	Source
	Died	Place	Source
	Buried	Place	Source
3	Name	Spouse	Source
	Born	Place	Source
	Christened	Place	Source
	Married	Place	Source
	Died	Place	Source
	Buried	Place	Source
4	Name	Spouse	Source
	Born	Place	Source
	Christened	Place	Source
	Married	Place	Source
	Died	Place	Source
	Buried	Place	Source

Key for source abbreviations

PK = Personal knowledge   **IF** = Information from (name of person or document from which information came)   **SE** = See enclosed papers

CHILDREN CONTINUED (Write under number at left if male [m] or female [f]. List all children in birth order. Mark "X" under number of direct-line child.)

5	Name		Spouse	Source
	Born	Place		Source
	Christened	Place		Source
	Married	Place		Source
	Died	Place		Source
	Buried	Place		Source

6	Name		Spouse	Source
	Born	Place		Source
	Christened	Place		Source
	Married	Place		Source
	Died	Place		Source
	Buried	Place		Source

7	Name		Spouse	Source
	Born	Place		Source
	Christened	Place		Source
	Married	Place		Source
	Died	Place		Source
	Buried	Place		Source

8	Name		Spouse	Source
	Born	Place		Source
	Christened	Place		Source
	Married	Place		Source
	Died	Place		Source
	Buried	Place		Source

9	Name		Spouse	Source
	Born	Place		Source
	Christened	Place		Source
	Married	Place		Source
	Died	Place		Source
	Buried	Place		Source

10	Name		Spouse	Source
	Born	Place		Source
	Christened	Place		Source
	Married	Place		Source
	Died	Place		Source
	Buried	Place		Source

HUSBAND

Born	Place	Source
Christened	Place	Source
Married	Place	Source
Died	Place	Source
Buried	Place	Source
Father	Mother	

WIFE

Born	Place	Source
Christened	Place	Source
Died	Place	Source
Buried	Place	Source
Father	Mother	Source

GENEALOGY
RESEARCH
ASSOCIATES

FAMILY GROUP RECORD

Husband is same as #___ on pedigree chart #___

Wife is same as #___ on pedigree chart #___.

CHILDREN (Write under number at left if male [m] or female [f]. List all children in birth order. Mark "X" under number of direct-line child)

1 Name / Spouse

	Source
Born	Place	Source
Christened	Place	Source
Married	Place	Source
Died	Place	Source
Buried	Place	Source

2 Name / Spouse

	Source
Born	Place	Source
Christened	Place	Source
Married	Place	Source
Died	Place	Source
Buried	Place	Source

3 Name / Spouse

	Source
Born	Place	Source
Christened	Place	Source
Married	Place	Source
Died	Place	Source
Buried	Place	Source

4 Name / Spouse

	Source
Born	Place	Source
Christened	Place	Source
Married	Place	Source
Died	Place	Source
Buried	Place	Source

Key for source abbreviations

PK = Personal knowledge   **IF** = Information from (name of person or document from which information came)   **SE** = See enclosed papers

CHILDREN CONTINUED (Write under number at left if male [m] or female [f]. List all children in birth order. Mark "X" under number of direct-line child.)

5	Name		Spouse	Source
	Born	Place		Source
	Christened	Place		Source
	Married	Place		Source
	Died	Place		Source
	Buried	Place		Source

6	Name		Spouse	Source
	Born	Place		Source
	Christened	Place		Source
	Married	Place		Source
	Died	Place		Source
	Buried	Place		Source

7	Name		Spouse	Source
	Born	Place		Source
	Christened	Place		Source
	Married	Place		Source
	Died	Place		Source
	Buried	Place		Source

8	Name		Spouse	Source
	Born	Place		Source
	Christened	Place		Source
	Married	Place		Source
	Died	Place		Source
	Buried	Place		Source

9	Name		Spouse	Source
	Born	Place		Source
	Christened	Place		Source
	Married	Place		Source
	Died	Place		Source
	Buried	Place		Source

10	Name		Spouse	Source
	Born	Place		Source
	Christened	Place		Source
	Married	Place		Source
	Died	Place		Source
	Buried	Place		Source

HUSBAND

Born	Place	Source
Christened	Place	Source
Married	Place	Source
Died	Place	Source
Buried	Place	Source
Father		Mother	

WIFE

Born	Place	Source
Christened	Place	Source
Died	Place	Source
Buried	Place	Source
Father		Mother		Source

GENEALOGY
RESEARCH
ASSOCIATES

**FAMILY
GROUP
RECORD**

Husband is same as #___ on pedigree chart #___

Wife is same as #___ on pedigree chart #___.

CHILDREN (Write under number at left if male [m] or female [f]. List all children in birth order. Mark "X" under number of direct-line child)

1 Name | Spouse | Source

Born	Place	Source
Christened	Place	Source
Married	Place	Source
Died	Place	Source
Buried	Place	Source

2 Name | Spouse | Source

Born	Place	Source
Christened	Place	Source
Married	Place	Source
Died	Place	Source
Buried	Place	Source

3 Name | Spouse | Source

Born	Place	Source
Christened	Place	Source
Married	Place	Source
Died	Place	Source
Buried	Place	Source

4 Name | Spouse | Source

Born	Place	Source
Christened	Place	Source
Married	Place	Source
Died	Place	Source
Buried	Place	Source

Key for source abbreviations

PK = Personal knowledge   **IF** = Information from (name of person or document from which information came)   **SE** = See enclosed papers

CHILDREN CONTINUED (Write under number at left if male [m] or female [f]. List all children in birth order. Mark "X" under number of direct-line child.)

5	Name		Spouse	Source
	Born	Place		Source
	Christened	Place		Source
	Married	Place		Source
	Died	Place		Source
	Buried	Place		Source
6	Name		Spouse	Source
	Born	Place		Source
	Christened	Place		Source
	Married	Place		Source
	Died	Place		Source
	Buried	Place		Source
7	Name		Spouse	Source
	Born	Place		Source
	Christened	Place		Source
	Married	Place		Source
	Died	Place		Source
	Buried	Place		Source
8	Name		Spouse	Source
	Born	Place		Source
	Christened	Place		Source
	Married	Place		Source
	Died	Place		Source
	Buried	Place		Source
9	Name		Spouse	Source
	Born	Place		Source
	Christened	Place		Source
	Married	Place		Source
	Died	Place		Source
	Buried	Place		Source
10	Name		Spouse	Source
	Born	Place		Source
	Christened	Place		Source
	Married	Place		Source
	Died	Place		Source
	Buried	Place		Source

HUSBAND

		Source
Born	Place	Source
Christened	Place	Source
Married	Place	Source
Died	Place	Source
Buried	Place	Source
Father	Mother	

GENEALOGY RESEARCH ASSOCIATES

FAMILY GROUP RECORD

Husband is same as #___ on pedigree chart #___

Wife is same as #___ on pedigree chart #___.

WIFE

		Source
Born	Place	Source
Christened	Place	Source
Died	Place	Source
Buried	Place	Source
Father	Mother	Source

CHILDREN (Write under number at left if male [m] or female [f]. List all children in birth order. Mark "X" under number of direct-line child)

1	Name	Spouse	Source
	Born	Place	Source
	Christened	Place	Source
	Married	Place	Source
	Died	Place	Source
	Buried	Place	Source

2	Name	Spouse	Source
	Born	Place	Source
	Christened	Place	Source
	Married	Place	Source
	Died	Place	Source
	Buried	Place	Source

3	Name	Spouse	Source
	Born	Place	Source
	Christened	Place	Source
	Married	Place	Source
	Died	Place	Source
	Buried	Place	Source

4	Name	Spouse	Source
	Born	Place	Source
	Christened	Place	Source
	Married	Place	Source
	Died	Place	Source
	Buried	Place	Source

Key for source abbreviations

PK = Personal knowledge   **IF** = Information from (name of person or document from which information came)   **SE** = See enclosed papers

CHILDREN CONTINUED (Write under number at left if male [m] or female [f]. List all children in birth order. Mark "X" under number of direct-line child.)

5	Name		Spouse	Source
	Born	Place		Source
	Christened	Place		Source
	Married	Place		Source
	Died	Place		Source
	Buried	Place		Source

6	Name		Spouse	Source
	Born	Place		Source
	Christened	Place		Source
	Married	Place		Source
	Died	Place		Source
	Buried	Place		Source

7	Name		Spouse	Source
	Born	Place		Source
	Christened	Place		Source
	Married	Place		Source
	Died	Place		Source
	Buried	Place		Source

8	Name		Spouse	Source
	Born	Place		Source
	Christened	Place		Source
	Married	Place		Source
	Died	Place		Source
	Buried	Place		Source

9	Name		Spouse	Source
	Born	Place		Source
	Christened	Place		Source
	Married	Place		Source
	Died	Place		Source
	Buried	Place		Source

10	Name		Spouse	Source
	Born	Place		Source
	Christened	Place		Source
	Married	Place		Source
	Died	Place		Source
	Buried	Place		Source

HUSBAND

Born	Place	Source
Christened	Place	Source
Married	Place	Source
Died	Place	Source
Buried	Place	Source
Father	Mother	

FAMILY GROUP RECORD

GENEALOGY RESEARCH ASSOCIATES

WIFE

Born	Place	Source
Christened	Place	Source
Died	Place	Source
Buried	Place	Source
Father	Mother	Source

Husband is same as #___ on pedigree chart #___

Wife is same as #___ on pedigree chart #___.

CHILDREN (Write under number at left if male [m] or female [f]. List all children in birth order. Mark "X" under number of direct-line child)

1

Name	Spouse	Source
Born	Place	Source
Christened	Place	Source
Married	Place	Source
Died	Place	Source
Buried	Place	Source

2

Name	Spouse	Source
Born	Place	Source
Christened	Place	Source
Married	Place	Source
Died	Place	Source
Buried	Place	Source

3

Name	Spouse	Source
Born	Place	Source
Christened	Place	Source
Married	Place	Source
Died	Place	Source
Buried	Place	Source

4

Name	Spouse	Source
Born	Place	Source
Christened	Place	Source
Married	Place	Source
Died	Place	Source
Buried	Place	Source

Key for source abbreviations

PK = Personal knowledge   **IF** = Information from (name of person or document from which information came)   **SE** = See enclosed papers

CHILDREN CONTINUED (Write under number at left if male [m] or female [f]. List all children in birth order. Mark "X" under number of direct-line child.)

5	Name		Spouse	Source
	Born	Place		Source
	Christened	Place		Source
	Married	Place		Source
	Died	Place		Source
	Buried	Place		Source

6	Name		Spouse	Source
	Born	Place		Source
	Christened	Place		Source
	Married	Place		Source
	Died	Place		Source
	Buried	Place		Source

7	Name		Spouse	Source
	Born	Place		Source
	Christened	Place		Source
	Married	Place		Source
	Died	Place		Source
	Buried	Place		Source

8	Name		Spouse	Source
	Born	Place		Source
	Christened	Place		Source
	Married	Place		Source
	Died	Place		Source
	Buried	Place		Source

9	Name		Spouse	Source
	Born	Place		Source
	Christened	Place		Source
	Married	Place		Source
	Died	Place		Source
	Buried	Place		Source

10	Name		Spouse	Source
	Born	Place		Source
	Christened	Place		Source
	Married	Place		Source
	Died	Place		Source
	Buried	Place		Source

HUSBAND

Born	Place	Source
Christened	Place	Source
Married	Place	Source
Died	Place	Source
Buried	Place	Source
Father		Mother	

WIFE

Born	Place	Source
Christened	Place	Source
Died	Place	Source
Buried	Place	Source
Father		Mother		Source

GENEALOGY RESEARCH ASSOCIATES

FAMILY GROUP RECORD

Husband is same as #___ on pedigree chart #___

Wife is same as #___ on pedigree chart #___.

CHILDREN (Write under number at left if male [m] or female [f]. List all children in birth order. Mark "X" under number of direct-line child)

1	Name	Spouse	Source
	Born	Place	Source
	Christened	Place	Source
	Married	Place	Source
	Died	Place	Source
	Buried	Place	Source

2	Name	Spouse	Source
	Born	Place	Source
	Christened	Place	Source
	Married	Place	Source
	Died	Place	Source
	Buried	Place	Source

3	Name	Spouse	Source
	Born	Place	Source
	Christened	Place	Source
	Married	Place	Source
	Died	Place	Source
	Buried	Place	Source

4	Name	Spouse	Source
	Born	Place	Source
	Christened	Place	Source
	Married	Place	Source
	Died	Place	Source
	Buried	Place	Source

Key for source abbreviations

PK = Personal knowledge   **IF** = Information from (name of person or document from which information came)   **SE** = See enclosed papers

CHILDREN CONTINUED (Write under number at left if male [m] or female [f]. List all children in birth order. Mark "X" under number of direct-line child.)

5	Name		Spouse	Source
	Born	Place		Source
	Christened	Place		Source
	Married	Place		Source
	Died	Place		Source
	Buried	Place		Source

6	Name		Spouse	Source
	Born	Place		Source
	Christened	Place		Source
	Married	Place		Source
	Died	Place		Source
	Buried	Place		Source

7	Name		Spouse	Source
	Born	Place		Source
	Christened	Place		Source
	Married	Place		Source
	Died	Place		Source
	Buried	Place		Source

8	Name		Spouse	Source
	Born	Place		Source
	Christened	Place		Source
	Married	Place		Source
	Died	Place		Source
	Buried	Place		Source

9	Name		Spouse	Source
	Born	Place		Source
	Christened	Place		Source
	Married	Place		Source
	Died	Place		Source
	Buried	Place		Source

10	Name		Spouse	Source
	Born	Place		Source
	Christened	Place		Source
	Married	Place		Source
	Died	Place		Source
	Buried	Place		Source

This form may be duplicated for personal use.
©1997 Genealogy Research Associates, Inc., www.GRAonline.com, phone: 1-801-280-3924

HUSBAND

Born	Place		Source
Christened	Place		Source
Married	Place		Source
Died	Place		Source
Buried	Place		Source
Father		Mother	

GENEALOGY RESEARCH ASSOCIATES

FAMILY GROUP RECORD

Husband is same as #___ on pedigree chart #___

Wife is same as #___ on pedigree chart #___.

WIFE

Born	Place		Source
Christened	Place		Source
Died	Place		Source
Buried	Place		Source
Father		Mother	Source

CHILDREN (Write under number at left if male [m] or female [f]. List all children in birth order. Mark "X" under number of direct-line child)

1	Name		Spouse	Source
	Born	Place		Source
	Christened	Place		Source
	Married	Place		Source
	Died	Place		Source
	Buried	Place		Source

2	Name		Spouse	Source
	Born	Place		Source
	Christened	Place		Source
	Married	Place		Source
	Died	Place		Source
	Buried	Place		Source

3	Name		Spouse	Source
	Born	Place		Source
	Christened	Place		Source
	Married	Place		Source
	Died	Place		Source
	Buried	Place		Source

4	Name		Spouse	Source
	Born	Place		Source
	Christened	Place		Source
	Married	Place		Source
	Died	Place		Source
	Buried	Place		Source

Key for source abbreviations

PK = Personal knowledge   **IF** = Information from (name of person or document from which information came)   **SE** = See enclosed papers

CHILDREN CONTINUED (Write under number at left if male [m] or female [f]. List all children in birth order. Mark "X" under number of direct-line child.)

5	Name		Spouse	Source
	Born	Place		Source
	Christened	Place		Source
	Married	Place		Source
	Died	Place		Source
	Buried	Place		Source

6	Name		Spouse	Source
	Born	Place		Source
	Christened	Place		Source
	Married	Place		Source
	Died	Place		Source
	Buried	Place		Source

7	Name		Spouse	Source
	Born	Place		Source
	Christened	Place		Source
	Married	Place		Source
	Died	Place		Source
	Buried	Place		Source

8	Name		Spouse	Source
	Born	Place		Source
	Christened	Place		Source
	Married	Place		Source
	Died	Place		Source
	Buried	Place		Source

9	Name		Spouse	Source
	Born	Place		Source
	Christened	Place		Source
	Married	Place		Source
	Died	Place		Source
	Buried	Place		Source

10	Name		Spouse	Source
	Born	Place		Source
	Christened	Place		Source
	Married	Place		Source
	Died	Place		Source
	Buried	Place		Source

HUSBAND

Born	Place	Source
Christened	Place	Source
Married	Place	Source
Died	Place	Source
Buried	Place	Source
Father	Mother	

GENEALOGY RESEARCH ASSOCIATES

FAMILY GROUP RECORD

WIFE

Born	Place	Source
Christened	Place	Source
Died	Place	Source
Buried	Place	Source
Father	Mother	Source

Husband is same as #___ on pedigree chart #___

Wife is same as #___ on pedigree chart #___.

CHILDREN (Write under number at left if male [m] or female [f]. List all children in birth order. Mark "X" under number of direct-line child)

1	Name	Spouse	Source
	Born	Place	Source
	Christened	Place	Source
	Married	Place	Source
	Died	Place	Source
	Buried	Place	Source
2	Name	Spouse	Source
	Born	Place	Source
	Christened	Place	Source
	Married	Place	Source
	Died	Place	Source
	Buried	Place	Source
3	Name	Spouse	Source
	Born	Place	Source
	Christened	Place	Source
	Married	Place	Source
	Died	Place	Source
	Buried	Place	Source
4	Name	Spouse	Source
	Born	Place	Source
	Christened	Place	Source
	Married	Place	Source
	Died	Place	Source
	Buried	Place	Source

Key for source abbreviations

PK = Personal knowledge   **IF** = Information from (name of person or document from which information came)   **SE** = See enclosed papers

CHILDREN CONTINUED (Write under number at left if male [m] or female [f]. List all children in birth order. Mark "X" under number of direct-line child.)

5	Name		Spouse	Source
	Born	Place		Source
	Christened	Place		Source
	Married	Place		Source
	Died	Place		Source
	Buried	Place		Source

6	Name		Spouse	Source
	Born	Place		Source
	Christened	Place		Source
	Married	Place		Source
	Died	Place		Source
	Buried	Place		Source

7	Name		Spouse	Source
	Born	Place		Source
	Christened	Place		Source
	Married	Place		Source
	Died	Place		Source
	Buried	Place		Source

8	Name		Spouse	Source
	Born	Place		Source
	Christened	Place		Source
	Married	Place		Source
	Died	Place		Source
	Buried	Place		Source

9	Name		Spouse	Source
	Born	Place		Source
	Christened	Place		Source
	Married	Place		Source
	Died	Place		Source
	Buried	Place		Source

10	Name		Spouse	Source
	Born	Place		Source
	Christened	Place		Source
	Married	Place		Source
	Died	Place		Source
	Buried	Place		Source

ASSIGNMENT 2: FILLING IN CHARTS AND FORMS

The following exercise will help you determine specifically what you need to learn about your own family by completing the two basic forms used by genealogy researchers.

1. In pencil, fill in the blank Pedigree Chart (page 2-13). At this point, try to remember the "rules" that you learned in this chapter for entering names, dates, and places. See how many generations you can enter from memory.

2. Complete the blank Family Group Records (pages 2-15 through 2-30). Do one record where you appear as a child with your parents. Then do one for each of your parents and grandparents, in which each appears as a child with his or her parents.

SELF-EVALUATION: Filling Out Basic Charts and Forms

How well did you do in filling out the Pedigree Chart and Family Group Records? Did you:

1. Capitalize the surname?

2. Write the dates in day-month-year format?

3. Include the name of the county for every location and enter the places with the smallest area designation first?

If you forgot about some of these, this little pre-exercise will remind you to be aware of these good research habits. Another good research habit to learn from the very beginning is to keep excellent records of all notes and to link them to the individuals to whom they belong. That is the subject of Chapter 4.

YOUR TURN ANSWERS

The Pedigree Chart

Imagine you were entering the locality "Cincinnati, Hamilton County, Ohio." Use only one letter per box; use one box for each comma, and leave a box blank for spaces.

Now assume that your sheet of paper was not large enough and you had to put the same information into half as many boxes. That is what happens when words are truncated.

| C | i | n | c | i | n | n | a | t | i | , | | H | a | m | i | l | t | o |

Of course, you want to be able to read the complete town and county. Most computer programs ask you if you want to eliminate the first part or the last part of the locality. If you eliminate the first part, you lose the town. If you eliminate the last part, you lose the state. Some programs eliminate what is in the middle, causing you to lose the county.

Recording Names

Print this person's name the way you should when you hand-enter onto a form: George Washington Johnson.

JOHNSON, George Washington or George Washington JOHNSON

Recording Dates

Write these dates in the correct format for genealogical forms:

A.   June 1, 1967   1 Jun 1967

B.   April 7, 1899.   7 Apr 1899

C.   May 23, 1776.   23 May 1776

Recording Places

Write these locations as they should be written on Pedigree Charts or Family Group Records.

A.   Born in Mother of Charity Hospital, New York City, New York County, New York.

New York City, New York, NY

B.   Died in Natividad Hospital, Salinas, Monterey County, California.

Salinas, Monterey, CA   (Put the name of the hospital in the notes.)

C.   Buried at Holy Cross Cemetery, Monterey, Monterey County, California.

Monterey, Monterey, CA   (Put the name of the cemetery in the notes.)

COMPUTER CHECKLIST #2

1. Check the "Preferences" option on your computer genealogy program. List here all of the preference options you have available.

2. Which options have you selected, and why?

WEB SITE

http://www.cyndislist.com
An alphabetical listing of genealogy Internet sites by topic.

BIBLIOGRAPHY

Rubincam, Milton, Editor. "Genealogy and Chronology." *Genealogical Research: Methods and Sources*. Rev. ed. Vol. 1. The American Society of Genealogists: Washington, D.C., 1980: 27-37.

Westin, Jeane Eddy. "First Step Backward: How to Take A Family History and Gather Available Records." *Finding Your Roots*. New York: Ballantine Books, 1990: 43-63.

CHAPTER 3

Becoming Acquainted with Your Genealogy Program

"Pursuing a research goal in genealogy is like a journey toward a distant horizon. The progress you've made isn't apparent until you look back and see how far you've come."

—Ray T. Clifford

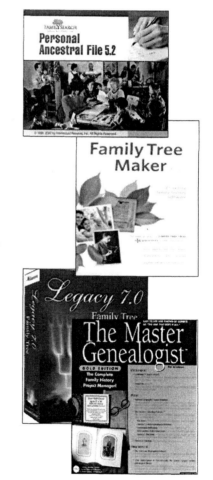

So far, you have been introduced to the principal techniques for successful family history research, including the Research Cycle. You have been instructed in ways to manually organize whatever family history information you could locate in family documents and among your relatives. Finally, you were asked to fill out a Pedigree Chart and Family Group Record on your own family. Another way to make your work more effective is through the use of a good genealogy computer program.

This chapter aims to demonstrate the effectiveness of using a computer to accomplish the above tasks, but since each of you may own a different program, this book will ask you to experiment as you go along. In addition, specific suggestions for using the various programs will be made available at our Web site, *http://www.GRAonline.com,* if you feel you cannot find a way to accomplish a specific assignment. This Web site "appendix," as we might call it, allows us to update your program's features as they are modified, due to the constant changes in genealogy computer programs, and to make specific suggestions pertinent to genealogy research.

ENTERING FAMILY INFORMATION

The first thing you want to do with any genealogical software program is to enter your own family information. Information for each individual in the family will include those vital records that uniquely identify his or her life. This includes information about birth, marriage(s), and death. Once an individual's information has been entered into the computer, you can **edit** or make changes to it at any time. In addition to this "vital records" information, you can enter sources and notes that will verify, or "document," the dates and places that you have entered—a very important part of good record keeping.

Terms to Understand

edit - To correct or change written material.

But entering dates and locations is only part of the value of a good genealogy computer program. This chapter will also help you to identify the features which are desirable in any good genealogy computer program.

EXCITING FEATURES OF GOOD GENEALOGY COMPUTER PROGRAMS

Using such a program aids in both organizing your information and in doing research. As we list some of the benefits, determine if the program you use can accomplish the tasks listed below:

1. As you enter vital records, you will internalize the information and begin to notice discrepancies in information.

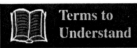

Terms to Understand

ac·tion e·vent ti·tles - Words used in the data entry of citations to focus on particular milestones, life happenings, and other events that occur in a person's life.

> **YOUR TURN**
>
> Does your genealogy computer program have a place to capture wrong or missing data? Does it provide a quick way to find notes you have made about discrepancies? How is that done?

2. As you link documentation to individuals you are entering, clues are revealed. Clues can be flagged with **action event titles,** such as "MIGRATION," to alert the researcher of movements to new areas where records may be kept. You might want to call them "new jurisdictions for records" in your notes.

> **YOUR TURN**
>
> Where would you enter migration clues into your genealogy computer program?

3. The program acts like a handy notepad and pencil where you can jot down any ideas that come to you, such as:

    A. Where was Uncle Joe buried?
    B. When did Aunt Mary and Uncle Jim marry? Where did they marry?
    C. Cousin Marvin might have a copy of this obituary. I need to ask him.

The Complete Beginner's Guide

These ideas can be flagged with action event titles, such as "TO DO," to indicate that work needs to be done, perhaps at a local **Family History Center**. Then either you, or those who will use your research after you are gone, can continue.

YOUR TURN

Where would you enter "TO DO" lists in your genealogy computer program?

Terms to Understand

Family History Centers - Genealogy research centers operated by The Church of Jesus Christ of Latter-day Saints in locations throughout the world, where individuals can search the center's own holdings, order genealogy materials on microfilm and microfiche through a loan program, and access a variety of genealogy databases.

4. Genealogy computer programs which automatically assign an ID number to every individual and Family Group Record ease the research and filing process. These same ID numbers can then be written in the upper right-hand corner of documents for ease in filing, since a number is faster to write and easier to keep track of than a complete name. Each number in your database is unique, while families often use the same names over and over again.

YOUR TURN

Determine whether your computer program assigns ID numbers for individuals and families. If it doesn't automatically do so, look at your genealogy computer program "preferences" options to see if you can assign ID numbers. How do you do it on your program?

Terms to Understand

da·ta - 1. Information organized for analysis or decision-making. 2. Information suitable for computer processing.

5. Good genealogy computer programs allow you to copy notes from one person to another to avoid excessive **data** entry.

Terms to Understand

GEDCOM - Acronym for Genealogical Data Communication, which is the standard proto-col for transferring data from one genealo-gy program to another. It was originally written to enable home users to receive data from the largest genealogical databases in the world main-tained by The Church of Jesus Christ of Latter-day Saints, which is constantly being updated. It has now become a standard transfer protocol for all major genealogy computer programs. GEDCOM files may also be submitted via the Internet at www.familysearch.org.

Terms to Understand

down·load - To trans-fer or copy data from one computer to anoth-er, or to a disk or peripheral device, or to be transferred or copied in this way.

6. Good genealogy programs have the ability to accept information data entered by others. Those programs which are **GEDCOM**-compatible can save typing time and typing errors by **downloading** information from others (such as

> **YOUR TURN**
>
> Read the instruction manual that came with your genealo-gy computer program to learn about the kinds of infor-mation it can accept and transmit to other programs. Briefly summarize what you learned.

information from *FamilySearch* at local Family History Centers or *World Family Tree*™ CDs).

7. Computer programs create Pedigree Charts, Family Group Records, descendancy charts, and other handy aids, both for visualizing the family history and for extending the research.

> **YOUR TURN**
>
> 1. Find the surname index in your program. Where is it located on the screen? What happens when you type in a name at the blinking cursor located at the top of the index?
>
> 2. Find out if you have a locality index. How do you use it?

YOUR TURN

What other kinds of charts does your program provide? List them.

8. Computer programs alphabetize and create multiple indexes, such as:

   A. Surname indexes in many varieties
   B. Record ID Number (RIN) or Marriage Record ID Number (MRIN) indexes
   C. Locality indexes by event
   D. Event indexes.

9. Additions or corrections made in one area can be carried over to other charts referring to that same person, eliminating hours of typing.

YOUR TURN

How do you make corrections to existing individuals and families in your genealogy computer program?

YOUR TURN

Do you have a "cut and paste," "copy," or "ditto" feature in your genealogy computer program? Which one(s)?

Terms to Understand

up·load - To transfer data or programs to a central computer on the Internet (or storage medium) to another computer.

Terms to Understand

FamilySearch - The umbrella name for the various records and research aids developed by The Church of Jesus Christ of Latter-day Saints. Many separate segments are included such as the Ancestral File™, the International Genealogical Index™, the Social Security Death Index, the Military Index (U.S. only), and several others.

Terms to Understand

World Family Tree - A collection of actual family trees submitted by users of the Family Tree Maker genealogy computer program. Many trees contain documented sources which are very helpful for continuing research. The contributors may be contacted.

10. Good genealogy computer programs have the ability to send information (**upload**) to databases (such as information to ***FamilySearch***™ at local Family History Centers, or ***World Family Tree***™).

11. Good genealogy computer programs have the ability to search all notes for a particular word or string of words, in order to look for an elusive clue that could tie two families together.

YOUR TURN

Is your genealogy computer program able to convert files completely? Yes No

Is it considered 100% GEDCOM compatible? Yes No

YOUR TURN

Can you locate a function in your genealogy computer program which will allow you to search and locate any word you have entered into your database for elusive clues you might have entered? Explain how this works in your program.

12. Good genealogy computer programs alert you when you make obvious errors, such as typing 1780 for 1980 or misspelling a name.

13. Good genealogy computer programs repeat places, dates and localities, when they are used more than once, to save typing time.

These are just some of the exciting features of a good genealogy computer program. They can be a great boost for the genealogist--especially for one who does not type very fast, or who finds writing by hand uncomfortable or slow. In addition, once you have entered your family data into a genealogy computer program, you can be assured that it will be printed out or transmitted in a neat, legible form.

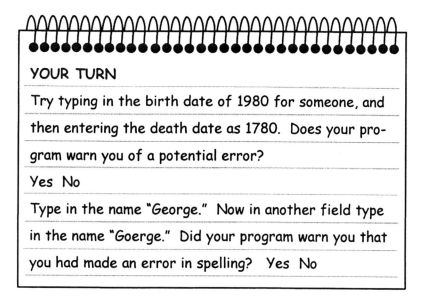

YOUR TURN

Try typing in the birth date of 1980 for someone, and then entering the death date as 1780. Does your program warn you of a potential error?

Yes No

Type in the name "George." Now in another field type in the name "Goerge." Did your program warn you that you had made an error in spelling?   Yes No

There are other reasons why computers are so popular today: they are fast, accurate and perform repetitive tasks very well. It is even possible to scan a typed manuscript directly into a computer through a separate scanning program, and then "cut and paste" the information into your genealogy computer program so that its database can index it for you.

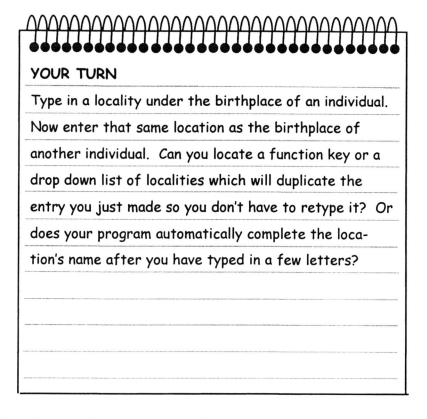

YOUR TURN

Type in a locality under the birthplace of an individual. Now enter that same location as the birthplace of another individual. Can you locate a function key or a drop down list of localities which will duplicate the entry you just made so you don't have to retype it? Or does your program automatically complete the location's name after you have typed in a few letters?

This chapter will get you started with your favorite genealogy computer program. If you have never used a genealogical software program, you may wish to choose one to begin with, then follow the tutorials given in this book and at our Web site *www.GRAonline.com.* As you become familiar with one program, you can expand your knowledge to other programs, and this will add to your capabilities. For now, you will be surprised to discover that, working with this text, you can learn how to use a genealogy computer program very quickly!

The information on the following pages and subsequent chapters will cover the basics of entering information into a genealogy computer program. It is important that time be spent learning these techniques properly from the beginning, in order to prevent unnecessary duplication of work.

JUST A REMINDER

Before you begin entering your materials on a computer, be aware of their frailties as well as their possibilities. Unfortunately, many beginning genealogists fail to protect their investment of time by:

1. Not making periodic backups of the data that has been entered into the genealogy computer program every 15 or 30 minutes. One easy way to do this is to use a separate file on the computer hard-drive, or a flash (or thumb) drive as shown in Illustration 3-1. When your computer crashes (and they all do one time or another), having the backup in a different place is just wonderful!

2. Not making a backup before trying to match and merge files or before importing information from an online site into your own data file. It is always so much easiet to go back to the beginning with the latest backup if you are dissatisfied with the results of the former actions.

3. Not storing the flash drive carefully, or losing it without a copy on the home computer.

CONCLUSION

Now that you have become familiar with your own genealogy computer program, you will be given an assignment to put together the "skeleton" for your family into that program. This includes data-entering the names, dates, and places. The next chapter will show you how to document the sources of your information and, if possible, to record every clue as you go back in time, in order to add "flesh" to that "skeleton."

THE MOST COMMON MISTAKES OF NEW COMPUTER USERS

1. **Neglecting to take seriously the basics of data backup care:**

Data can be damaged by excessive heat, direct sunlight, moisture, dust, and strong magnetic fields. Avoid placing flash drives on top of other electronic devices, such as a radio or television, as the data can be altered. And remember to take them with you when you leave your car. Disks can be damaged by direct contact with car radio stereo units, by the sunlight through windows, and from the heat in the glove compartment. FOR GOOD DATA CARE: Store the flash drive with its cover, or slide it closed with your thumb as in Illustration 3-1 which also protects it from being bent.

Remember: even if your flash drive "looks" fine, the data can be corrupted if it is not treated carefully. If this happens, you might not even realize that the information about third-great-Aunt Hortense has been altered or lost due to such damage.

2. **Inserting flash drives into USB ports incorrectly:**

Never force the disk in. If it does not go in smoothly, pull it out and try again. You may have it upside down. When information, or data, is being read from the disk or copied onto it, the light on the drive will be on and often flashing. As a general rule: NEVER REMOVE THE FLASH DRIVE WHILE THE LIGHT IS ON, and NEVER remove it during an operation. If you do remove the flash drive before it has finished its work, the information may become lost or garbled. Click on the "Safely Remove Hardware" icon before taking out of the USB port, or wait until the computer is turned off.

3. **Not understanding the difference between typewriter keyboards and computer keyboards:**

In some ways, computer and typewriter keyboards look alike, but there are several differences. Glance through the next page for specific examples if you are a brand new computer user.

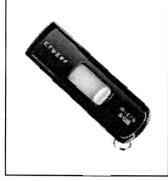

Illustration 3-1
Flash Drive
Also called a "thumb drive" because some versions can be opened and closed by pushing a plastic slider back and forth (shown in the illustration above in the middle as white). This exposes the metal part that is inserted into your USB port.

Illustration 3-2 The Most Common Mistakes of New Computer Users

HOW COMPUTER AND TYPEWRITER KEYBOARDS ARE ALIKE

The character keys are generally the same, but a cursor (a small, solid rectangle or flashing underline) shows you where on the screen the character will appear. The ⌗Shift⌗ key works like the shift key on a typewriter. When you hold it down while you press a character key, the upper character or uppercase (capital) letter will appear. The ⌗Caps Lock⌗ key will allow you to use all capital letters. You will still have to use the ⌗Shift⌗ key to display the top character on a number or symbol key. The ⌗Enter⌗ key and ⌗Tab⌗ keys on several programs are the same, in that they both start a new line of text or move you from field to field in the data entry portions of your program.

HOW THE COMPUTER KEYBOARD IS DIFFERENT

There is a distinct difference between the number 1 and the letter l, as well as the number 0 [zero] and the letter O. On the computer screen, the zero often has a line through it, making it look a little like the number eight. Using the lowercase L instead of a number 1 in a date like l936 will cause the program to give you an error message, and it won't continue until you correct it.

The *Space Bar* on the computer does more than move across text. It can erase the letters or characters in front of it, if it is not in "Insert" mode. The ⌗Ins⌗ (*Insert*) key lets you add characters to the left of the cursor. It pushes the rest of the characters forward.

Speaking of "spaces," these are very important on the computer. To the computer, there is as much difference between two spaces between words as putting three t's in the word PUTTTING. If you were to type in a surname field "_ _ Johnson," placing two spaces in front of the word, the computer would not alphabetize the word under Js but at the top of the entire surname list, because spaces come before the letter "A."

The ⌗Ctrl⌗ (*Control*) key is used, in conjunction with one or two other keys, in order to perform a specific function. It must be held down while the other key is pressed.

Computers are fast and accurate but they do not think for you. The only way they know you are finished with a task is for you to press the ⌗Enter⌗ key.

The ⌗Backspace⌗ key erases words as the cursor passes over them. The ⌗Del⌗ (*Delete*) key will erase the character under the cursor and move the remaining characters on the line one space backward. One character is erased each time you press the key.

Arrow keys (see Illustration 3-4) allow you to move the cursor around the screen without erasing information. See the illustration at the left.

Function keys do not put a character on the screen, but they do cause an internal operation to take place. The ⌗F1⌗ function key is often used to save changes, and then exit.

Most screens are like forms with fill-in blanks added. Pressing the ⌗Enter⌗ or ⌗Tab⌗ key will move you from one blank, or field, to another. *Up* and *down*, *left* and *right* arrow keys will move you from one field to another on the screen.

Illustration 3-3 How Computer and Typewriter Keyboards are Alike

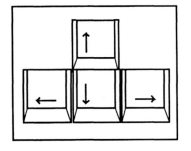

Illustration 3-4 Arrow Keys

ASSIGNMENT 3: ENTERING YOUR OWN FAMILY INFORMATION

You will need plenty of time to enter all the information you currently have on all of your family that you are interested in studying. Enter at least your parents, grandparents and, if possible, your great-grandparents.

Using the handwritten charts you filled out in Chapter 2, data enter your family information into your genealogy computer program. Remember the rules that you learned regarding surname capitalization, how to enter dates, and how to enter localities. Enter as many names as you have on all of your lines for at least four generations.

YOUR TURN ANSWERS

Personal preferences are allowed on all Chapter 3 responses.

COMPUTER CHECKLIST #3

1. Note that some programs automatically capitalize surnames. If not, you may set the preference for doing so. If you set the program to capitalize surnames for you, and then you also capitalize another kind of word, that word may be capitalized elsewhere when you don't want it to be. For example, the name BROWN, if capitalized, as a surname, might also end up capitalized when used as Brown County, Kansas.

2. Enter your name and dates into your genealogy computer program.

    A. Did you enter the birth date correctly, i.e. 1946 instead of 46?

    B. Did you enter the location correctly, i.e., city, county, state. If you know the hospital, put that information into notes. You want to maintain the consistency of three fields, for locations, not four fields, which is what would happen if you put the hospital before the city. This also would not allow you enough space on your pedigree chart for all the locations you need to continue your research.

3. What is necessary to "save" the information you just entered?

4. What must you do to link an individual to a family? CAUTION: You should never be required to enter the same person twice.

5. How can you look at a listing of everyone you have entered so far?

WEB SITES

This week Web sites that provide information on genealogy computer programs will be suggested. It is a good idea when you are starting to try out a couple of different programs as most have a free download you can use.

Programs That Work on MAC (Apple-based) Operating Systems
www.leisterpro.com/
Information on Reunion for MAC computer user, GEDCOM compatible. Creates large graphic tree charts and timelines; pictures, movies, sounds, pod cards, web output; book-style reports; wide range of custom reports; source documentation available; Cascading Style Sheets; Unicode support allows for multilingual text using different languages; and much more in Version 9.

www.myheredis.com
Requires Mac OS X version 10.3 or later. Features immediate display and access to all functions on one screen only; comprehensive data management; powerful search tools and database merging; integrated mode of visualization of your family in 3D; media associated with all types of data; sourcing capabilities; and pages and personal menus ready for integration on your website.

WEB SITES (cont.)

Genealogy Programs That Run on Windows Operating Systems

www.familysearch.org
Download Personal Ancestral File for free from their front page in several languages. Tutorials for using PAF 5.2 are available from the download page. A good beginning program for new genealogists and computer users. Data transfers easily to all of the programs below as user becomes more proficient.

www.ancquest.com
Information on *Ancestral Quest*. The programmer who developed this genealogy computer program donated the first Windows based program to the LDS Church, which evolved into their free *PAF* program (above). Today the *Ancestral Quest* program is more advanced than *PAF*, but has common functionality with more opportunities to share, match and merge, and collaborate with others. Immediate conversions from PAF files. Good tutorials online.

www.legacyfamilytree.com/
Information on *Legacy Family Tree* by Millennia Corporation. Imports data seamlessly from *PAF*, as well as importing GEDCOM files from other programs. Contains an excellent research guidance program. Once an individual has been imported into the program, research guidance will provide a list of websites, published sources, and repositories to solve a particular goal set by the researcher for that selected individual. Has research planners, a good program for printing reports and books, and various options to match the desires of individual users. It is advisable to purchase the set of training CDs or watch the online tutorials.

http://www.rootsmagic.com/
Information on *RootsMagic* and *Personal Historian*. *Rootsmagic* imports data from *PAF* and other major genealogy programs. It has a superior feature for publishing your family history easily on the Web or in traditional paper format. Has advanced features for citing sources, creating user-defined facts, scanning images, and merging. The newest version allows you to run the program on a thumb drive so you can take it anywhere you do research that has a Windows Operating system and an available computer.

www.ancestry.com/ or *www.FamilyTreeMaker.com*
Information on *FamilyTreeMaker*. This program is easy to use. It centers around the www.Ancestry.com databases and publishing possibilities so it can search the Ancestry.com databases and automatically import the citations from positive searched into the program. When the data in this program is imported to the Ancestry.com publisher, a lovely, professionally-bound book can result. It does not share data easily with other genealogy computer programs, but data is shared at it's fee-based site at a reasonable price, however.

www.whollygenes.com/
Information on *The Master Genealogist* for Windows users. Provides many opportunities to look at data from all angles. Good training tutorials are available and needed because this program provides many advanced options for users. It is not for the complete beginner without some help, but those who grow up with this program really appreciate its features. Excellent help available when needed. Study its Web site and make comparisons.

More comparisons available at *www.GRAonline.com* under "Resources."

BIBLIOGRAPHY OF SOURCES STUDIED FOR THIS CHAPTER

Ancestral Quest. For Windows. Incline Software, LC, South Jordan, Utah, *http://www.ancquest.com,* 2010.

Family Origins is owned by *RootsMagic,* 2010..

FamilyTreeMaker is owned by *Ancestry.com,* Provo, Utah, 2010. *www.ancestry.com* or *www.familytreemaker.com* whose parent company is *MyFamily.com.*

RootsMagic. For Windows. RootsMagic, Inc., Springville, Utah, 2010. *http://www.rootsmagic.com/*

Genelines. For Windows. Progeny Software Inc., Nova Scotia, Canada, 2010.

Generations Family Tree Software, Beginners Edition is no longer available.

Legacy Family Tree. For Windows. Millennia Corporation, Duvall, Washington, 2010, *http://www.legacyfamilytree.com/.*

The Master Genealogist. For Windows. Wholly Genes Software, Columbia, Maryland, *http://www.whollygenes.com/.*

PAF Mate: Charts and Reports for PAF. For Windows. Progeny Publishing, Inc., Wolfville, Nova Scotia, Canada.

Personal Ancestral File, Version 5.2. For Windows. The Church of Jesus Christ of Latter-day Saints, Salt Lake City, Utah, 2010, *http://www.familysearch.com/.*

Reunion: The Family Tree Software. For Macintosh users. Leister Productions, Inc., Mechanicsburg, Pennsylvania, *http://www.leisterpro.com/.*

CHAPTER 4

Why Document?

There is no life of a man, faithfully recorded, but is a heroic poem of its sort, rhymed or unrhymed.

—*Thomas Carlyle*

Have you ever said, "If I could only find that clue that led me to believe that. . . " or, "I wonder if I have already searched this book for the wife's side of the family, or did I only look for the husband's side?" For these reasons and others which follow, it is important to record the sources you use as you are searching for your family, by providing complete **citations**, **documents** and evaluations. The purpose of this chapter is to help you understand the great significance of this aspect of family research.

YOU'LL WANT TO DOCUMENT BECAUSE

- It saves time and helps you to avoid duplication of research.

- Your work is accepted as credible.

- Others who follow your lead will seek out, or provide, new resources you lack because they know where you have traveled.

- You are able to **synthesize** an abundance of information more readily when it is organized and linked to the individual or family to whom it belongs.

- If your documentation has been appropriately entered from the beginning, you will need to do very little editing when you decide to publish a book on your family.

Today's computer genealogy programs can help you document your sources as you enter your family's vital statistics, and they even enable you to attach sources to the events to which they refer. Although it is possible to do research without the aid of a computer, keeping track of documentation is the greatest benefit of a good genealogy computer program.

 Terms to Understand

ci·ta·tion - A polished reference to a particular authority; or a quoting of an authoritative source for substantiation.

 Terms to Understand

doc·u·ment - A written or printed paper that bears the original, official, or legal form of something and can be used to furnish decisive evidence or information.

 Terms to Understand

syn·the·size - To study all the facts and combine the information in your mind to form a new, more complex idea.

There are many ways to data enter documentation into your computer genealogy program, and it's important that you learn the methods and strategies that will work best for you. Remember, you're providing an important "paper trail," not only for yourself, but for those who will follow your work. Consequently, just as you will hope to find sources which will give you the information you need, you should provide the same courtesy to others by supplying:

- Complete citations, so that you or those who read your information can track down the original sources for other clues.

- What you found and what you did not find, so that you and others won't need to spend time searching irrelevant sources.

- Your evaluation of the materials, as well as the evaluation of others, so that you and others can see if your opinions agree.

- Suggestions of what to do next, in case you or others might want to continue the quest.

THE ELEMENTS OF A COMPLETE CITATION

Experienced researchers can think back to the information they hoped to receive when they were doing research. They wanted to know who wrote or gathered the information, what the information contained, when it was gathered or written, where it can be found in its original form, how it was put together, what information the document itself contained, and an evaluation of the materials based on previous research or experience. Imagine how much further along we would all be if all of these questions had been made available in the genealogies that have already been published. Such information would have streamlined the process

Items covered	Description of items covered
WHO?	The author, compiler, publisher and/or provider of the information.
WHAT?	A description of the source:the title of the book, a description of the collection, or an index to other records.
WHEN?	A specific date or span of time covered by the source, whether it is a records collection, book, film, or fiche. Example: Wills, 1834-1910.
WHERE?	The places covered by the source, as well as the addresses of the publisher, the person providing information, or the repository where the information is stored.
HOW?	The format of the source, e.g., book, film, fiche, electronic media.
THE DOCUMENT	Whether the document you used is a photocopy, scanned copy, transcript, abstract or extract.
WHY?	The researcher's evaluation, the historical background, and societal customs, all of which may provide the evidence to prove a point.

Illustration 4-1 Important Items to Include

The Complete Beginner's Guide

for all of us, permitting us to move on and discover the answers to new questions, instead of having to verify the information left by others.

In the past, not only was information less readily available than it is today, but the space available to record information was limited on Family Group Record forms. Because of this, little information regarding sources was provided. With today's technology, however, we can pretty much put in all the information we need in order to adequately document our sources. The most important items we should include in any records we produce in our genealogy computer programs are those you see listed in Illustration 4-1.

Illustration 4.1 indicates various parts of your documentary **evidence** and **analysis.** The who, what, when, where, and how describe the location, condition, format, and provider of the information. The next area is lightly shaded to refer to the act of capturing the actual document itself. Whether we make a photocopy, **extract, abstract, transcription** or scanned image of the document, we need to preserve the information in some way in order to evaluate this piece of evidence. But the last and most important item (shaded the most in Illustration 4.1) is our evaluation of the information. Why do we think that this document has solved or guided us to a conclusion in our research? What does it guide us to?

MAKING YOUR RESEARCH MORE EFFECTIVE

Record What You Have Done to Avoid Duplication of Research

Documenting your sources includes more than indicating the citations for the materials found. Your documentation should also include what was searched and not found. When you are recording your documentation, you can use a variety of places in your computer program to record what you have searched and what you have done. The locations preferred by most researchers include:

- Research planners or calendars (a sample research planner is reproduced on pages 4-5).

- Written reports.

- The "Notes" field of the computer genealogy program.

Research planners or calendars are filled out in advance of the work. They record what we "hope" to locate as we travel to various repositories. When, finally, we are able to look at the sources we have recorded on our planners, it's important to record the date of the search and the extract number; once we have done this, the planner then becomes a "table of contents" to the copies of our notes about the records we have gathered. Our research planner can also be the place where we record the code to the repository, the call numbers for the sources, the name of the individual or family for whom we're searching, what we want to find, and where we should record that information (such as under a Family Group Record) after we return home.

Document "As You Go"

Experienced genealogists will tell you that you can simplify your work if you will take the time to document each source as you record its information. And as you begin to amass information from a variety of sources, you will discover that each piece of documented information adds to every other piece, helping you to put together a much more complete picture than you thought possible.

While there is not, as yet, a universally accepted, "standard" documentation format, certain elements should always be included, such as those indicated in Illustration 4-1. Ideally, all facts and clues pertaining to an individual would be recorded with that individual as well.

Terms to Understand

ev·i·dence - Some documentary or oral statements or material objects helpful to forming a conclusion or judgment.

Terms to Understand

a·nal·y·sis - The separation of an intellectual whole into its constituent parts for individual study.

Terms to Understand

ex·tract - A passage from a document; an excerpt.

Terms to Understand

ab·stract - A written summary of the most important parts of a document.

Terms to Understand

tran·scrip·tion - A written or typewritten copy of materials, as from notes or archived documents.

YOUR TURN

Imagine, for example, that everything you knew about your grandfather, James, was recorded, as in Illustration 4-2. In your family he had always been known as James "M." Nelson, but no one knew what his middle initial represented. What does the following documentation tell you?

COMPUTER DOCUMENTATION SAMPLE

1897 BIRTH: WI, Milwaukee Co., James M. Nelson entry, Milwaukee County Births, Vol. 1, page 346, microfilm no. 1275678, item 2, Family History Library [FHL], Salt Lake City, Utah.

James M. Nelson, son of George O. and Mary Elizabeth Nelson, of Milwaukee Heights, born 4 May 1897.

1900 CENSUS: WI, Green Co., Monroe Twp, George O. Nelson household, 1900 U.S. census, Greene County, Wisconsin, population schedule, township of Monroe, enumeration district [ED] 43, supervisor's district [SD] 1, sheet 13A, line 14; National Archives micropublication T00, roll 32.

George O. Nelson, white, male, 40 years old, born Jun 1860 OH, father born OH, mother born NY, can read and write, owns home freely, occupation farmer; Ellie [Mary Elizabeth's nickname was Ellie], white, female, wife, age 38, born Sep 1862 Canada, parents born NY, housekeeper, can read and write; George, 18, born Nov 1882 OH, father born OH, mother born NY, farmer laborer, can read and write; Mary, 16, born Oct 1884 IL, father b. OH, mother b. NY, going to school . . . Monroe, son, age 3, born May 1897 WI, father b. OH, mother born Canada.

1905 LETTER: Letter from George O. Nelson to his wife, dated 14 June 1905 from Medicine Lodge, Kansas. Copy in possession of Mr. John Browning, 12566 How'd He Do It Drive, Hoe, CA 98435:

". . . Sweetheart, found a wonderful new farm outside of Medicine Lodge...will be there in two weeks with the boys to pick up the household goods . . . Jim Boy can even have a swing in the big tree we've found for him here . . . love George."

Illustration 4-2 Computer Documentation Sample

Research Planner

Remember to have only *one goal* per Research Planner.

Goal _____

_____

Surname/Subject _____   Researcher _____

Area _____   Client _____

Source Location		Description of Source	Object	Time	Remarks		
Date source searched	Library or repository & call #	(State, county, type of record, and time period of record)	(Person's name or what is sought)	(Person's age or date of event)	Comment or ID # of family	Index	File

Genealogy Research Associates, Inc., www.GRAonline.com, Phone: (801) 280-3924

Illustration 4-3 Research Planner

Terms to Understand

vi·tal re·cords - Documents which contain information about births, marriages, and deaths.

Terms to Understand

chron·o·log·i·cal or·der - Events arranged in order of time of occurrence.

Terms to Understand

time·line - A linear representation of significant events shown in chronological order.

Answers

Did you notice that:

- James was born in Milwaukee, Wisconsin on the 4th of May 1897, and lived in Milwaukee Heights.

- His family moved to Greene County, Wisconsin when he was 3 years old.

- James had two older siblings who were from a different mother. Their mother was born in New York, and his mother was born in Canada.

- His father was born in Ohio, and his paternal grandparents were born in Ohio and New York.

- His father could read and write and was financially secure, for he owned his own farm. His mother, Ellie, was born September 1862 in Canada, but her parents were born in New York.

- James had a middle name, Monroe. When James Monroe was eight years old, his family moved to Kansas. He was called "Jim Boy" and obviously liked to swing.

- By the time James Monroe was twenty-two years old, he had moved to California.

- He married Sarah Marie Brown at her home in Salinas, Monterey County, California, where he, too, was a resident in 1920.

You can see that more can be discovered about a person's life once you have recorded the full documentation, rather than simply saying, "Oh, I found him in the **vital records**, on a census, and in family correspondence."

Another miracle happens when we data enter our materials into a computer. We think of other things we could be doing to solve our problem. If we keep track of ideas and unanswered questions which evolve as we enter our documentation, the next phase of our research will be clearly mapped out.

YOUR TURN

1. Write one piece of information you hope to find as a TO DO note.

2. Enter your TO DO note at the end of your other notes, as shown in Illustration 4-4.

A Tip About Chronology

Notes entered in **chronological order** are most effective in the research process. The sequence may be a simple chronology or a complicated sequence of cause and effect. Such **timelines** help us to understand and remember

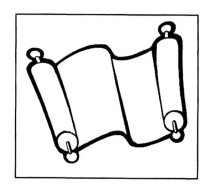

sequential relationships; they act as visual aids to promote the mental arrangement of events in their proper order; and they help us to reconstruct history. When our family timelines are accurate, they provide the maximum amount of information in the minimum amount of time. They reduce the critical elements necessary for family history—events, times and places—to an understandable conclusion.

A tip about evaluating the source: If a document is torn, difficult to read, missing parts, or in some way different from others in the same series, that fact should be noted as well. Many computer genealogy programs today allow an area to make a comment about the quality of the source, as well as what the source contained.

IMPORTANT: To be most effective as a research tool, as well as a register, notes should be comprised of source citations of the original document and complete abstracts of what information was included in those original documents.

TO DO:

1. Order death certificate in California, perhaps Monterey County, for James Monroe Nelson. Maybe it will tell the year he moved to California.

2. Search the 1910 census index for California and/or Kansas for James Monroe Nelson, via his father, George.

3. The 1920 census would give Sarah's birthplace. Maybe her obituary, in Mom's scrapbook, would tell me more. Ask Mom to read it to me over the phone.

4. What happened to the brother and sister of James Monroe? They were quite a bit older than he was, and the census says their mother was born in New York, and that James' mother was born in Canada. Did his father marry once before, in Kansas?

Illustration 4-4 TO DO notes

Terms to Understand

cite - To quote as an authority or example, to mention or bring forward as support, illustration or proof.

TRANSCRIBING AND ABSTRACTING

The beginning genealogist is often surprised to find that a source citation is not enough to document a family history. While it was customary, in genealogies written in the past, to include a minimum of information, technology has changed all that. In electronic formats, the space limitations are not nearly as restrictive as the short forms of the past. We are not only able to **cite** sources, but we can also transcribe or abstract text, keep track of the sources we have searched, and include our individual skill, knowledge and experience in a personal interpretation of the materials within our documentation.

All of this should be entered in a format which would keep all three parts distinct: the citation, the document itself (in whatever format it is recorded), and the researcher's evaluation. Transcripts, abstracts and interpretations of the record should be part of the documentation, along with the citation. Abstracting, extracting, transcribing or copying the record that you have cited into your computer genealogy program provides a valuable service for the reader or researcher who is building on your work.

Fortunately, there are guidelines to help you avoid pitfalls when you are data entering this aspect of a complete documentation reference. For example, when you are extracting the essential information, remove only the extraneous, redundant words, but keep all of the essential Who, What, When, Where, Why, and

Terms to Understand

au·thor·i·ta·tive - Of acknowledged accuracy or reliability.

Terms to Understand

un·a·bridged - Containing the original content; not condensed.

How elements. If you encounter something unusual, record it as you find it. Important: Never "correct" names, dates, signatures, spelling or punctuation; you must copy the record as you see it. You can then add any necessary explanatory remarks in brackets, which look like this: [ ]. For example, if the spelling of a word or name is unusual, or if the grammar is out of the ordinary, you may follow the word or phrase with the Latin term *sic* in brackets, signaling the reader, "I see that this is not usual, and I am noting the fact."

Ellipses

Use ellipses (three periods, with spaces between) to indicate that part of the original text is being omitted. The ellipses will indicate to any other reader that you have left out non-essential information, such as legal verbiage or redundant sentences. An example of this is found in Illustration 4-2, above, where the entire letter is not transcribed, only those parts pertaining to Jim Boy and his dad:

. . . Sweetheart, found a wonderful new farm outside of Medicine Lodge . . . will be there in two weeks with the boys to pick up the household goods . . . Jim Boy can even have a swing in the big tree we've found for him here . . . love George.

Brackets

Brackets are used to signify that material not found in the original is being added, such as a point of clarification or an alternative transcription of a hard-to-read word. A point of clarification was added to a nickname given to Mary Elizabeth in this census record from Illustration 4-2.

George O. Nelson, white, male, 40 years old, born Jun 1860 OH, father born OH, mother born NY, can read and write, owns home freely, occupation farmer; Ellie [Mary Elizabeth's nickname was Ellie], white, female, wife . . .

Evaluations, Impressions, Insights and Working Notes

Besides including basic sources to substantiate the vital information entered into individual data fields, you can use the "Notes" field as a place to enter impressions about what records to search the next time you have an opportunity to go to a repository, or to identify conflicting or missing information.

The evaluation of any document, in light of the objective or goal for using that particular document to prove a point, requires that the interpretation of data be placed either in a separate report or in a separate area of the note field in order to prevent confusion with the original document. The original document, as well as the evaluation, is likely to be used by others who will rely on your work. You could also put this information in brackets if the genealogy computer program you are using does not have a separate place to record the researcher's evaluation notes.

Because social customs and terminology have changed over time, a proper explanation of terms used in documents would be helpful. By consulting **authoritative** sources, such as *Black's Law Dictionary*, or by referring to historical information in order to understand how the definitions of phrases have shifted over time, or by examining **unabridged** dictionaries for multiple definitions, you can more accurately verify relationships and events, placing them in the context of the times in which they occurred.

Not only will citations and abstracts help others, once they are listed in their entirety, they will guide you and future researchers to other sources and lead to additional clues. As sources are constantly coming to light with the help of computer-aided inventory processes, electronic copying technologies, heightened public awareness of genealogy, involvement by businesses in disseminating information, and faster and more efficient preservation methods, many of these new sources require new citation guidelines. There are, however, certain basics with regard to source citations—the Who, What, When, Where, Why guidelines you learned about earlier in the chapter—that are unlikely to change, no matter what source or medium you use.

GENEALOGY DOCUMENTATION GUIDELINES

Several genealogy documentation guides are included in the closing bibliography. But we should remember that documentation can vary according to the medium in which it is being written (e.g., pen, typewriter, or computer), as well as the type of computer genealogy program being used (i.e., the program's features). Documentation requirements may also vary, depending on whether the information is to be published in an article, book, or electronic database, and it can vary depending on our current purposes. Often, what we start out doing (e.g., having fun entering our family into a computer program for Christmas), is not what we end up doing (publishing a history for a family reunion), and you will discover that information you prepared for one purpose is often needed for another medium or publication format.

Since this is the case, it would be extremely helpful if we could have a couple of basic sample formats for entering our sources. However, to be sure the format is what we have in mind, it's also important for us to know how the information will look when it is printed out. For example, do you want your sources to be printed directly below the individual to whom they apply, including all the source elements (the citation, the abstracted information, and the researcher's evaluation notes), or would you prefer that the citation for a major event be given as a footnote or endnote?

The Documentation Guideline forms which follow will allow you to practice in pen or pencil the recording of the information that you can eventually put into your computer program. The form entitled *Documentation Guidelines for Notes* (Illustration 4-5) is used to practice the free-form method that is my personal preference and placed in the general notes field. This would print out like the examples shown in our James Monroe Nelson example, Illustration 4-2.

The *Documentation Guidelines for Source Entries* (Illustration 4-6) provides you with a chance to practice entering sources which would be picked up as abbreviated footnotes or endnotes. Each genealogy computer program has its own formats for printing these items, but they are always linked to an event (such as birth date, birthplace, marriage date, marriage place, death date, death place, burial date, burial place, name, etc.). Rarely will a genealogy computer program allow you to include more than a few sentences under the "Comments" field, but they do allow entry for your own cautions or warning about a record. Each user will need to decide for him/herself which is best.

Whether you use a free program downloaded from the Internet, or a more robust Windows program, ranging in price from under $75, you should be sure that it contains the basic elements necessary to document sources properly.

In the general notes area, you should have the flexibility of recording your notes in any way you want. This option, however, has its good and bad points. If you enter your notes every which way:

- your final report will not be orderly;

- it won't be easy for others to read;

- you will have difficulty finding information; and

- if you change computer programs, it will be difficult to transfer your sources.

From Your Computer Screen

1897 BIRTH: WI, Milwaukee Co., James M. Nelson entry, Milwaukee County Births, Vol. 1, page 346, microfilm no. 1275678, item 2, Family History Library [FHL], Salt Lake City, Utah.

James M. Nelson, son of George O. and Mary Elizabeth Nelson, of Milwaukee Heights, born 4 May 1897.

1900 CENSUS: WI, Green Co., Monroe Twp, George O. Nelson household, 1900 U.S. census, Greene County, Wisconsin, population schedule, township of Monroe, enumeration district [ED] 43, supervisor's district [SD] 1, sheet 13A, line 14; National Archives micropublication T00, roll 32.

George O. Nelson, white, male, 40 years old, born Jun 1860 OH, father born OH, mother born NY, can read and write, owns home freely, occupation farmer; Ellie [Mary Elizabeth's nickname was Ellie], white, female, wife, age 38, born Sep 1862 Canada, parents born NY, housekeeper, can read and write; George, 18, born Nov 1882 OH, father born OH, mother born NY, farmer laborer, can read and write; Mary, 16, born Oct 1884 IL, father b. OH, mother b. NY, going to school . . . Monroe, son, age 3, born May 1897 WI, father b. OH, mother born Canada.

1905 LETTER: Letter from George O. Nelson to his wife, dated 14 June 1905 from Medicine Lodge, KS. Copy in possession of Mr. John Browning, 12566 How'd He Do It Drive, Hoe, CA 98435:

". . . Sweetheart, found a wonderful new farm outside of Medicine Lodge...will be there in two weeks with the boys to pick up the household goods . . . Jim Boy can even have a swing in the big tree we've found for him here . . . love George."

1920 MARRIAGE: CA, Monterey Co., Salinas, James Monroe Nelson, State File Number 45723, California Department of Health Services, State Registrar of Vital Statistics, Sacramento, CA:

James Monroe Nelson, age 22, and Sarah Marie Brown, age 19, both of Salinas, were married at the home of the bride, on 14 February 1920.

TO DO:
1. Order death certificate in California, perhaps Monterey County, for James Monroe Nelson. Maybe it will tell the year he moved to California.

2. Search the 1910 census index for CA and/or KS for James Monroe Nelson, via his father, George.

3. The 1920 census would give Sarah's birth place. Maybe her obituary, in Mom's scrapbook, would tell. Ask Mom to read it to me over the phone.

4. What happened to the brother and sister of James Monroe? They were quite a bit older than he was, and they said their mother was born in New York, while James stated his mother was born in Canada. Why?

General Notes Free-form Style
(see Illustrations 4-2 and 4-4)

Source Notes Step 1

Source Notes Step 2

Documentation Guidelines for Notes

Event Year	Event	Foreign Country	State/Shire
County		Town/Parish	

Title of Source

Author	Publisher		Copyright Date
Vol., Folio or ED.	Page #, House, or Line #	Repository Address or Person:	
Call #	Item #		

Abstract/Extract/Transcript/Scanned Image:

Evaluation of Materials

Documentation Guidelines for Source Entries

Source Title

Author

Publication Information

Copyright Date   Source Call #

Repository (address and telephone or person)

Individual Reference (certificate #, volume or page)

Date of Entry

Actual Text (Abstract/Extract/Transcript/Scanned Image)

Comments (Evaluation of Material)

Illustration 4-6 Documentation Guidelines for Source Entries

On the positive side, if you know the rules of good notes entry, this free-flowing open option allows you to:

- enter your notes in chronological order;

- indicate locations and dates in a way that is required for research purposes;

- copy and paste blocks of information from one individual to another;

- copy and paste blocks of information from one program to another; and

- create a place to data enter information that applies to more than one person since these notes are printed below the individual in the body of the text.

Why, then, do computer genealogy computer programs provide two places to cite sources? The most obvious reason is that individuals are unique and desire a variety of choices. But this is coupled with the possibilities available when source "fields" are set up for information. Fields can be sorted and linked to other items, as technology improves. Once information is entered into a field, it can be duplicated in other fields without more data entry. This also allows for limited standardization of sources, so that they can be brought into other programs more easily.

Therefore, once a repository such as the Oregon State Board of Health, with its appropriate address and phone number, is data-entered, it will never need to be entered again. Likewise, once a film obtained from the Family History Library containing the vital records of the parish of Viipuri, Finland is entered, it will not need to be entered again except to change the page number or the content.

All of these labor-saving features are welcome, but as you begin your family research, be sure that whatever program you select has a place for unlimited note-keeping abilities and that your notes and family vital record data can be transferred to more sophisticated programs as you move along. The most common transfer program in genealogy is called GEDCOM, and you will want to look for 100% GEDCOM compatibility in any genealogy computer program you use. In this way, the source citations that prove the vital information in your family lines, and the family data you have worked so hard to collect and record, can be automatically transferred to more advanced programs and large databases of shared information, either on disk or through the Internet.

The problem is that no two genealogy programs work the same. Therefore, a GEDCOM transfer patch would need to be made between each program that wants to communicate with another. So far, the only common transfer field between GEDCOMs is the general notes field. Therefore, many teachers opt to put all sources in the general notes field because they know their students will eventually experiment with other programs.

What if you want to be able to scan your documents and pictures into your computer genealogy program? Are there programs to do that as well? Yes. But when programs link their data files directly to their image files, scanned images quickly take up computer file space and limit the ability to send files online. I save those scanned images in a separate file that can later be copied into the genealogy computer program when I'm ready to publish something. For now, don't permanently link the image and data files.

The time will quickly come when you will publish either a Web site, a traditional book, or even make an iPod download. Since this will add to our overall understanding of an individual, it's no wonder that we want to use greater technology to capture all that we know about those we are researching. Our focus now, however, is to standardize our documentation methods, in order to produce the best possible results from our research and in our reporting.

A GUARANTEED GUIDE FOR EXCELLENT DOCUMENTATION

The steps that follow will help you to keep your documentation succinct, yet inclusive, of all pertinent information (whether you enter it at first by hand, or directly into your computer):

Steps for Computer Entry

1. Place documentation in chronological order, based on the date of the information contained within each transcript, abstract or extract--not the date of publication. So your first entry for an item should be the date. For example, if your goal is to verify the birth year of an individual, and a marriage certificate indicates that this person was born in 1847, you should begin the citation with the year of birth, not the year of the marriage certificate. Remember: the purpose for this entry is to prove documentation for the birth year.

EXAMPLE: **1847**

2. Give each event a one-word **event title** (if possible), to quickly pinpoint what events are included and what events have yet to be found (e.g., those not having a title). Again, this word should describe the event, not the source from which it originated.

EXAMPLE: **1847 BIRTH:**

3. Next, show the **geographical** location in this order: the country (if outside the U.S.), state (two-letter postal abbreviation since these can be changed automatically by the computer later to full state names), county (with the word "county," abbreviate the letters to "Co."), and town/parish/township, post office, river courses or other geographical designations. In other words, go from the largest jurisdiction down to the smallest (this is exactly the opposite of the way that information is entered into the individual entry fields in most genealogy programs).

EXAMPLE:

1847 BIRTH: OH, Hamilton Co., Cincinnati, California Twp.

1850 CENSUS: KY, Jefferson Co., Louisville, District 2.

1860 CENSUS: IN, Vanderburgh Co., Evansville, Rosse P.O.

The purpose of entering the data in this manner is to make it as easy as possible to interpret the chronological life events of an individual. The examples (which include only part of the citation portion of a complete, three-part documentation) demonstrate the ease with which a researcher may see both the years and the movement within a county, from state to state, or from country to country.

Can you see, in the example above, how the available collected notes on one individual lists a movement pattern from Ohio to Kentucky, and finally Indiana?

Terms to Understand

e·vent ti·tle – A brief introductory word or two to signify an important milestone or occurrence in an individual's life (see Illustration 4-8).

Terms to Understand

ge·o·graph·i·cal – Relating to the topography of a specific region, or to the study of physical features of the earth's surface.

Terms to Understand

im·mi·gra·tion - The act of entering a country to which one is not a native, to settle permanently.

Terms to Understand

nat·u·ral·i·za·tion - To grant full citizenship to one of foreign birth.

PRIVATE INVESTIGATOR

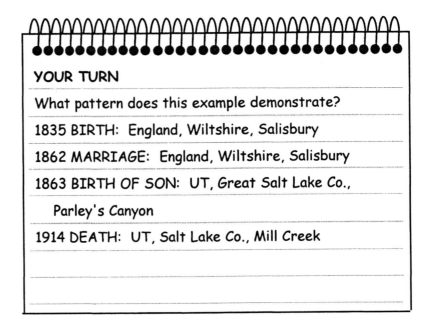

YOUR TURN

What pattern does this example demonstrate?

1835 BIRTH: England, Wiltshire, Salisbury

1862 MARRIAGE: England, Wiltshire, Salisbury

1863 BIRTH OF SON: UT, Great Salt Lake Co., Parley's Canyon

1914 DEATH: UT, Salt Lake Co., Mill Creek

Answers

Did you recognize that the "Your Turn" example portrays the movement of an individual from England to Utah, all taken from the collected notes of that person?

Calling Sherlock Holmes . . .

Notes listed in chronological order can also help you determine what sources were not searched. The next example shows you how a quick glance can suggest to a researcher other, unused, easy-to-acquire resources which should be searched to contribute evidence regarding children, dates of **immigration** and **naturalization,** previous marriages, etc.

EXAMPLE 3:

1835 BIRTH: England, Wiltshire, Salisbury

<u>1841 CENSUS: England</u>

<u>1851 CENSUS: England</u>

<u>1861 CENSUS: England</u>

1862 MARRIAGE: England, Wiltshire, Salisbury

1863 BIRTH OF SON: UT, Great Salt Lake Co., Parley's Canyon

<u>1870 CENSUS: UT</u>

<u>1880 CENSUS: UT</u>

<u>1900 CENSUS: UT</u>

<u>1910 CENSUS: UT</u>

1914 DEATH: UT, Salt Lake Co., Mill Creek

The underlined type illustrates the sources which you can research for further information. (We are not suggesting that these be entered into their appropriate place until they have actually been researched; this is only to show you how to go about discovering missing information.)

Terms to Understand

fiche - A microfiche, or a card or sheet of microfilm capable of preserving a considerable number of printed pages in reduced form.

YOUR TURN

Can you tell that the underlined items suggest that the researcher look at the 1910, 1900, 1880, and 1870 federal census records of Utah? What records should be searched in England from this brief list?

Did you also notice that a full location citation, such as "UT, Great Salt Lake Co., Parley's Canyon," is more descriptive than just Salt Lake County? Which records would permit you to search for the precise location where the individual you're researching lived?

We must learn to list the major parts of the citation, using one of the major guidelines for bibliographical formats (see the bibliography at the end of this chapter, or use as a guideline the methods of an experienced researcher). In Illustration 4-1, "Items Covered in Documentation," the various segments of the citation were described. Each one attempts to answer one of the following questions: Who? (the author, compiler, etc.); What? (description of the source which may be the title of a book, the description of a collection, or an index to other records); When? (a specific date, a span of time for this record collection—but not the event year); Where? (the places covered by this book, collection, or item, which may include a geographical location, as well as the actual repository for the item being used); and How? (book, film, **fiche,** electronic media, etc.).

Evaluate, Evaluate . . .

The "why" question is part of the evaluation process, and it is the most neglected aspect of the research process. Begin now to develop the habit of evaluating each document in light of your objective or goal; your use of that document should be included in the data entry process. Although not every item you data enter will require an evaluation statement (a marriage document obviously gives the marriage date), other entries will need an explanation (that same marriage document may list the witnesses to the ceremony, which may provide important clues to family members or close friends).

Other Helpful Tips

• All facts and clues pertaining to an individual should be recorded with that individual. (When you keep notes on different individuals, be sure to use separate sheets of paper; don't combine surnames on one page. If you have three names on one sheet of paper, under which name will you file it?)

• Keep track of ideas and unanswered questions which evolve as you record what you have found. (Use the same term again and again, such as TO DO!)

PROBLEM TO OVERCOME	POSSIBLE SOLUTION
Something unusual is found (misspelled name, wrong date, etc.)	Record the entry as you find it. Names, dates, signatures and punctuation are never corrected. Put needed explanatory remarks in brackets [ ]. *Example: "John Moore" [sic: transcription error; should be Moon]*
Document is torn, difficult to read, or has missing parts	Record the entry as you find it. Put explanatory remarks, or added material not found in the original, in brackets [ ]. *Example: "Th[omas]" or [court date was torn but the document was placed between others in the court ledger dated 1794].*
Interpretation of the data is necessary	Separate the interpretation from the actual document by entering the interpretation below the document, either all in capital letters or in a separate paragraph surrounded by brackets. Consult authoritative sources to interpret the meaning of phrases, terms of relationship, or legal terms. *Example: [The term son-in-law in his will does not mean his daughter's husband, but rather his stepson, or son "by" law, which was a meaning of the word during this time period. See* Webster's Unabridged Dictionary, *p. 1678 (. . . include full citation . . .). Further evidence: He stated he had no daughters in his pension papers].*
Document is full of redundant legal verbiage	Use ellipses . . . (three dots, with spaces between to signify that part of the original text or title is not being cited). *See sample above.*

Illustration 4-7 Rules for Entering Evaluation Comments in the Computer

- Give each Family Group Record its own ID number. You won't have to worry about this last detail if you are using the PAF program. The program automatically assigns a Family Group Record number, called an MRIN (Marriage Record Identification Number), each time you enter a family. That number appears at the center top of the record when you print information on your families, and it is titled "Family Group Record #." You should also use this number to identify items you have entered onto your research planner.

- When I return from a research trip, I place Post-It notes, with MRIN numbers, on the documents I have brought back, in order to remind myself where I should enter them. Once they are entered, I jot down, LIGHTLY IN PENCIL somewhere on the actual document (usually the upper right-hand corner), the Family Group Record (FGR/MRIN) number where I entered the data. This aids in filing the document later.

Remember to Analyze the Information You Have Gathered

- Notes listed in chronological order can help you to determine *what sources were not searched*, as well as which sources were located.

- Evaluation of the document, in light of the objective or goal (the purpose for which you searched for and copied the document), should now be undertaken.

- Although an evaluation statement is not necessary with every item that has been data entered, some documents require explanation.

SAMPLE EVENT TITLES

BIRTH	EDUCATION	OCCUPATION
BURIAL	IMMIGRATION	PROBATE
CENSUS	LAND	RELIGIOUS ACTIVITIES
CHRISTENING	LIFE EVENTS	RESIDENCE/MIGRATION
CITIZENSHIP/NATURALIZATION	MARRIAGE	TAX
COURT	MEMBERSHIP	
DEATH	MILITARY	

Illustration 4-8 Sample Event Titles

ASSIGNMENT 4: FILLING OUT DOCUMENTATION GUIDELINE FORMS

1. Use the Documentation Guideline for Notes form on page 4-10 to record, in pencil or ink, one of the sources listed below.

   A. First as a citation;
   B. Then as an abstract of the actual document;
   C. Finally, evaluate or interpret the information you have recorded.

   The repository you visited:
   Family History Library
   35 North West Temple Street
   Salt Lake City, Utah 84150

   The individual you were looking for and the record you found:
   John Bassett, age 43, male, white, farmer, real estate $ 1500, personal $ 100, born VA; Nancy, 33, f, w, keeping house, b VA; Joshua, 7, w, m, at home, b VA; Mary, 5, f, w, at home, b VA; John D., 2, m, w, at home, b VA; Charles A., 1, m, w, at home, b VA.

   The individual you were looking for and the record you found:
   Elijah D. Hundley, found in a book by George Calvin Waldrep called *Halifax County Cemeteries.* Published Nathalie, Va.: Clarkton Press, 1984. A three-volume collection. He was found in volume 1, page 188.

   Hundley Family Cemetery (Old Christ Episcopal Church). This cemetery, located on Rt. 736 north of Clover, VA, was part of Christ Episcopal Church. The graves, about 75, are unmarked, with the exception of the Carringtons. The Hundleys are in a fenced plot on the cemetery lot. "Elijah D. Hundley, B. 4 Sept 1798, D. 1 Jan 1873."

   Repository you visited:
   You were driving in Henry County, Virginia when you found a cemetery which you were later told was the Vaughn-Philpott-Morris Cemetery.

   Individual you were looking for and the record you found:
   Tombstone for Benjamin R. Wells, found in the Vaughn-Philpott-Morris Cemetery, Henry County, Virginia.

   "Benjamin R. Wells b. 20 Aug 1897, d. 8 Sept 1898."

2. Enter source notes and free-form notes under at least three different individuals in your family file.

3. Go into the general notes area for one person you are working on. Start a line with the words TO DO. Now enter a note to make a phone call, in order to ask a relative for information, or a reminder regarding a repository you heard about that might have information on this person, or some other information you want to remember.

YOUR TURN ANSWERS

Those pages not listed below are appropriate for personal preference responses.

What does Illustration 4.2 tell you about the middle initial of James M. Nelson?

The 1900 census indicates that the initial stood for Monroe because the 3-year-old boy born in May agreed with the May 1897 birth date in the birth record. The 1920 marriage certificate substantiated the census record when the groom was listed as James Monroe Nelson.

What pattern does this example demonstrate?

It indicates a movement of the family from Wiltshire, England to Salt Lake County, Utah.

What records should be searched in England from this brief list?

The 1861, 1851, and 1841 British census records for Salisbury, Wiltshire, England.

COMPUTER CHECKLIST #4

1. What keystrokes are necessary to enter "source notes" for events in your program?

2. What keystrokes are necessary to enter "general notes" for individuals in your program?

WEB SITES

http://www.msoe.edu/gen_st/style/stylguid.html
This Web site provides guidelines which follow the *Chicago Manual of Style*.

http://www.mla.org/set_stl.htm
This Web site provides guidelines for the *MLA Style Manual*.

http://www.columbia.edu/cu/cup/cgos/idx_basic.html
This Web site provides guidelines for the *The Columbia Guide to Online Style*.

WEB SITES

Citing Your Sources by Monterey Peninsula College
http://www.mpcfaculty.net/library/citing.htm

Using Modern Language Association (MLA) Format by The Purdue Online
Writing Lab *http://owl.english.purdue.edu/handouts/research/r_mla.html*

MLA Writing Style: *http://www.mla.org/style* by The Modern Language
Association*: http://www.mla.org/*

Citing Sources Electronically -
http://www.wisc.edu/writing/Handbook/elecmla.html by The Writing Center,
University of Wisconsin-Madison
http://www.wisc.edu/writing/Handbook/Documentation.html

Chicago/Turabian Documentation by The Writing Center, University of
Wisconsin-Madison
http://www.wisc.edu/writing/Handbook/DocChiWorksCited.html

Modern Language Association (MLA) Citation Guide by The Ohio State
University *http://library.osu.edu/sites/guides/mlagd.html*

Chicago Manual of Style Citation Guide -
http://library.osu.edu/sites/guides/chicagogd.html by The Ohio State University

Style Sheet for Citing Sources Electronically by University of California-
Berkeley *http://www.lib.berkeley.edu/TeachingLib/Guides/Internet/Style.html*

Assembling a List of Works Cited in Your Paper by Duke University Libraries
http://www.lib.duke.edu/libguide/cite/works_cited.htm
http://library.duke.edu/research/citing/

BIBLIOGRAPHY

Chicago Manual of Style. 14th ed. Chicago: University of Chicago Press, 1993.

Gibaldi, Joseph. *MLA Style Manual.* 2nd ed. New York: The Modern Language Association of America, 1999.

Mills, Elizabeth Shown. *Evidence! Citation & Analysis for the Family Historian.* Baltimore: Genealogical Publishing Co., 1997.

Turabian, Kate L., John Grossman and Alice Bennett. *A Manual for Writers of Term Papers, Theses, and Dissertations.* 6th ed. Chicago: University of Chicago Press, 1996.

Walker, Janice R. and Todd Taylor. *The Columbia Guide to Online Style.* New York: Columbia University Press, 1998.

Wylie, John Vincent. "Richard Lackey Died Too Soon: How to Document Modern Media and Online Sources." *In Your Ancestors' Image.* The Federation of Genealogical Societies and The Rochester Genealogical Society, 14-17 August, 1996; Rochester, New York, F-80.

CHAPTER 5

Printing Your Records

Hold fast the form of sound words.

—2 Timothy:13

Now that you have entered the individuals in your direct line (with their spouses and children), and you have started your documentation, you are ready to print your materials. Thus you can determine if your notes are printing out the way you expect, you can make corrections, and you can begin to assemble a research notebook in which to store printed documents and finding aids. One of the greatest benefits to using a genealogy computer program properly in your personal research is the ability to produce many kinds of reports using data that you entered just once.

BEFORE YOU PRINT

Do you want one of those nifty-looking family trees you've always associated with genealogical research? It can be yours at the press of a button. How about a fancy fan-style chart that looks good enough to frame? You can have that, too. Or do you want a business-like genealogical overview of current research that includes your notes and sources in order to send off to a **family association**, **genealogical society** or **fraternal** organization? It's all yours, as long as you've entered the information into your computer program. But as you will see, there are questions to ask yourself before printing. Let's consider some of these basic questions before pressing that print button:

1. What is my purpose in creating a particular document?
2. Who will see this chart or report? What information do they need in order to understand my information and to accept my research findings?
3. How do I, or my readers, expect the report to look when it's printed?
4. What information should be included? Just names? Dates and locations? Notes and sources?
5. Should I print the report to paper, display it on a screen, or save it electroni-

Terms to Understand

`fam·i·ly`
`as·so·ci·a·tion` - An organization of individuals who study and research a particular family or families. Such organizations often produce newsletters and published histories, organize "family reunions," and promote the gathering of information on their particular lines.

Terms to Understand

`ge·ne·a·lo·gi·cal`
`so·ci·e·ty` - An organization of individuals who gather to promote family history research within their locality, among a particular ethnic group, or focused on a particular subject.

Terms to Understand

`fra·ter·nal` -
Brotherly, benevolent.

Terms to Understand

cus·tom set·ting - A form on a computer program which has the ability to be adapted or modified to fit the user.

Terms to Understand

date cal·cu·la·tor - In a genealogy computer program, this calculator allows you to put in two of three dates, and the one date left out will be calculated. For example, if you enter the date of death as well as the person's age, the calculator can provide you with the date of birth. You could, likewise, enter the person's birth date and age, and the calculator would give you the date of death.

Terms to Understand

re·pos·i·to·ry list - A listing of every repository you have entered into your particular genealogy computer program.

Terms to Understand

sound·ex cal·cu·la·tor - This genealogy computer program feature converts a surname to its proper Soundex equivalent (see Chapter 14).

cally in order to send it as an e-mail or to save to a portable devise?

6. Do I want to print all of the pages of the report or only selected pages?

7. What **custom settings** are possible to add before printing?

A wide variety of reports in the form of charts, trees, data error lists, and indexes can be produced using your specific genealogy computer program. Also various research tools are possible (depending on the program you are using), but they may include some of the following: **date calculators**, **repository lists**, **soundex calculators**, research guidance features, mapping features, geographical locators, and many other options.

YOUR TURN

Explain the various keystrokes for producing the following using your genealogy computer program:

1. Pedigree Charts

2. Family Group Records

3. Descendant Charts or Trees

4. Lists

5. Research Tools (such as **date calculators**, **repository lists**, research logs, **soundex calculators**, etc.)

6. Custom Reports

PEDIGREE CHARTS

Pedigree Charts can be printed individually, in groups, or for the entire data file. You can determine how many generations to include, as well as how many generations per page – 4, 5, or 6 (six generations per page can present the problem of leaving out vital dates and places). Other options include whether to print a record ID number for each individual; whether to print a Pedigree Index (an alphabetical list of each person on the selected Pedigree Charts); and whether to include **LDS ordinance** or other custom field information. You can also opt to print Family Group Records which will correspond to the Pedigree Chart(s) being printed. Similar charts are labeled differently by different programs. See sample programs and contact information in Illustration 5-1.

Pedigree Family Group Records Only. This option will print only Family Group Records within a selected pedigree **range**–for example, from your own grandchildren to your Great-Grandfather Anderson. You simply stipulate how many generations you want, beginning with the last specific individual. This option will not print the entire Pedigree Chart(s), it will only print Family Group Records, and it includes many of the features available on Family Group Records. No Family Group Records would be printed for siblings, aunts and uncles, however.

Pedigree Index Only. This prints an alphabetical list of each person within a selected pedigree range. You specify how many generations, beginning with a specific individual.

Blank Pedigree Chart. The Pedigree Chart is printed without family records data. It is just a blank form for hand-entering information.

Ancestry Chart. This is just another name for a Pedigree Chart. Larger versions of a Pedigree Chart or Ancestry Chart can be printed to run vertically on a standard page size, or it can be printed on a larger scale (pages must be taped together after printing).

At this point in the evolution of genealogy programs, the appearance of charts and reports differ, depending on the program. Some programs offer boxes around each individual name/date/location area, as well as around the charts themselves. Other programs provide the option of shading and color within the boxes that contain names, or other ways to make charts more attractive. Some, like free *PAF 5,* have programs to enhance the appearance of printed charts and reports. *PAF Companion,* for example, converts data to a Windows format for more attractive reports and for plain charts. Once you have entered three or four generations, take the time to experiment with your print options in display mode.

Fan Charts. A fan chart is a kind of Pedigree Chart which, because of its configuration, allows many more generations of a family to be viewed at once.

FAMILY GROUP RECORDS

The Family Group Record is at the heart of every genealogical report. Without the nuclear family—father, mother and children—there is no genealogy. And if the information for that family is not accurate or complete, the genealogy as a whole cannot be accurate or complete. So it's crucial that you keep careful track of every family in your database by printing out current copies of Family Group Records for your files. When you print a Family Group Record, it may also include the following custom options:

Print spaces for additional children. If selected, this option allows the Family Group Record to be printed with empty children's sections (these fill the remainder of the page), making it possible for you to fill in "newly discovered" children, by hand, as you do subsequent research.

Other marriages listed in notes. If an individual has multiple marriages, the other spouses can be included in the "Notes" section.

Terms to Understand

LDS - An abbreviation for The Church of Jesus Christ of Latter-day Saints.

Terms to Understand

or·di·nance - Refers to baptisms, endowments, and sealings, as mentioned in Matthew 16:19, performed for deceased relatives by members of The Church of Jesus Christ of Latter-day Saints with the purpose of identifying and linking one's entire family. When used in the phrase "LDS ordinance field," it means those computer fields which record the dates of the ordinances.

Terms to Understand

range - A quantity or specific order of something, e.g., a range of MRINs would include only those MRINs selected by an individual.

Name and Online Location	Training Availability	Free Trial Versions and Cost
	Programs for Windows Users	
Personal Ancestral File 5.2 from www.familysearch.org While developed by the Family History Library (FHL), PAF is not being update in the future.	Follow the links at the home page of Complete online training available at website. Good beginning program.	Program is free at www.FamilySearch.org Available in many foreign languages. : Click on *Download PAF* on homepage
NOTE: See *FHL Affiliates* below for those programs tested to work with New FamilySearch	See www.familysearch.org for affiliate status of programs below. See New FamilySearch features in chapters 10 and 11 of this book	www.familysearch.org is free but not a genealogy computer program for individual users. Affiliates fulfill that job.
Ancestral Quest 12.1 from www.ancquest.com/orders.htm *FHL Affiliate Status*	Free Online Training for excellent review at website. Producer donated work to PAF so similiar in look and feel. Good relative coordination features.	Yes - see website
Family Tree Maker 2010 www.ancestry.com click on the SHOP button.	After buying can attending online training. Program upgrades yearly in order to be able to help clients search their databases. Program pulls in sources via ancestry.com databases	None found, upgraded yearly. If you already own older version of this program you can usually upgrade at a lower price.
Legacy 8.0 www.legacyfamilytree.com Video Tour of new features *FHL Affiliate Status*	Legacy for Beginners training online is good and available before purchase. Robust program. Program has built-in Research guidance linked to data in files.	Yes: Less functional version is free and good for overview.
The Master Genealogist www.whollygenes.com	Primer training book for TMG DVD training excellent; Super Bundle (4 DVDs and 1 CD training) Robust program.	30-day free trial, see current costs online
RootsMagic 4.0 www.rootsmagic.com *FHL Affiliate Status*	www.rootsmagic.com/overview.htm and free video training with purchase of program Program can work from a thumbdrive.	Yes, Web site gives free demo and a version with limited data & less functional ity of the full program to test out.
	Programs for Apple Users	
Reunion www.leisterpro.com for Mac OSX 10.3.9 or newer	Demo online, Forum, Reunion for iPhone	Free Demo Mode allows 50 people to be entered. Current costs are posted on their Web site

Illustration 5-1 Genealogy Computer Program Comparison Chart

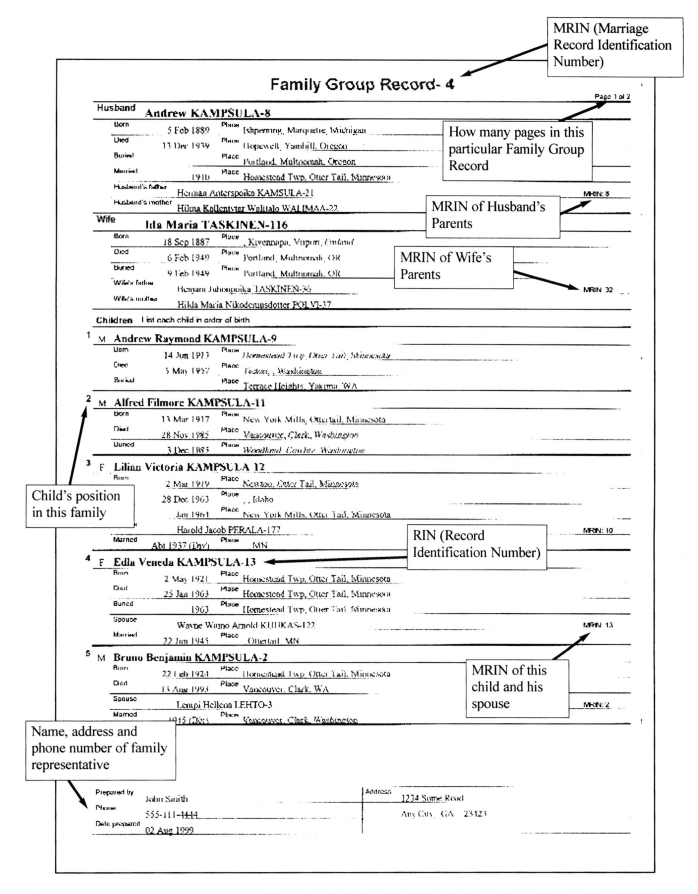

Illustration 5-2 Completed Family Group Record Printed from PAF 5

Terms to Understand

MRIN - An abbreviation for Marriage Record Identification Number.

Terms to Understand

de·scen·dant - The offspring of a particular individual.

Record Identification Numbers (RINs). A number used to identify an individual in your program. It is handy to use when you have multiple people with the same name. These can be included in any of your printouts, if you set your program preferences to include them.

Notes to Print. Programmers give various definitions to what they consider to be a note. It is good to know what your specific genealogy computer program's notes refer to and when the program will allow the notes to print. For example, your program might have general notes that serve all purposes, historical notes, research notes, and health notes. Usually you can choose to print: 1) all notes in a record, 2) only specific notes, or 3) no notes.

Sources to Print. Some programs have separate templates and/or fields for notes that will be used as sources for documentation of evidence. The templates may allow you to choose to print: 1) the the full source, 2) part of the source, or 3) no sources. If you include the full source, you may be able to select whether to include all comments, some comments, or no comments.

Print LDS Ordinance Information. The LDS ordinance information can be included or omitted on the record.

Pedigree Chart Reference Number. This option is used when you have many pedigree charts and wish to quickly locate someone. It indexes by Chart # and Position #.

Range of Family Group Records. You can print a range of Family Group Records (abbreviated **MRINs)** automatically with our without notes or sources.

Blank Family Group Records. Blank Family Group Records with or without LDS ordinance fields, are handy when you're doing research in a library.

YOUR TURN

Select the options you want for your Family Group Records and list them below.

OTHER CHARTS AND FORMS

Descendancy Chart

A Descendancy Chart shows all of the **descendants** (children, grandchildren, great-grandchildren, etc.) of a selected individual. Choose the number of generations, if you want the RINs and MRINs to be displayed, and how much detail provided on each person. An Index of Descendants is also available.

Individual Reports

This report includes an individual's name and information found in his or her Individual Report and Marriage Record, as well as all of the notes and sources pertaining to that individual. You can choose to print one or more Individual Reports, or you can choose to print only the notes when you use this option.

Printed Lists

Your genealogy computer program can generate many kinds of lists, but since each program offers a slightly different variety, it's important for you to explore what lists are available to you.

The best way to find out what each list offers is to print them out, using your own family file. In addition, many of these lists offer the same customizing options available with Pedigree Charts and Family Group Records. Below are sample lists you may find helpful on your genealogy computer program:

Alphabetical, or *Name Sorted List.* This is an alphabetical list of all individuals in a data file. It can be set up to includes each individual's record ID number, birth and/or christening date(s), death and/or burial date(s), parents' MRIN, and the spouse's (or father's) name. It can then become an index to your research notebook that could be organized by family groups.

Place Sorted List. This report lists all place names included in the data file, alphabetically, by location. Place Sorted Lists can help you check for inconsistencies in place-name formatting (e.g. Los Angeles, L.A., LA, etc.), though many programs handle formatting automatically. A Place Sorted List also provides a key to the locations of vital events for all individuals in the data file.

Source List. This permits you to print all of the sources you have cited in your data file only if you data entered your sources individually.

ID Sorted List. If your computer genealogy program provides identification numbers, you can list all records in your data file by their ID numbers.

Possible Record Problems or **data error lists** can be very helpful, pointing out possible conflicts within your records, such as a death date that occurs before the birth date, or a child's birth date which comes before the mother's birth date. You should check this feature periodically, as you add new records to your file. Some programs automatically catch the most common types of errors as they are entered.

Research Tools and Forms. Genealogy programs include many other features, such as blank forms, correspondence **logs**, research logs, relationship charts and research process forms—all helpful in keeping your research organized and written down. For example, the **relationship chart** can be used to determine the family relationships between two individuals, such as first cousins, second cousins, aunts, uncles, etc.

Custom Reports. Several programs allow you to create custom reports from data already entered. Others permits you to include additional information, or to change **fonts**, or to change frame outlines or boxes around forms and charts, etc.

PRINT DESTINATION

When printing forms or reports, you always have the option to "print" to:

1. various printers,
2. the screen,
3. a file (meaning an electronic or digital file).

When you want your materials organized in a manner that will help you analyze connections, but you don't have a printer available, **screen printing** works well. This is also particularly helpful when you want to evaluate how a new chart or form will look without wasting paper.

NOTE: When printing to the screen or preview mode, some charts and reports may only appear in pieces, because the monitor cannot display the entire report at one time (for example when viewing a wall-size chart). Use the arrow keys to view the remainder of the report.

Terms to Understand

data er·ror list - A grouping of mistaken entries put into your particular genealogy program.

Terms to Understand

log - A list of resources usually recorded after they have been searched.

Terms to Understand

re·la·tion·ship chart - A genealogy diagram which describes the familial connections between individuals.

Terms to Understand

fonts - The various typefaces, or type styles, produced by your computer program.

Terms to Understand

screen print·ing - The ability of a computer program to produce a report on the screen rather than on paper.

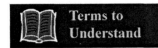

Terms to Understand

re·trieve - To open a file in a computer program, whether it was saved in that program or in a different program.

Printing to file or a portable device such as a thumb drive allows you to print and save your notes into an electronic format. and saving the data to a to a folder on your computer or portable device. This then allows you to **retrieve** the notes into a "spell check" program, if you genealogy computer program does not have one built in, to correct spelling errors and/or rearrange data which can then be cut and pasted back into your genealogy computer program.

This is also a handy feature for pulling reports into another word processing document. For example many programs produce "book" files in an .rtf (rich text file) format that can be imported into a publishing program like Adobe's *InDesign* for a professional publication look.

However other Window's based genealogy computer programs print your file with a ".prn" extension which can only be utilized by a printer (and not a program) when you select the "Print to File" option.

It is also a good idea to learn how to interrupt a print job, in case you find that you have opted to print 500 pages and you only wanted five! Don't worry: the printer may take a minute or two in order to finish printing what was already stored in its memory, so it probably won't stop right away. But it will stop.

CONCLUSION

As you will soon discover, various report formats help you analyze your family history data more effectively in preparation for setting good research goals. For example:

1. Reports containing partial localities can alert you that preliminary work needs to be done to determine the complete names of a locality during the time of an event.

2. Problem lists can alert you to erroneous dates in your program, which may require research to locate the proper resolution to the issues.

3. Approximate dates warn you that research is needed to locate the actual date of the event.

4. Alphabetical indexes can point out where you might have data entered the same family previously so that matching and merging of information is in order.

Therefore, you should practice the various print options available while you have a smaller number of names with which you are very familiar in your genealogy computer program. Due to this familiarity, you are more likely to see problems and to understand where the developer of your program has determined the output of your results should be in the reports you produce. You will then be prepared to use these results, as necessary, throughout your research and reporting experiences. Or you may decide it is worthwhile to explore different programs for other features. And that is really no problem, if you are consistent in your own work.

Many researchers use multiple programs to give them the results they desire. And most programs make it possible to import and export the majority of information, except items under notes and sources. This is why many researchers use their general notes field to enter all information because all programs accept that field. Until you learn more about publishing and sourcing, it is a good idea as a beginner to use your general notes field for entering your research notes and personal evaluation experiences.

ASSIGNMENT 5: PRINTING YOUR OWN FAMILY INFORMATION

1. Using the source notes and free-form notes you entered in Assignment 4, print out a Family Group Record, including all notes.

2. Print a copy of your Pedigree Chart.

3. Print an alphabetical list of all individuals in your family database.

YOUR TURN ANSWERS

Personal preferences are appropriate for all answers in this chapter.

COMPUTER CHECKLIST #5

1. Did you find all of the reports listed below, under #2, in your program? Make a list of additional reports that are available in your program besides those named under question #2.

2. For each report you have named in response to question #1, write down the computer command(s) necessary to access it.

   Pedigree Charts

   Family Group Sheets

   Descendant Charts or Trees

   Lists

   Research Tools (these vary greatly, depending on the program you are using, but they may include some of the following: date calculators, birthplace distribution lists, repository lists, soundex calculators, data error lists, etc.).

   Custom Reports

3. Locate the options in your program for printing to screen. What keystrokes must you use?

4. Locate the options in your program for printing to an electronic file. What keystrokes must you use?

5. Locate the options in your program for printing to paper. What keystrokes must you use?

6. Can you change the font sizes? How do you do that?

7. What type of research reports can you print with your program?

WEB SITES

http://Genealogy-software-review.toptenreviews.com
This site has good comparative charts for printing and other features of various genealogy programs.

BIBLIOGRAPHY

Rodgers, Maxine. "Writing and Publishing Family Histories." *Genealogical Journal* 15, no. 2 (1987): 50-66.

Check the online training materials for the genealogy computer programs listed in Illustration 5-4 for information on using each of these new programs.

CHAPTER 6

Your Family History Notebook

Rejoice, ye dead, where'er your spirits dwell,
Rejoice that yet on earth your fame is bright,
And that your names, remembered day and night,
Live on the lips of those who love you well.

—Robert Bridges

Now that you have printed out the materials from your first data-entry work, you will need a place to **archive** your personal family history materials. A simple three-ring binder system is quick and easy to put together and allows you to find anything in a matter of minutes if you are consistent in your filing strategies.

The purpose of this chapter is to instruct you on a unique filing system that caters to genealogy computer users who can have Family Group Record numbers and **RIN** printed on their pages. Filing pages in numerical order is much faster than filing (with duplicate surnames and given names) in alphabetical order. Plus, each Family Group Record acts as a cross-index to other pages in the notebook as shown in Illustration 6-5, and the Pedigree Chart acts as a table of contents because of cross-referenced numbers printed on them (see Illustration 6-6).

YOUR FAMILY HISTORY NOTEBOOK AND FILING SYSTEM

You can easily create a Family History Notebook by following these simple steps:

Materials Needed

(How many you need will be determined by how much information you have gathered.) Begin by purchasing the following:

1 or 2 - Two-inch, three-ring binders with see-through covers
2 or 3 - Packages of colored index tabs (8 per package)
4 to 8 - Packages of clear index tabs (8 per package) or 1 package of pre-numbered tabs 1 to 99.

 Terms to Understand

ar·chive - A place or collection containing records, documents, or other materials of historical interest; a repository for stored memories or information.

 Terms to Understand

RIN - An abbreviation for Record Identification Number used in computer programs (e.g. *Personal Ancestral File*).

Illustration 6-1 Document Protectors

Terms to Understand

`MRIN Tab` - A label on a notebook separator used to divide one Family Group Record from another. Family Group Record Numbers are also called MRINs or Marriage Record Identification Numbers in genealogy computer programs.

A RULE OF THUMB

Break down documentation whenever you cannot find something quickly.

In addition, you will need clear sheet protectors suitable for the three-ring binders to store documents. A three-hole punch will also facilitate the filing process.

YOUR TURN

1. Open the two-inch, three-ring binder.

2. Make a basic set of dividers using one package of colored index tabs. (As you need others you may add them, but A-E below provides a basic guide to your notebook(s) which will expand over the years.) Label them as follows:

   A. Research Planners (placed as a reminder to do them)

   B. Pedigree Charts

   C. Pedigree Chart Index

   D. Alphabetical Index (on some programs known as a Family Group Index)

   E. Descendancy Charts

3. Using clear index tab dividers, label them starting with the number 1 and going to at least the number 20.

You may soon have hundreds of Family Group Record (**MRIN**) **tabs**. CAUTION: *Do not try to outdo your computer program by trying to force these numbers to match a particular surname.* Just file the Family Group Record you have printed behind the MRIN tab to which it applies. (MRIN or Family Group Record 3 would be filed behind Tab 3.) You will have many more clear dividers than colored ones.

NOTE: *PAF* 5.2 no longer maintains the same MRIN numbers when you transfer or upgrade your data using *GEDCOM.* One way to get around this is to import an earlier version, such as *PAF* 4.0 to *PAF* 5.2 into *Legacy*, and click the option in *Legacy* to maintain the same MRIN numbers. PAF 5.2 is no longer being supported by *FamilySearch.org*, so you won't need to be updating it. However, you might want to move your data to a more advanced program, such as *Ancestral Quest, RootsMagic,* or *Legacy* as those programs will keep your current family group record numbers as they are generated in the program.

If you want to change the MRIN numbers when you move to these other programs, make a GEDCOM of just the families you want to move and import the file without telling the program to maintain the Family Group Record number. The family group records will start over with #1 if a brand new file, or with the next available number if you import the data to an existing file.

Illustration 6-2 Example of Pages Filed Behind an MRIN Tab

YOUR TURN

1. Add the printed charts created in Assignment 5 to your notebook behind the appropriate tabs (e.g. Family Group Records in numerical order).

2. File original documents, print-outs of census records, photographs, etc., behind the Family Group Record where the individual APPEARS AS A MARRIED ADULT UNLESS he/she never married, in which case the documentation, photos, and miscellaneous materials pertaining to that individual would be filed behind the parents' Family Group Record.

Miscellaneous completed Research Planners, abstracts, notes, copies, etc., that do *not* tie in at the moment to a specific Family Group Record, are filed under colored tabs in a section behind the numbered tabs or in a separate three-ring notebook as your records expand. They are filed under surname tabs or locality subdivisions if there are too many documents to place under one surname. For example, a hundred pages of notes on CANNON families (some from Montgomery County, Virginia; some from Henry County, Virginia; and some Virginia with no county as yet known), could be filed behind tabs labeled *Cannon, VA, Montgomery; Cannon, VA, Henry; and Cannon, VA Rule of thumb: break down documentation whenever you cannot find something quickly.*

Mixed surnames on the same page of a compiled history, a census or book index, and other combined locality sources would be kept under tabs by locality (e.g. NC, Hyde Co, Histories). Once an item has been determined to apply solely to one Family Group Record, however, file it behind that record so you can find the information on each person quickly.

Illustration 6-3 Tabs by Counties Filed Behind MRIN Tabs or . . .

YOUR TURN

File miscellaneous completed Research Planners, abstracts, notes, copies, etc., that do NOT tie in at the moment to a specific family group record under colored tabs behind the clear numbered tabs or in a separate 3-ring notebook. File them under surname tabs or locality subdivisions.

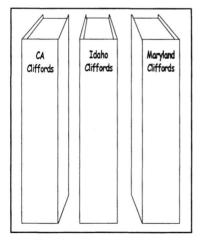

Illustration 6-4 . . . Separate Notebooks for Miscellaneous Papers

Terms to Understand

Name Sort·ed Lists – Groups of individuals arranged in various ways by given name or surname, in order to accomplish some purpose such as locating and separating into two groups a similar surname. For example, all the American-born side of the family called themselves Kampsula, while the Finnish-born side called themselves Kamsula (see Illustrations 6-5 and 6-6).

A computer-generated family history notebook is arranged so that you can quickly locate not only direct-line families but collateral lines and those not related (as yet) individuals who are in the process of being researched. *Your genealogy computer program cannot assist in your analysis if it doesn't have all the facts.* Therefore, don't forget to add everyone to your database from your family materials.

The reports filed behind the first five colored tabs act as a guide to all family groups in your Family History. As thousands of names are added to the Family History, you will find that many people have the same names. This is why it is so helpful for the computer to automatically assign the RIN to each person. (The RIN number is to the right of the individual's name in *PAF*.) The program can also produce **Name Sorted Lists** to help you keep track of the individuals you have entered into your program, their birth and death years, and their spouse or parents' names.

Also, as people are connected to families, an MRIN is assigned to each family. This number becomes the Family Group Record number as well. The families in your notebook are in numerical order, according to their Family Group Record (also known as MRIN). This MRIN number is given directly to the right of the marriage date in the Pedigree Chart in *PAF* (see Illustration 6-6). So, for example, <u>if you wish to locate the brothers or sisters of any direct-line individual, all you need to do is turn to the numbered tab which has the same number as that listed across from the marriage date on the Pedigree Chart.</u>

YOUR TURN

File the appropriate forms behind the appropriate tabs (e.g., Pedigree Charts behind the Pedigree Chart tab).

A. Research Planners

B. Pedigree Charts

C. Pedigree Chart Index

D. Alphabetical Index

E. Descendancy Charts

PEDIGREE CHARTS

Pedigree Charts list in order the parents, grandparents, great-grandparents, etc., as far as is known for the person listed as #1 (to the left of the name) on Pedigree Chart #1. See Illustration 6-7.

Every person on the chart is given a chart number, which is to the left of the person's name. So person #1's maternal grandfather would be 6. Person #1's father would be 2. The blank chart, prenumbered, would look like Illustration 6-7.

As individual families go beyond the four generations found on the standard Pedigree Chart (or in other words, beyond #1's great-grandparents), a new chart is assigned for each great-grandparent. Now person #8 will be found on Chart No. 2, person #9 on Chart No. 3, etc. The chart number is indicated in the upper right-hand corner.

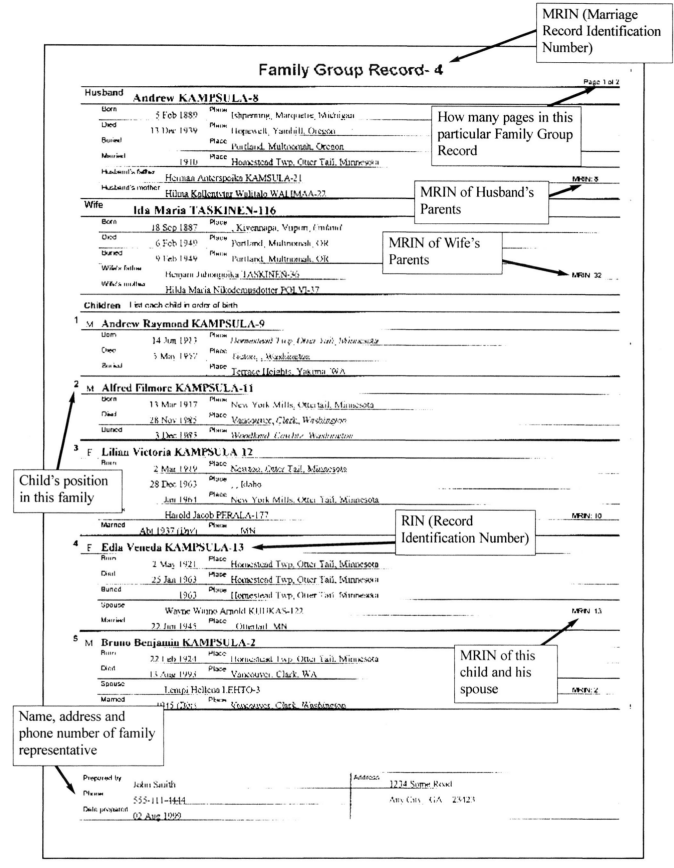

Illustration 6-5 Completed Family Group Record Using PAF

Pedigree Chart

Chart no. 1

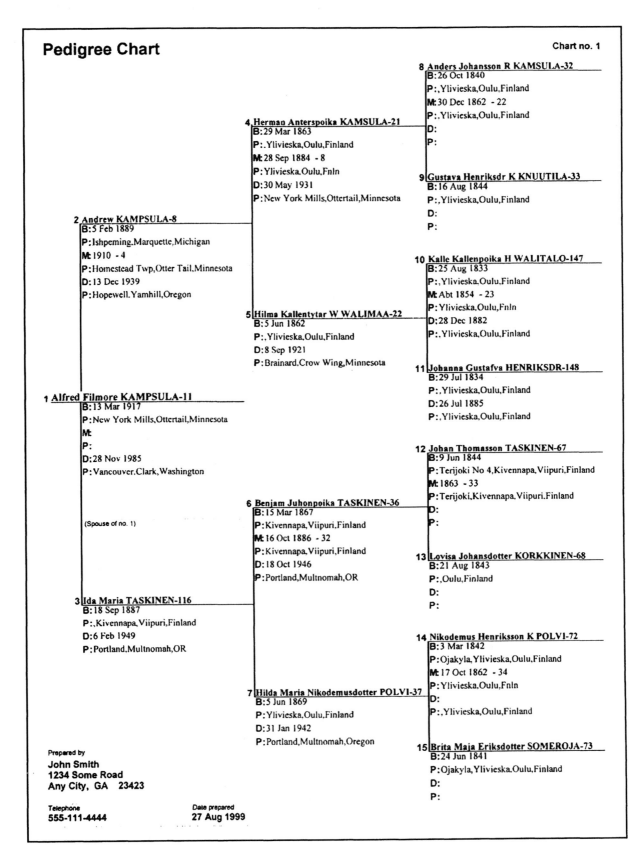

8 **Anders Johansson R KAMSULA-32**
B: 26 Oct 1840
P:, Ylivieska, Oulu, Finland
M: 30 Dec 1862 - 22
P:, Ylivieska, Oulu, Finland
D:
P:

4 **Herman Anterspoika KAMSULA-21**
B: 29 Mar 1863
P:. Ylivieska, Oulu, Finland
M: 28 Sep 1884 - 8
P: Ylivieska, Oulu, Fnln
D: 30 May 1931
P: New York Mills, Ottertail, Minnesota

9 **Gustava Henriksdr K KNUUTILA-33**
B: 16 Aug 1844
P:, Ylivieska, Oulu, Finland
D:
P:

2 **Andrew KAMPSULA-8**
B: 5 Feb 1889
P: Ishpeming, Marquette, Michigan
M: 1910 - 4
P: Homestead Twp, Otter Tail, Minnesota
D: 13 Dec 1939
P: Hopewell, Yamhill, Oregon

10 **Kalle Kallenpoika H WALITALO-147**
B: 25 Aug 1833
P:, Ylivieska, Oulu, Finland
M: Abt 1854 - 23
P: Ylivieska, Oulu, Fnln
D: 28 Dec 1882
P:, Ylivieska, Oulu, Finland

5 **Hilma Kallentytar W WALIMAA-22**
B: 5 Jun 1862
P:, Ylivieska, Oulu, Finland
D: 8 Sep 1921
P: Brainard, Crow Wing, Minnesota

11 **Johanna Gustafva HENRIKSDR-148**
B: 29 Jul 1834
P:, Ylivieska, Oulu, Finland
D: 26 Jul 1885
P:, Ylivieska, Oulu, Finland

1 **Alfred Filmore KAMPSULA-11**
B: 13 Mar 1917
P: New York Mills, Ottertail, Minnesota
M:
P:
D: 28 Nov 1985
P: Vancouver, Clark, Washington

(Spouse of no. 1)

12 **Johan Thomasson TASKINEN-67**
B: 9 Jun 1844
P: Terijoki No 4, Kivennapa, Viipuri, Finland
M: 1863 - 33
P: Terijoki, Kivennapa, Viipuri, Finland
D:
P:

6 **Benjam Juhonpoika TASKINEN-36**
B: 15 Mar 1867
P: Kivennapa, Viipuri, Finland
M: 16 Oct 1886 - 32
P: Kivennapa, Viipuri, Finland
D: 18 Oct 1946
P: Portland, Multnomah, OR

13 **Lovisa Johansdotter KORKKINEN-68**
B: 21 Aug 1843
P:, Oulu, Finland
D:
P:

3 **Ida Maria TASKINEN-116**
B: 18 Sep 1887
P:, Kivennapa, Viipuri, Finland
D: 6 Feb 1949
P: Portland, Multnomah, OR

14 **Nikodemus Henriksson K POLVI-72**
B: 3 Mar 1842
P: Ojakyla, Ylivieska, Oulu, Finland
M: 17 Oct 1862 - 34
P: Ylivieska, Oulu, Fnln
D:
P:, Ylivieska, Oulu, Finland

7 **Hilda Maria Nikodemusdotter POLVI-37**
B: 5 Jun 1869
P: Ylivieska, Oulu, Finland
D: 31 Jan 1942
P: Portland, Multnomah, Oregon

15 **Brita Maja Eriksdotter SOMEROJA-73**
B: 24 Jun 1841
P: Ojakyla, Ylivieska, Oulu, Finland
D:
P:

Prepared by
John Smith
1234 Some Road
Any City, GA   23423

Telephone
555-111-4444

Date prepared
27 Aug 1999

Illustration 6-6 Completed Pedigree Chart Using PAF 4.0

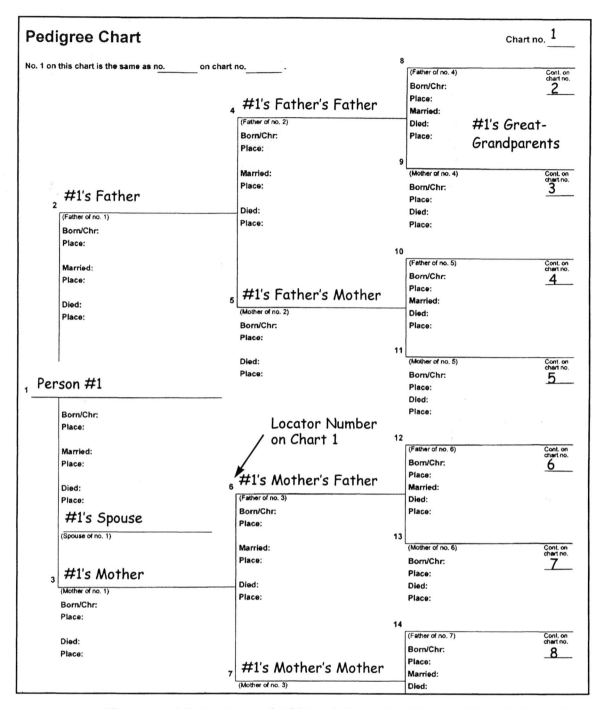

Illustration 6-7   Position and Additional Charts Identified on a Blank Pedigree Chart

PEDIGREE CHART INDEX

By the time you have traced a family back eight generations, there are 135 different surnames on the Pedigree Charts alone (unless cousins marry). Therefore, the next tab in the Family History is the Pedigree Chart Index. The names are given in alphabetical order on this index, and each Record Identification Number or RIN is shown immediately to the right of each person's name. Also the year they were either born or christened, died or buried is provided to help you select the person you are seeking.

The chart number is then listed, which is the number in the upper right-hand corner, as indicated in Illustrations 6-6 and 6-7. The person's number on that particular chart is then listed. Remember that the chart number appears to the left of the person's name, while the RIN number is to the right of the name.

Finally, the person's parents' Family Group Record number, or MRIN, is given to aid you in locating further information. In some computer programs, such as *PAF*, the Pedigree Chart default option is set not to print the index. Therefore, it won't even show as an option unless you go into your Report options and change that default.

Name	RIN	Born/ Chr	Died/ Bur	Chart Number	Person Number	Parent MRIN
BROWN, John E.	421	1854	1921	1	5	4
CHATWIN, William	13	1902	1992	1	3	2

Illustration 6-8   Pedigree Chart Index

YOUR TURN

Print a copy of a Pedigree Chart Index from your computer program. Is your index as described here, or is there a difference in your computer genealogy program's index? What differences do you see?

ALPHA INDEX OR FAMILY GROUP SORTED LIST

If there are 135 parents and grandparents by the time only eight generations are listed, you can imagine how many aunts, uncles, cousins, brothers, sisters and in-laws are included. Fortunately, an easy-to-use, every-name index is available. It has different names in different programs, such as Alphabetical Index, or Family Group Sorted List.

Since all of your direct-line people, as well as the majority of your collateral lines, will appear on at least two Family Group Records, one as a child and one as a parent, this list can help locate them.

Terms to Understand

De·scen·dan·cy Chart - A list of the off-spring and their chil-dren for one particu-lar individual.

YOUR TURN

Print a copy of an Alphabetical Index from your genealogy computer program.

DESCENDANCY CHART

While Pedigree Charts list direct-line ancestors from the present person back to the earliest ancestor, **Descendancy Charts** start with the earliest ancestor on a line and come to the present. All related people in the computer files are includ-ed, such as nieces, nephews, step-children, etc. On a Descendancy Chart, a per-son's RIN is given to the right on *PAF* and those programs using the same option, but the birth, christening, or death date is also given (e.g., PERSON-875 as shown in Illustration 6-9.)

To the left of each name on a Descendancy Chart is a number indicating what generation removed an individual is from the starting ancestor. (Note: The let-ters "sp" mean "Spouse.") Many of these charts, such as those in the *Family Tree Maker* programs, can be customized to contain as much information (including the birth, marriage, and death dates and locations) as you desire.

```
                        DESCENDANCY CHART

Date Chart Printed                              Page of Chart
------------------------------------------------------------------
1-- Oldest PERSON-989 (1669)
    2-- Oldest Person's Eldest SON-877 (1695)
      sp-Oldest Person's Eldest Son's WIFE-876 (1698)
        3-- Oldest Person's GRANDSON-875 (1740)
          sp- Grandson's WIFE-945 (1745)
            4-- Oldest Person's Grandson's DAUGHTER-766 (1771)
            4-- Oldest Person's Grandson's 2nd DAUGHTER-767 (1773)
        3-- Oldest Person's 2nd GRANDSON-876 (1742)
```

Illustration 6-9 Descendancy Chart Printout

(This would continue for as many generations as you wish, or to the end of the computer genealogy program's files.)

YOUR TURN

Print a copy of a Descendancy Chart from your geneal-ogy computer program.

Once you have this printed out, it would complete the files to be placed behind the five colored tab indexes at the front of the Family History Notebook (see Illustration 6-11). Let us now look at the Family Group Record layout.

FAMILY GROUP RECORDS

As you can see in Illustration 6-5, Family Group Records contain many numbers. These allow for an easy cross-reference to any other record in the collection. See if you have discovered the key to using the numbers printed on the MRIN records, also known as Family Group Records.

YOUR TURN

Using Illustration 6-5, identify the following:

1. The MRIN for this family is number _____.

2. The Andrew Kampsula, who was born in 1889, has a Record Identification Number of _____.

3. The Andrew Kampsula, who was born in 1889, is the son of _____.

4. The Andrew Kampsula, who was was born in 1889, would be found as a child on MRIN number _____.

5. Ida Maria Taskinen would be found as a child on MRIN _____.

6. Edla Veneda Kampsula, RIN 13, would be found with her husband on MRIN _____.

7. Bruno Benjamin Kampsula, RIN _____, would be found with his wife on MRIN _____.

8. Who is the wife of husband of Edla Veneda Kampsula? _____

Also, you may have noticed that much more room is allowed for each location field so words do not have to be truncated as they might need to be on Pedigree Charts. The biggest advantage to Family Group Records is the opportunity to print out all your source notes, comments, and TO DO lists. (See Illustration 6-10.)

Family Group Record

Husband
> **ANDREW KAMPSULA**

Wife
> **IDA MARIA TASKINEN**

Notes

Andrew Kampsula provided the date and place of his birth on his children's birth certificates. His parents were recent immigrants from Finland when he was born in Ispeming, which is located in the upper peninsula of the state of Michigan, in the county of Marquette. There his father worked in the lumber and mining industries as he waited to become a U.S. citizen so he could apply for a Homestead. His parents were located on the following U.S. federal census records:

1900 CENSUS: Minnesota, Otter Tail Co, Homestead Twp, T-1053-85 Vol 39 Ed 144, line 12, sheet 5:

Andrew Kampsula, son, white, male, born Mar 1890, age 10, single, born Michigan, Fa born Finland, Mo born Finland.

1910 CENSUS: Minnesota, Otter Tail Co, Homestead Twp, ED #9, sheet 3A:

Andrew Kampsula, age 21, single, born Michigan, parents born Finland, occupation farm work, home farmer.

His marriage information came from the personal knowledge of Alma Niemela, Andrew's sister who was present at his wedding in Herman Kampsula's home. They were married by Rev. Nissila. The marriage record is stored in a bank vault in New York Mills, Minnesota, in custody of the Apostolic Lutheran Church, but I have not been able to get permission to look at it.

I wrote the family history of Andrew Kampsula with that of his son, Bruno. But one little glimpse into his life from that book was that Andrew would dance around with Ida, his wife, if she was mad at him to get her over the anger. Ida had a stroke when the children were young which paralyzed her face. She later recovered. Andrew was very mild mannered. Ida did the disciplining. Andrew died of lung cancer in Portland, Oregon, just months after moving there from Minnesota, on the advice of doctors. He was buried at the Lincoln Memorial Cemetery in Portland, where his wife, his daughter-in-law, Helen, and other members of his extended family are also buried.

TO DO

1. Pull in the family history stories from the previously published works into this database.
2. Locate pictures of Ishpeming, Michigan.
3. See if the Lutheran marriage certificate can now be obtained.

Illustration 6-10 A Printout of Family Group Record Notes

Terms to Understand

ta·ble of con·tents - Provides a listing of the chapters or other divisions at the front of a book, database, or other compilation, along with locator guides, such as page numbers.

Terms to Understand

an·ces·try - The people from whom you are descended, i.e., your parents and grandparents.

Terms to Understand

Ahnen·ta·fel Charts - Lists of direct-line ancestors displayed by generation in a basic numbering formula, in which an individual's paternal (father's) lines are two times the number of the child, and the maternal (mother's) lines are two times plus one the number of the child. The word Ahnentafel comes from a German word meaning "Ancestor Table."

OTHER TABS

For research purposes, many other charts and forms are possible, but they may or may not be included in your **"Table of Contents"** in the front of your personal Family History Notebook. Use those most helpful to your person research. Some charts would include:

Ancestry Wall Chart
Ahnentafel Chart
Place Sorted Index
RIN Numbers in Order
MRIN Numbers in Order
Individuals with Notes
End-of-Line Individuals
Possible Data Entry Problems
Duplicate Individuals
Surname Frequencies
Incomplete Ordinance Forms

YOUR TURN

Experiment with your computer program by printing out various formats and filing them, as directed above.

CONCLUSION

This Family History Notebook will be constantly expanding. Not only will it record ancestors long gone, it will record more recent events. It is a good idea to periodically update the information in your binder(s), as people are born, pass away, marry or move. Just pencil the information in as you learn about it and later update your files.

There are a great variety of forms which may be created by you, the genealogy computer operator, to help visualize or solve research problems. Also, many documents, lists, notes, letters, etc. contain information that involve many families that are of the same surname, or that are connected to that surname by marriage, geography, religion, etc.

Those that apply to a specific family are filed at the back of the correct Family Group Record after the notes (see Illustration 6.2) If the information belongs to multiple family groups of the same surname they would be filed behind a colored SURNAME tab as shown in Illustration 6-11). When necessary, due to the volume of information you have collected, you can break down materials even further into smaller units, such as a particular surname in one state or one county as shown in Illustration 6-3 or in different binders as shown in 6-4.

You will also find papers in your possession with multiple surnames but in one locality such as when you search a death index for everyone who died in the same state. Those can be filed under state-wide locality tabs for multiple surnames.

Now, take all the information completed in the YOUR TURN sections and assemble your Family History Notebook, as explained in Assignment 6, and label the spines with the number of Family Group Recordsincluded in that volume as shown in Illustration 6-11 inset.

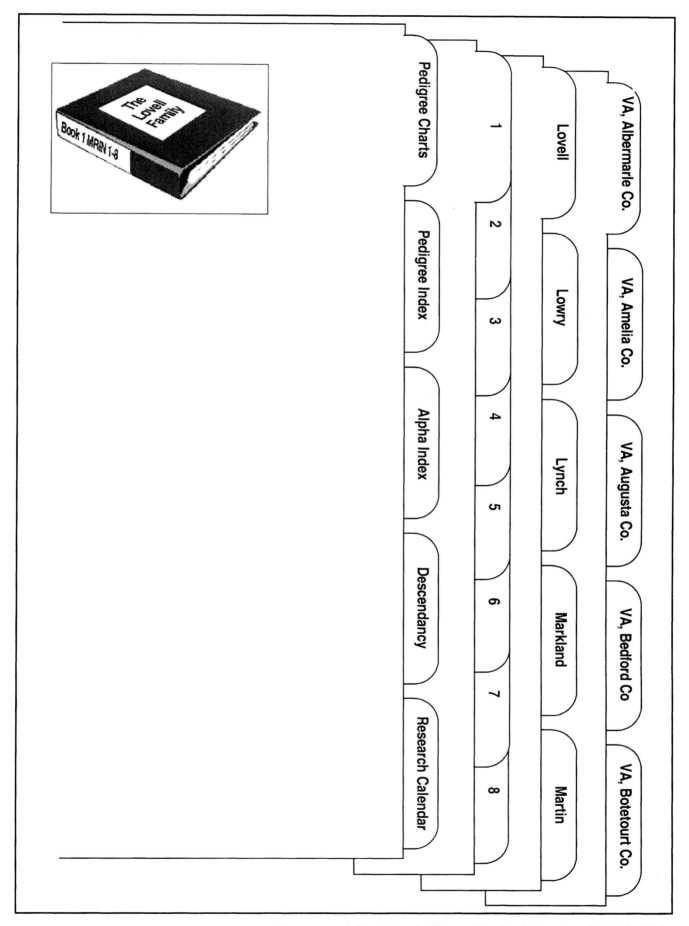

Illustration 6-11 A Family History Notebook (inset) with Labeled Tabs

ASSIGNMENT 6: ASSEMBLING YOUR FAMILY HISTORY NOTE-BOOK

1. File your Family Group Records, any documentation pages, copies of documents, pictures, and originals (in acrylic sleeves) behind the appropriate clear Family Group Record tab in the family history notebook according to chapter instructions. Each Family Group Record is filed behind its own MRIN number, which cross-indexes to each other record.

2. File the Pedigree Charts, Pedigree Chart Index, and miscellaneous surname materials, as indicated in Chapter 6, behind their appropriate colored tabs.

3. Make a title page to slip behind the clear cover of the notebook, and then make a spine cover to indicate the Family Group Record series that appear in this notebook. You may be very creative in designing your own personal cover. Don't forget to add your own name as the compiler.

YOUR TURN ANSWERS

Analyzing the Family Group Records

Page 6-10 answers:

1. The MRIN for this family is number 4.
2. The Andrew Kampsula who was born in 1889 has a Record Identification Number of 8.
3. Andrew Kampsula born in 1889 is the son of Herman Anterspoika KAMSULA and Hilma Kallentytar Talitalo WALIMAA.
4. Andrew Kampsula born in 1889 would be found as a child on MRIN 8.
5. Ida Maria Taskinen born in 1887 would be found as a child on MRIN 32.
6. Edla Veneda Kampsula, RIN 13, would be found with her husband on MRIN 13.
7. Bruno Benjamin Kampsula, RIN 2, would be found with his wife on MRIN 2.
8. Who is the husband of Edla Veneda Kampsula? Wayne Waino Arnold KUUKAS.

COMPUTER CHECKLIST #6

1. Computer programs can produce various reports that help in the filing and retrieval process. Look at your program for such options, and list them here.

2. Describe how each one can help you.

WEB SITE

http://www.FileYourPapers.com
This Web site presents free information on setting up your genealogy computer program in *PAF*, *Legacy*, *Ancestral Quest*, and *RootsMagic* as well as other programs that can produce family group record numbers so that you can file as explained in this chapter.

BIBLIOGRAPHY

Ames, Stanley Richard. *How to Write and Publish Your Family History Using WordPerfect® DOS Versions 5.1 and 6.0.* Interlaken, New York: Heart of the Lakes Publishing, 1994.

CHAPTER 7

Developing a Sense of Our Ancestors' Environment

A normal adult never stops to think about problems of space and time. These are things which he has thought about as a child. But my intellectual development was retarded, as a result of which I began to wonder about space and time only when I had already grown up.

—*Albert Einstein*

Genealogists, it turns out, also think a lot about space and time. Like Einstein, we continue to wonder about who we are, where we came from, and what forces of time and space came together to create us and our current **environment.** We understand that our lives and the lives of our ancestors are both the creations of our history and the creators of history for the next generation.

In addition, as we learn more about who our ancestors were and how they lived, we come face-to-face with this great truth of history: *history is the product of the relationship between time and events, in sequence.* The challenge for us as genealogists is to uncover that relationship and the way it functions in the lives of our ancestors. And when we begin to follow the clues to our ancestors' lives, we may discover a sequence which is a simple chronology—a puzzle easily solved. On the other hand, those clues may lead us to a complicated cause-effect scenario, complete with genuine mysteries, fascinating stories, and surprises we never dreamed of.

 Terms to Understand

en·vi·ron·ment - The circumstances and complex social and cultural conditions that surround an individual.

 Terms to Understand

se·quence - The following of one thing after another; an arrangement that is related or continuous.

Terms to Understand

dec·ade - A period of ten years.

Terms to Understand

cen·tu·ry - A period of one hundred years.

Terms to Understand

e·ra - A period of time as reckoned from a specific date, which serves as the basis of a chronological system.

Terms to Understand

Pre-Rev·o·lu·tion·ar·y per·iod - American history prior to 1776.

Terms to Understand

ma·ter·nal - Related through one's mother.

MAPPING YOUR ANCESTORS' LIVES

Einstein wouldn't be a bit surprised to learn that, in order to discover the events in our ancestors' lives, it is necessary for us to develop two key traits: a sense of historical time and a meaningful knowledge of historical periods.

If you can determine the basic time concepts, such as the year, the **decade,** and the **century** that included the events in your ancestors' lifetime, then capture the historical events of that **era** on paper, you will be able to use this information to help plot, or map, your family's activities.

Such a study is made easier by the fact that certain periods in time are naturally divided by historical events. The most significant of these for U.S. researchers include the **pre-Revolutionary** period, the Westward Movement, the Civil War era, the two world wars, and the Great Depression; in fact, you may already know about the effects of one or more of these events on your own family. Since trade, travel, education, and the price and availability of real estate are affected by great historical events, and each individual family is therefore affected to some degree by these forces, you can see that it's important to understand the events that occurred during the times in which your family was living.

YOUR TURN

In order to make good use of the ideas you jotted down as you did your data entry and to add to your "TO DO" lists, here are examples of the kinds of questions a good researcher should ask.

What do you really know, for example, about the place your **maternal** grandfather was born? You were told he was born in such and such state, but in what town? In fact, what do you know about all of the people who appear on your Pedigree Chart? What has been substantiated in your family history? Begin the process of substantiating the facts in your family history by writing down one thing that you do not know about a geographical locale for one of your ancestors.

The development of such a sense of geography and chronology begins at a very basic level—we must constantly evaluate and re-evaluate our information. For example, think about what you know about the geographic locality of all those ancestors you have entered on your Pedigree Chart. If your answer is "Not much," or "Those details didn't seem very important," then you need to pay particular attention to the next exercises.

Most of the time, records are filed, catalogued and located at the *county level* in the United States with the exception of **independent cities**–such as Richmond, Virginia, and towns within the New England states (Massachusetts, Connecticut, Rhode Island, Vermont, Maine, and New Hampshire.) Therefore, you need to know the county jurisdictions in non-New England states and you need to know the towns in the New England states. Other countries have similar procedures. In the British Isles, Europe, Mexico, South America, and Scandinavia, for example, you must identify a parish or village name because vital records and church records are kept at the local level. Road **atlases,** maps (both current and historical), and **gazetteers** are all methods whereby we can find the names of counties and towns as they exist today.

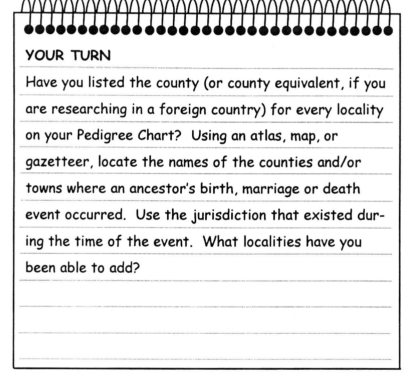

YOUR TURN

Have you listed the county (or county equivalent, if you are researching in a foreign country) for every locality on your Pedigree Chart? Using an atlas, map, or gazetteer, locate the names of the counties and/or towns where an ancestor's birth, marriage or death event occurred. Use the jurisdiction that existed during the time of the event. What localities have you been able to add?

Perhaps the map you consulted does not show the town in question. At times like this, a **postal directory** or **shipping guide** is helpful because they list all of the little localities that are not listed on maps. We must once again re-evaluate the county formation date for the location we have just obtained. For example, if you were to look at a map or gazetteer for a particular locality, published close to the time of the event you are researching (these are also known as historical maps and gazetteers, if they were made to show an earlier time period), you might find that the locality name has changed. This is very common everywhere, and yet records are kept at their original point of creation.

Since many place-names have changed over the years, there are several resources for obtaining the original name for a locality. *The Handy Book for*

Terms to Understand

in·de·pend·ent cit·ies - Cities which are self-governing and free from affiliation or control by a county jurisdiction.

Terms to Understand

at·las - A collection of maps in book form.

Terms to Understand

gaz·et·teer - A geographical dictionary or index; which contains word descriptions of localities, including population, distance from large towns, how to get there, what the town is known for, etc.

Terms to Understand

post·al di·rec·to·ry - A book containing an alphabetical listing of post offices.

Terms to Understand

ship·ping guide - A book containing an alphabetical listing of places to which items could be transported by wagon, ship, train, etc.

YOUR TURN

Were the counties and towns you recorded on your

Pedigree Chart actually in existence at the time of the

birth, marriage, or death events? List an event (birth,

marriage, or death) for one of your grandparents or

great grandparents and include the name of the loca-

tion at the time of that event using the sources just

mentioned.

Genealogists, the *Map Guide to the U. S. Federal Censuses, 1790-1920,* and *Ancestry's Red Book* are three basic genealogy books which provide this information.

Once you find the name of the county where an event occurred, you must find out from which other county it may have been formed. This original county is called the "parent" county. If the parent county was formed after the date of the event, then you must look at the county from which that parent was formed and so forth until both the county and date range match. In the documentation area of your genealogy computer program that is connected with the person you are researching, or on a copy of the print-out for that person (to be data entered later), you should enter or write a note about the county's formation, so you will not have to look it up again. If you have no idea where your relative came from, consider who else in your family might have that information and record that information on your "TO DO" list.

YOUR TURN

In the documentation area of your genealogy computer

program connected with the person you are research-

ing, enter or write a note about the county's formation

for the event in the previous "Your Turn" assignment.

Becoming a Better Family Historian

Have you noticed that the terms "genealogy" and "family history studies" have been used rather interchangeably thus far? Many people do not know the meaning of the word *genealogy* and this can cause a great deal of misunderstanding. The following incident happened a few years ago, but it is a perfect illustration of the kind of thing that can happen.

We had arranged for commercial bus transportation, and the driver had been notified to pick up fifty enthusiastic genealogists at 7:00 a.m. sharp for a field trip to various repositories. Many of these family historians were elderly, and they gingerly stepped aboard the bus with briefcases, totebags, and notebooks in hand. Because they were dressed for speed and efficiency at the repositories we were visiting, some wore cobbler's aprons, some had on sleeve guards, and some sported fanny packs.

Our driver, I later discovered, had misunderstood the communication involving who he was picking up. He thought we were "geologists" and was amazed at the agility of the group of "rock collectors" who boarded his bus, as well as at their attire. But imagine our driver's confusion when he heard, "I hired a professional to eliminate one of my grandparents. He charged me $3,000. One thousand dollars for the report and $2,000 to have it hushed up."

After a chuckle, another "geologist" retorted, "I've been trying unsuccessfully to dig up my great-grandfather for over twenty years. Do you think they'll have him at Sutro Library?" And across the aisle, someone leaned over and asked me, "Karen, if you'll run down the Wheelers, I'll pay you double."

By this point, our driver must have thought he was chauffeuring a busload of desperadoes. After the bus pulled up in front of San Francisco's wonderful Sutro Library, the driver expressed his confusion, and we all had a good laugh over the misunderstanding. But it was quite understandable. There are always new words and phrases when you approach a new field of study.

In Chapter 1, we briefly looked at the distinction between the terms genealogy, with its greatest concern being primarily kinship and matters of descent, and family history, which we consider an extension of genealogy, but with more depth. "Meat on the bones," is what we called it. As you move back in time in your family history studies, you will be continually confronted with terms and localities of which you may not be aware. The personal family historian is interested in all aspects of time and place that affect his subjects. He or she doesn't just identify ancestors. The family historian tries to answer why they did what they did, where they went, what routes they took to get there, the political conditions of the time and place, and other seemingly insignificant aspects of the environment, such as words that were common but are unusual to us (this is why a good dictionary becomes invaluable). You begin to see that people, places, their language and customs really are inseparable. This is why it is so important to obtain an environmental perspective on our ancestors' lives.

Terms to Understand

Sut·ro Li·brar·y – One of the ten largest genealogical libraries in the United States. It is located in San Francisco, California.

YOUR TURN

Look at Illustration 7-1, "Environmental Influences on Research," and ponder the history surrounding the individual you selected to study for the previous two "Your Turn" assignments.

1. What world, national, state, county or local events were impacting upon his or her life?

2. Could these events provide clues to further research? Identify two areas of research that you can add to your TO DO list, as a result.

3. Might these same events have impacted upon his neighbors? How?

4. If one individual's records were lost, could not his neighbor's records provide insights? If so, how?

A GEOGRAPHICAL PERSPECTIVE

While history provides part of the background to a person's life, geography provides an even clearer picture. For example, knowing that rivers were the early "highways" of this nation, and that they were probably one of the ways your ancestors traveled, makes knowing their whereabouts important. Why? Because the records providing clues about your ancestors will be found among the documents originally recorded along the banks of these well-traveled rivers, and such original sources may be only counties removed from where you know your ancestor lived.

ENVIRONMENTAL INFLUENCES ON RESEARCH

	INFLUENCES	IMPLICATION ON RESEARCH
	TOPOGRAPHY Land configurations, waterways, and geographic barriers affected settlement and movement of individuals.	Finding family dwellings and later migrations involves an understanding of specific geographical settings for families being studied.
	JURISDICTION The power, right or authority exercised by an individual or governing body, to legislate, interpret, and apply civil and religious law.	Civil and religious records are maintained by different jurisdictions. Knowing where to find these important genealogical records is half the battle in family history research.
	LIFE EVENTS Occurrences in most individual's lives involving their family, government, religion, social interactions, and private affairs.	Life events took place in specific jurisdictions, during specific time periods in the existence of individuals, and often involved other associates.
	TIME Life events occur during specific time periods. People marry at certain ages, have children soon thereafter, may serve in the military during certain time periods, etc.	Maintaining records chronologically, and comparing the results with history, directs the researcher to jurisdictional events, specific locations, and original records.
	HISTORY Accounts of many individual life events and individual involvement with others constitutes "history."	Studying the history of specific periods of time leads to associations, relatives, motives for movement, involvement in common enterprises, and new sources to search.

Illustration 7-1 Environmental Influences on Research

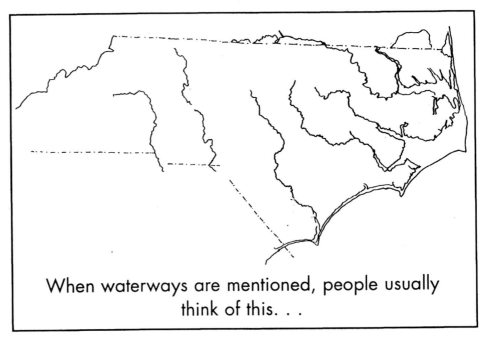

When waterways are mentioned, people usually think of this. . .

Illustration 7-2 Map with Simple Waterways

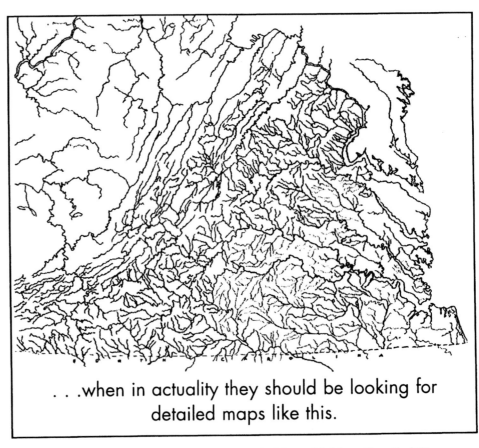

. . .when in actuality they should be looking for detailed maps like this.

Illustration 7-3 Map with More Detailed Waterways

People in the past were not very different from people today. If a town was closer to home, even if it was over the state line, it was probably the place where your ancestors' family shopped, attended church, or even filed property records. Similarly, if a mountain stood between their village and the next, your ancestors may have decided to travel by boat to a church in a neighboring parish, much further in miles, but quicker and easier to reach.

In addition, since people took the path of least resistance to handle their daily chores, these very movements may have contributed to actual jurisdictional changes in county and state boundaries. So while your ancestor may never have moved, his records might be found in several areas depending on the religious or political jurisdictions under which he lived. Consider this example from North Carolina, as described by historian Dr. Adelaide L. Fries, in writing about the Moravian community of Wachovia in North Carolina:

> The Moravians selected their lands in Anson County; they settled in Rowan County; they went through the Revolutionary War in Surry County; they lived through the War of 1812 and the Mexican War in Stokes County; they experienced the Civil War in Forsyth County—and they always stayed where they started! (Extracted from a letter dated April 17, 1941 from Adelaide L. Fries, Archivist, to Mrs. Braun.)

Finally, events played an important part in each person's life. The death of a spouse might cause a movement elsewhere. Wars, fires, floods, drought and hostile neighbors could provide a "push" away, while lower living costs, the promise of free land, or the encouragement of friends might have caused a "pull" to another area.

The Value of Maps

Where our ancestors were, *when* they were in a particular place, and *why* they were there all tell us a great deal about the conditions of their lives. And that is why, as genealogists, we must learn to think not only about time, but also about space. As a consequence, successful genealogists know that it's important to study geographical maps of the areas where our ancestors lived and traveled. Maps often provide us with "the picture that is" worth a thousand words, both in terms of the events and forces that motivated our ancestors.

Maps not only help us to understand movement patterns and interpersonal relationships, but they also help us to recognize the significance of causes and effects, both in terms of geography and in terms of the times in which they were living. But first, you must know what to look for in the maps you are studying, and you must find maps that reflect the period you are interested in.

It's important to look first at a map's **legend** in order to understand the distance between the localities being examined. That information can then be combined with what we know about the modes of travel available at the time, along with a sense of the speed of that travel. As you study maps for clues, be sure to watch for features of the landscape that might also have *facilitated travel*— canals, navigable rivers and railroads, for example. While it may appear at first glance that the Hartmann and Young families couldn't possibly have met in 1852 because one family lived in New York and the other in Ohio, a quick map study will tell you that the two states are actually less than fifty miles apart at one point. In addition, a researcher who consults a map can see at a glance that Ohio and New York are connected by the nineteenth century's version of a freeway--a navigable waterway. And since the Hartmanns lived in the northeast corner of Ohio and the Youngs lived in the far northwest corner of New York, both along the shore of Lake Erie, our researcher would be able to see right away that a meeting between members of the two families was entirely possible.

Terms to Understand

leg·end - Definition of symbols listed on a map.

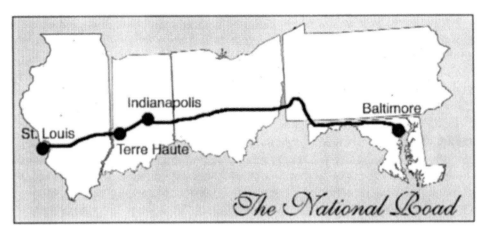

Illustration 7-4   Map of the National Road

Similarly, you will also need to look for mountains, rivers, or other natural *barriers to common travel.* As an example, let's take a look at the Thompsons and Odells whose Western North Carolina villages appear to lie only ten miles apart. In this case, a researcher can't assume that the two families could meet in the middle, since a closer study of the map will reveal a high and densely forested range of mountains between the two villages. As a consequence, travel from the Odells' village to the Thompsons' village would have required a journey *around* the mountains and rivers--over 150 miles.

But our ancestors were not so easily discouraged. When the opportunity to trade or the chance to settle on new land presented itself, people found alternate routes around the obstructions, and this is why information about routes, such as navigable rivers, valleys, mountain passes and coastal routes is important for us to know about.

The road to Pittsburgh, for example, became a major artery of travel, and its value to travelers was increased by the easy descent of the Ohio River. And the National Road (also called the Cumberland), which ascended the Potomac in Maryland, extended across southern Ohio and ended at Vandalia, Illinois, provided one of the shortest routes to the west.

As a result, the National Road was one of the most heavily traveled routes in the nineteenth century. When it came to travel, then, our hardy ancestors were not very different from people today. They followed the easiest, safest, fastest routes they could find, just as we do, and as a result, most people crowded on to the same rivers and roads, just as we do today.

How do people find the fastest routes to a destination today? Right! They use the Internet to find maps, to plot their route, and to find unknown locations. You can use the Internet in your research as well. Visit the Websites listed at the end of each chapter. Learn other methods for using the Internet in your research under "Resources" at *www.graonline.com.*

The World Wide Web is the most convenient "repository" available from your home, school, or place of work for accessing the information available on historical maps, understanding the meaning of historical terms, and locating time lines of historical events. The Internet should become your powerful assistant to locating background information on your ancestor's environment.

YOUR TURN

1. On a contemporary map, locate the path of the National Road.

    a. What is it called today?

    b. Through what states does it pass?

2. Locate the Ohio River.

    a. Through what cities does it pass?

    b. Where does it end?

3. What does this tell you about its importance as a major route of travel?

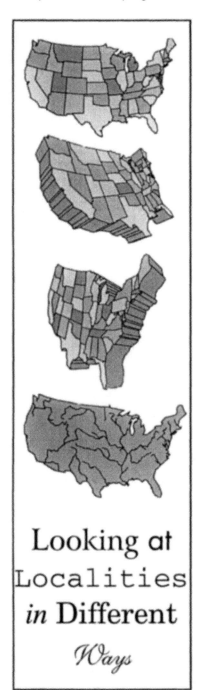

Looking at Localities *in Different* *Ways*

Illustration 7-5 Looking at Localities in Different Ways

On the Hunt for the Vanishing Ancestors . . .

Although each of our ancestors' moves from one place to another presents new challenges, the fact that people traveled the same routes may make it easier to trace their journeys, even across the continent. Let's imagine that your ancestors disappeared from Pennsylvania after one census and turned up on a land record in Illinois, six years later. Knowing this much, you can be pretty sure that they followed a proven route, like the National Road, to reach their goal. So when you're trying to figure out where your ancestors might have been in the years between the Pennsylvania census and the Illinois land purchase, the most likely places to look would be along one of those heavily traveled routes.

The Effectiveness of Maps

One reason maps are so effective is that the information they provide can be more appealing and easier to understand than pages of text. When maps are accurate, they provide a maximum amount of information in a minimum amount of time. Historical maps and atlases are my favorites. They reduce the critical elements necessary for family history--events, time, and place, to an understandable conclusion.

Maps also show features that may have existed during key historical periods, but which no longer exist. An example is the network of canals that existed through much of the eastern U.S. At one time, it was possible to travel, using canals, from upstate New York to Southern Ohio. Yet if you look for those canals on a current map, you won't see them. With the advent of faster and cheaper modes of transportation, travel by canal fell out of favor and the canals fell into disrepair, so that only remnants of this great system remain. A good historical map would tell you about where this canal system was located and even provide the dates it was active. Therefore, information about your ancestors can actually be obtained from maps as they become sources of information as well as devices for understanding events.

Illustration 7-6 Map of New York Canals

Good maps portray changes such as migration, emigration, immigration, transportation, and the growth of towns. They provide an area for research, the shape of the land, and how its topography might affect movement and, thus, the locality of records. So a good map can provide not only a place for your research, but also insights into what that place is like. Since history is time in recorded sequence, maps illustrate an event before it happens and after it happens, and they help us to understand the consequence of various incidents. This is graphically

illustrated by looking at the dramatic changes illustrated in a topographical map
of Mt. St. Helens, before and after its 1980 eruption.

Some Historical Background

Some of the first maps produced on this continent were of the coastal areas,
since ships plying the Atlantic between Europe and America provided the lifeline
that kept isolated settlers connected to British and European civilization. In addition to the arrival of new settlers, goods of all kinds were shipped across the
Atlantic, and they were paid for by the export of American furs and other natural
resources.

Because ships and their cargo were so important to the fragile society in
America, shipwrecks were disasters of major proportions, and those on both
sides of the Atlantic were anxious to minimize the risks. So map makers were
engaged, early in our history, to provide accurate maps to sailors so that ships
could arrive safely. Imagine being commissioned to draw the coastline of
America with none of the technology we have available today. This is why you
may not find old maps of the area you are seeking without considerable, or at
least directed, effort.

Away from the coast, early maps served dual purposes: military and political. George Washington, a surveyor himself, understood that accurate maps were
important for military campaigns, and he used his knowledge during the
Revolutionary War. While military mapping was not pursued with vigor until the
Civil War, and while many small, local surveys were quietly being conducted as
towns were established and public lands opened up, there were also some noted
early survey projects: the Lewis and Clark explorations in 1803, the Zebulon
Pike expedition to the Rocky Mountains in 1805, and several geologically-orient-
ed field trips to the Ozark Mountains in the 1830s. In the 1850s, formal surveys
for wagon roads, railroad routes to the Pacific and international boundaries were
begun. During the Civil War, an unprecedented demand for maps strained the
resources of the government. Defense surveys were performed around major
northern cities, and they played important roles in Grant's campaign at Vicksburg
and Sherman's march to the sea.

Illustration 7-7   The First Transcontinental Railroad, 1869

Terms to Understand

pla·ni·met·ric map - A flat map showing no physical attributes of the land.

Terms to Understand

top·o·graph·ic map - A map showing physical attributes of the land.

YOUR TURN

1. Choose a small town where your ancestors settled and write down the town, county, and state.

2. Now locate the town on a U.S. Geological Survey (USGS) or other topographical map. (Many such maps are available on the Internet: go to http://www.usgs.gov.)

3. Either make a photocopy, print it out, or describe in detail, giving the names of features such as lakes, hills, and other towns that are nearby.

Then, because of the westward migration following the Civil War, a great need arose for detailed information about the resources and natural features of the country. And as national, state and county boundaries changed, those, too, had to be mapped. In 1881, Congress authorized and financed a twenty-year program which, over time, became the U.S. Geological Survey. Having relatives engaged in engineering by the government, I've seen the equipment and pictures of the strenuous activities necessary to map this country.

Anyone involved in Tennessee research can tell you about the great changes brought about by the establishment of the Tennessee Valley Authority in 1933. But before those changes were put into effect, the government had to have map coverage of the entire area. **Planimetric** maps of the area, using five-lens aerial photographs and radial-line plotting methods, filled this need. **Topographic** and planimetric maps are very helpful for those doing Tennessee research.

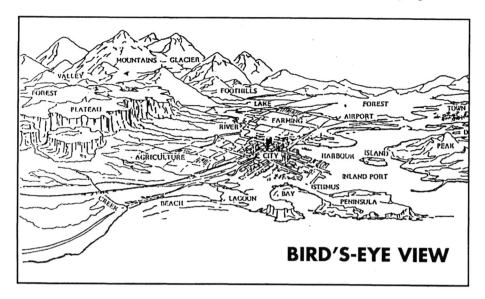

Illustration 7-8 Bird's-eye View Style Map

Illustration 7-9 Topographical Map

HOW TO USE MAPS EFFECTIVELY IN YOUR RESEARCH

In this section, we'll explore some of the ways that maps can provide a knowledge of topography, jurisdictions, historical background, and clues to available sources. No map on its own can provide all of the information you need to solve a specific genealogical problem, but your use of maps can become part of a back-and-forth, reciprocal process with original documents. Original documents, such as census, legal and church records, usually provide more substantive information. But maps act as invaluable guides to help us interpret the information we gather, just as our knowledge of the history of the place and era we're researching helps us interpret the information we find in maps.

Before you begin to study a map, *always* read the explanatory information provided about it. If the map has been published in a book, you will often find that information in the book's Foreword or Introduction. If the map is not part of a book, you will find the explanatory information located in one or more corners of the map itself along with the map's legend, scale and list of abbreviations.

Terms to Understand

dem·o·graph·ic – Relating to the study of the characteristics of human population, size, growth, density, distribution, and vital statistics.

YOUR TURN

Locate a good map of the United States and record below the kinds of information it provides, such as:

1. What features are shown in the legend?

2. What measures does it use for distance?

3. What other information does it provide?

Often, collections or series of maps cover specific topics, such as religious migrations, the historical background of a region, or occupations. These publications are filled with rich bibliographies of source materials which can aid the family historian in finding information and sources. Some maps are even developed with the help of **demographic** studies, and as part of the information they provide, contemporaries of your ancestors may be listed. Ultimately, *maps relinquish their secrets best to those who are best equipped to appreciate their information,* so the most powerful combination is the use of maps, historical texts, and original documents.

As a researcher, try to establish relationships between what you see on the map and what you know about an event. Make contrasts and comparisons. Seek to establish patterns of sequence and movement.

Maps Most Beneficial to Genealogists

There are several types of maps which are most beneficial to genealogists, including those which:

- depict the topography of the surface of the earth, so that we can understand how geography might have affected the movements of people,

- portray *political jurisdictions* created by government so we know where to find records,

- illustrate *religious boundary divisions* which might be affected by topography, or politics, so we can ascertain the location of church records,

- outline the stage upon which our ancestors played out their lives, including all the above, as well as occupational pursuits, distances from trading posts, and migration trails.

Maps Depicting Topography

Events are easier to understand when the nature of a place is known.
Physiographic maps illustrate with colors and symbols, features such as elevation, population, or rainfall. They indicate why the Rocky Mountains were a formidable barrier to land travel and commerce, and why the deserts had no great concentration of population until air conditioning and water were available. It is not surprising, then, to see the cradle of civilization in our country centered around seacoasts, waterways, valleys, and plains. Favorable environments attracted early settlers.

Terms to Understand

phys·i·o·graph·ic map - A map that uses colors and symbols to illustrate elevation, population, and rainfall.

Illustration 7-10 The United States During the Revolution

Maps Depicting Political Jurisdictions

The early sovereigns of Europe possessed confused ideas about the size of this country and the location of its rivers and resources. It is not surprising, therefore, that their patents and grants of land overlapped, causing confusion and conflicts generations later. Seeing the maps that were drawn at the time helps us to understand the disputes that arose. When a map points out the boundary of another country, this guides us to resources in other nations which may solve our research problems.

In the early years of America, as populations grew and people learned more about the land, it was not uncommon for boundaries to shift, place names to change, and one governmental jurisdiction take over for another. The result was that *our ancestors may have thought they were living in one place, while in fact, they were actually in another.* For example, George Campbell and his family lived for some years on a farm in the newly formed county of Schuyler, Illinois. At some point, the county line was shifted slightly, and the Campbells discovered that they had "moved" to neighboring Hancock County, even though their farm had remained at the same physical location. A map or series of maps which show the boundary shift might be the only way a researcher could tell for sure what had happened 150 years before.

It's also important that you *establish relationships* between jurisdictional conflicts on the large scale (national and international) and your own research. The early power struggle over America reveals the impact of European politics on our ancestors' efforts to hold on to their newly formed colonies and territories. The earliest maps of America show France and Spain with grand discoveries in America, while England claimed only a small cluster of colonies. However, as history points out, the very concentration of settlement becomes a source of close support when struggles with other nations began. While other nations extended themselves over more land than they could manage and ultimately lost their foothold on this continent, the English colonies survived, and the French and Spanish languished or failed altogether.

As some foreign governments relinquished their lands, ownership by individuals was a major factor in the growth and significance of federal power. Therefore, we would expect many records to be kept at a federal level, and we could reasonably expect that they might include the names of our ancestors. Cargo routes from many coastal ports guide us to immigration paths, and maps would show us those. The appearance of forts on those maps could indicate the blocked thrusts of competing nations over such items as furs and skins, and it would suggest the recording of militia or military records which might include your ancestors. Maps, then, represent the changes in political boundaries and, through dating, show us the approximate dates of these movements and events.

Maps Depicting Historical Geography

Maps of historical geography reveal the difference between today's culture of instant gratification and the stretch of time it took for mail to travel from one coast to another when the nation was young. For example, to make distances easier to travel involved the efforts of hundreds of thousands of people, including our ancestors, who provided the labor to build the roads, canals, and railroads. So maps showing the development of these arteries infer the existence of occupational records in certain localities.

Since transportation was more difficult at higher elevations, migration trails developed on rivers, down valleys, passes, and along the coast. Frontier towns became important points of supply for those traveling westward. For a time, steamboats became more important than roads, and then canals became cheaper for moving goods than steamboats. All of these changes are recorded on maps. So maps that depict historical geography show the movements of a restless people going off to new locations, causing conflicts with existing residents, starting brush wars, arriving at solutions—all of this resulting in the cycle of changed boundaries and jurisdictions.

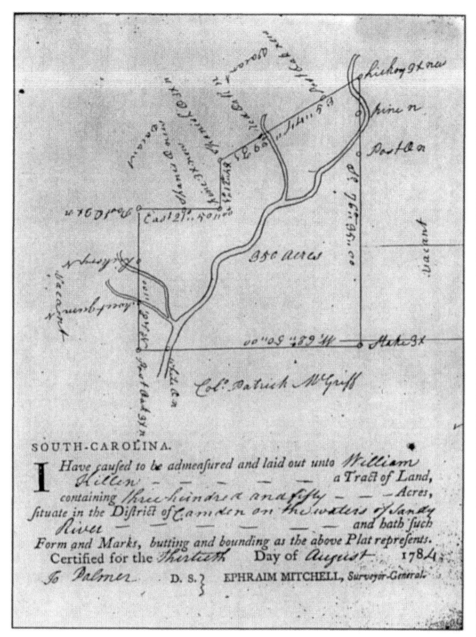

Illustration 7-11   Land Survey Map

Terms to Understand

`town·ship map` - A descriptive outline sketch of land boundaries with the owners' names written on each section so that neighbors can easily be seen and each owner's distance from other places can be calculated.

Terms to Understand

`mil·i·tar·y dis·trict` - A division of an area administered by the armed forces sent there to protect the area.

Terms to Understand

`ca·das·tral map` - A survey map relating to land boundaries.

Other Resources

As we trace the growth of the nation, especially in the Midwest, **township maps** help to distinguish one area from another. When they are used with county histories, these maps help to plot the proximity of one family to another. In the South, **military district** maps, **cadastral** maps, and **land surveys**, used in conjunction with land and property records, provide important clues for locating otherwise obscure information, such as the maiden names of female ancestors.

Terms to Understand

`land sur·vey` - Determines the boundaries, areas, and elevations of the earth's surface by means of measuring angles, distances, riverways, and neighbors.

Terms to Understand

fire in·sur·ance map and bird's-eye view – Sketched drawings which show how the details of a town, or surrounding area appear from above.

Terms to Understand

ses·sion – A meeting of a legislative body for the purpose of transacting business.

Illustration 7-12   Township Map

In New England, town maps provide clues for migration movements and the location of records. In Europe, historical maps and gazetteers, used together, provide parish and religious data which can, in turn, help you to locate vital records on your ancestors. These European maps also provide information on political boundary changes and census enumeration districts, which help locate families in unindexed sources. For many of the same reasons, **fire insurance maps** and **bird's-eye view** maps provide a great deal of help to those doing urban research.

Just as it's important to understand the foundation principles in genealogy, it's also important to understand the original sources which form the basis for the marvelous electronic genealogy mapping aids we now have available. Today, more than ever before, you can find thousands of maps, both on the Internet and drawn by computer programs. But, as in all things, the result may not be what you expect or need. For example, the electronic map might be far less detailed than you need, or it might focus on a time period that is not helpful to your particular research. This is when you find yourself asking, "Where did the originals come from?" And then you will be glad that you know how to locate and understand the original sources and how they work. With this background, you will then be able to go back and check the original sources.

Laws created during specific legislative **sessions** are the chief authorities for county creations, changes and boundary descriptions. By carefully reading these session laws from the colonies, territories and states, maps evolved. The laws, previous maps, and other primary and secondary sources added to the creation of new historical maps. This long study resulted in few sources as conclusive as the *Historical Atlas and Chronology of County Boundaries, 1788-1980*, by John H. Long. In five volumes, it condenses the study of laws and county formations to help historians and others understand the jurisdiction of records. Sometimes, maps covering the exact location you are concerned with are in error. By returning to the session laws, you might be able to determine the true location, and thus jurisdiction, for the creation of the record you seek.

By taking that information a bit further and placing the information into electronic format, we have the development of a computer program which depicts, year by year, each boundary change, chronologically. **Animap**™ is the best-known jurisdiction mapping program for the computer, and it is a great aid to the genealogist. Combined with the original maps of the area we are studying, we can then compare the information from both with our research findings. These original maps are located in major university libraries, state and federal archives, Family History Centers, microfilm and microfiche collections available in public libraries, and on the Internet.

Terms to Understand

Animap™ - A computer mapping program showing the changes in jurisdictional boundaries over time.

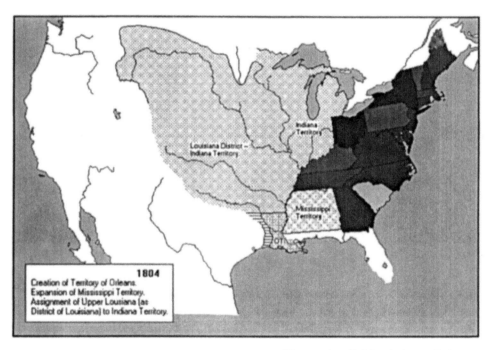

Illustration 7-13   Animap Printout

YOUR TURN

1. During what period of time did your ancestor (the individual you used as the example for the previous exercise) live?

2. Approximately when did your ancestor's parents marry?

3. When was your ancestor born?

4. How old was your ancestor when a major historical event occurred? What was the event?

5. Can you identify when your ancestor moved from one place to another?

A CHRONOLOGICAL PERSPECTIVE

A chronological study of your ancestors' lives can also help you find out what happened to them during those six years between the census in Pennsylvania and the land purchase in Illinois. One way to develop a sense of chronology is to *enter your notes in chronological order*. This way, your information will be most effective in the research process.

Time lines of events also help us understand and remember sequential relationships. They are visual aids that seem to promote the mental arrangement of events in their proper order. Think of these examples: presidential elections, major national wars since the American Revolution, the development of the railroad across the nation, the movement of Native Americans from the East to the

West along the Trail of Tears. Each one of these is a major touchstone in American history, and mentally arranging events in your ancestors' lives in relation to them helps you to see not only their place in that history, but the impact of major events on their movements and choices. There are several sources available to aid in compiling a time line of your family. Some are included in the chapter bibliography.

AMERICA'S INVOLVEMENT IN WAR

Colonial Wars

King Philip's War, 1657-76
King William's War, 1689-97
  European name: War of the Palatinate
Queen Anne's War, 1702-13
  European name: War of Spanish Succession
King George's War, 1744-48
  European name: War of Austrian Succession
French & Indian War, 1754-63
  European name: Seven Years' War

Revolutionary War, 1775-83

Post-Revolutionary Wars

War of 1812 (President Madison), 1812-14
Indian Wars (several presidents), 1817-58
Mexican War (President Polk), 1846-48
Civil War   (President Lincoln), 1861-65
Spanish-American War (President McKinley), 1898

Modern Wars

World War I (President Wilson), 1917-18
World War II (President Roosevelt), 1941-45
Korean War (Presidents Truman & Eisenhower), 1950-53
Vietnam War (Presidents Kennedy, Johnson, & Nixon), 1961-73
Persian Gulf War (President Bush), 1991

Presidents were involved in wars and so were your ancestors . . . in one way or another.

Illustration 7-14   America's Involvement in War

Cause-Effect Relationships

Once you begin to mentally place your ancestor within these time periods, you are ready to recognize the possible causes for, and the effects of, his or her actions. Let's imagine that you know your earliest ancestor in America was a member of the denomination known as the Quakers. You know he settled in Pennsylvania, but you don't know where he was before that. However, in the course of your research you learn that the Quakers of that period were forced, because of their beliefs, to leave the predominately Catholic area of Maryland and go to Pennsylvania. Aha! Now you know to check for that Quaker ancestor in Maryland during the period prior to his settling in Pennsylvania.

YOUR TURN

1. In the text example, what is a possible cause and what is a possible effect in the life and movements of the Quaker from Maryland?

2. See Illustration 7-14 on "America's Involvement in War." Do you see any dates when one of your male ancestors would have been between 16 and 30 years of age? Identify the ancestor and describe the event.

3. What does this suggest about what your ancestor might have been doing during all or part of this period?

4. How would this have affected his family's well-being?

Conclusion

Since every event takes place both in space and in time, each occurrence has an historical, chronological and a geographical aspect, and these can be better understood with maps of the time and place. Chronological arrangements of events (as outlined in Chapter 4) also provide a sequential relationship for events–"maps" of a different kind. Developing an environmental awareness of your ancestors' history will also result in greater success in locating sources for solving research mysteries as you will discover in the following chapters.

ASSIGNMENT 7: ORGANIZATION OF HISTORICAL EVENTS

Part I: Organization of historical events, as well as vital records, is important. Organization conserves the mind for other tasks. Furthermore, events in history may affect your research goals if you are aware of them. Select one ancestor. Try to answer these questions about his/her life. If you don't know the answer to the question, use the sources indicated below the question to find the answers.

1. When was the town you are researching organized?
   (County histories give this information.)

2. When was the county in which the town lies established?
   (*The Handy Book for Genealogists* and *Ancestry's Redbook* give this information.)

3. When did the state receive statehood?
   (The sources under #2 answer this question.)

4. What counties was your county formed from?
   (The sources under #2 above or the *Map Guide to the U.S. Federal Censuses, 1790-1920* can help.)

5. What groups of people lived in this town, this county?
   (County histories give this information.)

6. What motives attracted settlers to this area?
   (County histories, state histories, and general U.S. histories can help.)

7. What religion or peculiar local customs did the people of this town, or county, have?
   (County histories, state histories, and general U.S. histories can help.)

8. Did any major war take place during the lifetime of the ancestor you are studying?
   (County histories, state histories, and general U.S. histories can help.)

Part 2: Once these questions are answered, the dates which are involved and the event should be placed in the documentation area for the individual upon which you are concentrating your efforts. Have you become aware of other sources for finding information on this ancestor?

YOUR TURN ANSWERS

Analyzing the Environment

1. On a contemporary map, locate the path of the National Road.

   A. What is it called today? Hwy 70.

   B. Through what states does it pass? Illinois, Indiana, Ohio, Pennsylvania, Maryland.

2. Locate the Ohio River.

   A. Through what cities does it pass? Paducah, Illinois; Evansville, Kentucky; Owensboro, Kentucky; Louisville, Kentucky; Warsaw, Kentucky; Maysville, Kentucky; Covington, Kentucky; Cincinnati, Ohio; Portsmouth, Ohio; Gallipolis, Ohio; Marietta, Ohio; Moundsville, West Virginia; Wheeling, West Virginia; Parkersburg, West Virginia; Huntington, West Virginia; Georgetown, Pennsylvania; Beaver, Pennsylvania; Pittsburgh, Pennsylvania.

   B. Where does it end? In Pittsburgh, Pennsylvania when it meets with the Allegheny and the Monongahela Rivers.

3. What does this tell you about its importance as a major route of travel? Since it passes through so many states, it could be a major migration route for all the states mentioned above.

Cause and Effect

1. In the example above, what is a possible cause and what is a possible effect in the life and movements of the Quaker from Maryland? The cause for his movement could have been the persecution caused by his beliefs. The effect on his life was that he moved from Maryland and started a new life in Pennsylvania where he was welcome. The records of that area should be searched.

The other YOUR TURN assignments in this chapter are appropriate for personal preference answers.

COMPUTER CHECKLIST #7

1. Is there a way to enter notes chronologically in your computer program to aid in your development of a sense of chronology? What method will you use to provide chronological notes?

WEB SITES

www.usgs.gov
U.S. Geological Survey National Mapping Information.

www.lib.utexas.edu/maps/historical/index.html
The Perry-Castaneda Library Map Collection at the University of Texas at Austin. Includes maps of all areas of the world, not just Texas.

scarlett.libs.uga.edu/darchive/hargrett/maps/maps.html
Rare map collection from the Hargrett Library at the University of Georgia Library covering 500 years, from the sixteenth through the twentieth century.

http://familyhistory.byu.edu
This is the family history center at Brigham Young University. Select "Resources" at the Home Page. Then select "Internet Resources" from the list that's given. Scroll down to maps.

BIBLIOGRAPHY

Cerny, Johni and Wendy Elliott. *The Library: A Guide to the LDS Family History Library.* Salt Lake City: Ancestry, 1988.

Church of Jesus Christ of Latter-day Saints. *Family History SourceGuide.* CD-ROM. Salt Lake City: Church of Jesus Christ of Latter-day Saints, 1998.

Eichholz, Alice. *Ancestry's Red Book.* Rev. ed. Salt Lake City: Ancestry, 1992.

Everton, George B., Sr. *The Handy Book for Genealogists.* 9th ed. Logan, Utah: Everton Publishers, 1999.

Schlesinger, Arthur M., Jr. *Almanac of American History.* New York: Putnam, c1983.

Thompson, Morris M. USGS. *Maps for America, U.S. Geological Survey.* 3rd ed. U.S. Department of the Interior, 1989.

Welsey, Edgar B. *Our United States...Its History in Maps.* Chicago: Denoyer-Geppert Company, 1957.

For various state and county histories, consult:

Meyerink, Kory. *Printed Sources.* Salt Lake City: Ancestry Inc., 1998.

The US Government Printing Office has printed a free 12-page booklet by the US Department of the Interior and the US Genealogical Survey entitled *Maps Can Help You Trace Your Family Tree: How to Use Maps in Genealogy.* Write to: US Geological Survey, National Cartographic Information Center, 507 National Center, Reston, VA 22092.

U.S. Gazetteers

Abate, Frank R., ed. *American Places Dictionary: A Guide to 45,000 Populated Places, Natural Features, and Other Places in the United States.* 4 vols. Detroit: Omnigraphics, 1994.

Abate, Frank R., ed. *Omni Gazetteer of the United States of America: Providing Name, Location, and Identification for Nearly 1,500,000 Populated Places, Structures, Facilities, Locales, Historic Places, and Geographic Features in the Fifty States.* 11 vols. Detroit: Omnigraphics, 1991.

de Colange, Leo. *The National Gazetteer.* London: Hamilton, Adams, and Co., 1884.

A Bibliography of Gazetteers:

Sealock, Richard B., ed., et al. *Bibliography of Place- Name Literature, United States and Canada.* 3rd ed. Chicago: American Library Assoc., 1982.

Postal Directory

Bullinger's Postal and Shippers Guide for the United States and Canada: Containing Post Offices and Railroad Freight Stations with the Nearest Post Offices and Railroads on which Every Place or the Nearest Communicating Point is Located and the List of Railroads and their Terminal Points. Westwood, NJ: Bulllinger's Guides, 1871-. Annual.

CHAPTER 8

Resolving Conflict

"Confusion is a word we have invented for an order which is not understood."

—Henry Miller

Have you ever played the game "Telephone"? You sit in a circle, and the first person reads something written on a piece of paper, and then whispers what he or she has read to the person on right. Player #2 whispers what he or she hears to the next person on the right, and so on. By the time this "information" reaches the last player in the circle, it contains some of the original statement, but much is lacking. There may even be some brand-new information added, based on what players thought they heard. "Telephone" is only a game, but chances are quite high that misinformation—because people passed on what they thought they heard—has happened in the passing-down of your family history. Because so much of our family history is passed on orally, it's understandable that people will mishear, misreport—even embellish that history.

Parlor Games

RESOLVING CONFLICT

Now that you have all your "bits and pieces" of family trivia, documents, and traditions organized, sorted, separated, entered, alphabetized, documented, cited, and filed in notebook form, you have completed the organizational phase, and you can find anything in minutes! Now it's time to resolve conflicts, see what information others have, and decide what to do next.

If your ancestry goes back to the early decades of European settlement in America, chances are high that at least one of your family lines has been researched. Perhaps a book has even been published, or is in the process of being published. Whether this is the case or not, it's time for you to move on to the next phase of your research in order to see if others have been working on your line, compare what you have with other available information, and resolve any conflicts. Others may have clues you need, but until you have followed these steps you may not be able to recognize those clues. The first step is to review the research cycle.

Family Documents

Terms to Understand

boun·ty lands - Territorial or public property given to an individual as a reward, inducement, or payment by a government for acts deemed beneficial to the state such as enlisting for military service.

Terms to Understand

plague - A widespread, highly infectious, usually fatal, epidemic disease.

Terms to Understand

ter·ri·tor·ies - An area of land or water under the jurisdiction of an external government.

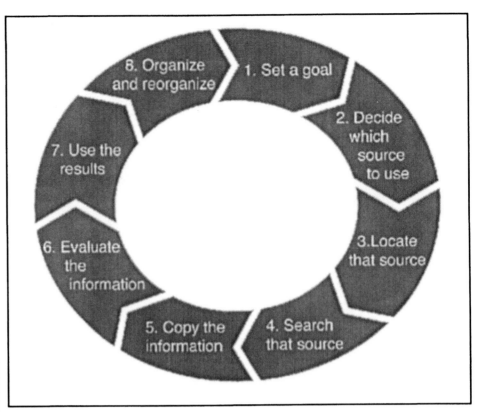

Illustration 8-1   The Research Cycle

Goals

According to Step 1 in the Research Cycle, we must first set a goal. One way to do this is to look at your Pedigree Chart and ask yourself, "What is one specific piece of information I want about one individual on my chart?" Since under the notes for that person you have already listed everything you already know about him/her in chronological order, the new information you want to know now becomes the goal.

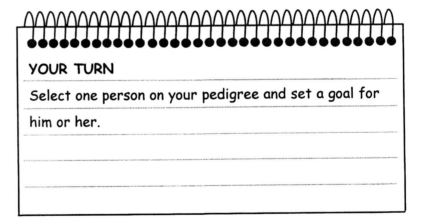

YOUR TURN

Select one person on your pedigree and set a goal for him or her.

Dates

Now look at the dates on both your Pedigree Chart and your chronological notes list. Are any of these dates associated with a significant historical event? Use the resources in the previous chapter to arrive at significant dates, watching for wars, droughts, famines, **plagues**, the acquisition of new **territories**, openings of canals, availability of **bounty lands**, migration, etc.

The Complete Beginner's Guide

Do any of these dates raise questions in your mind? Was this person of marriageable age; could he/she have been married before; was the death date of one spouse so early as to cause the other spouse to marry again in order to provide for the needs of young children?

Now ask yourself if any of these facts are possible research topics. For example, since Henry Butler was 12 years older than his wife Katherine, could this be his second marriage? Since their first child was born in Boone County, Kentucky, might they have been married in Boone County as well?

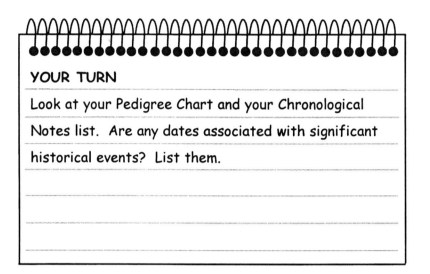

YOUR TURN

Look at your Pedigree Chart and your Chronological

Notes list. Are any dates associated with significant

historical events? List them.

> **Terms to Understand**
>
> **lo·cal·i·ty an·al·y·sis** – The act of locating the jurisdiction of a particular place at the time of an event, and for the present day.

Where to Go for Answers to Your Questions

Since you are new to the experience of using genealogical sources for answering your questions, use the Guide to Sources for Extending Your Pedigree (Illustration 8-2) to tell you where to look. This guide provides some of the *sources most commonly used by genealogists* to fill in those missing holes.

INITIAL TECHNIQUES FOR SEARCHING SOURCES

As you begin to search the sources listed in the guide, you should observe the following techniques:

1. Go from the *known* to the *unknown*.

2. Don't skip any *generations or sources*.

3. *Within reason*, get *all* of them. (For example, get those individuals of the same surname in the same locality, neighbors who may have traveled with your ancestors for several generations, and relatives who appear on one record or another. On the other hand, you wouldn't want to get all of the Smiths in New York City; in such cases you have to decide what is within reason.)

4. Find the *present county jurisdiction* for the location where your ancestors lived.

5. Now find the *county of jurisdiction at the time of the event.* They are often different. This is called a **locality analysis.** It is very important that you are looking in the correct place at the time of the event, since records are kept in the county where they were originally created or filed. Use gazetteers of the time period, geographical dictionaries, maps, and books to guide you in the state, county or town information you seek.

GUIDE TO SOURCES FOR EXTENDING YOUR PEDIGREE

INSTRUCTIONS: Line up the goal in the left column with the date of birth or death. Then search the record groups listed under the heading "Key to Record Groups." *(This is only a GUIDE. There can be exceptions.)*

GOAL	PRESENT-1910	1910-1880	1880-1850	1850-1790
Find parent's names	1, 2, 3, 4 & 3 again, or 7, 18	7, 11, 8, 9	13, 11, 8, 9, 19	13, 16, 11, 20, 8, 9
Find birth date/place	1, 2, 14, or 7	7, 14, 8, 9, 12	7, 6, 8, 9, 11, 19	8, 14, 20, 17, 9
Find marriage	1, 6, 9, 14 or use 7 for clues	1, 8, 9, 11, 14, 19	8, 9, 10, 11, 14, 17, 19	6, 8, 10, 14, 17, 20
Find death date	1, 3, 5, 9	8, 14, 5, 9, 12	5, 12, 8, 15, 14, 9, 19	5, 12, 9, 8, 14, 20
Find spouse's maiden name	1, 3, 6, 4	11, 12, 8, 9, 10, 14	11, 8, 9, 10, 12, 14, 19	11, 8, 9, 10, 12, 14, 20
Find death place	1, 4, 3 and use clues in 7	5, 8, 9, 10, 14	15, 14, 12, 9, 8, 5, 19	12, 5, 16, 17, 10, 20
Find siblings	4, 18, 9	5, 8, 9, 10, 12, 14, 18	5, 8, 9, 10, 12, 14, 18	5, 8, 9, 10, 12, 14, 16, 18, 19

KEY TO RECORD GROUPS

1. Check family records.
2. Order birth certificate from state of birth.
3. Order death certificate from state of death.
4. Check Social Security Death Index at FamilySearch.org.
5. Check probate index from county of death--both wills [testate] and administrations [intestate].
6. Check marriage record from the state where first child was born.
7. Locate an 1880 to 1930 federal census record closest to person's birth date: 1) search everyname index at Ancestry.com, FamilySearch.org, or ProQuest if place unknown, or search 2) the county and state.
8. 1) find ancestors on census records; 2) then search county, state, occupational and religious histories.
9. Locate obituaries in communities where ancestors may have died.
10. Check land and property records in counties where the ancestor lived just before he appeared in census records.
11. Check marriage record indexes in the county in which the first child appears on federal or state census records.
12. Check death and/or cemetery records in the county where the ancestor was last located in federal or state census records, or tax records.
13. Check statewide printed census indexes, or online census records under #7 above for years person alive.
14. Look for church records where person found on census records.
15. Check federal census mortality schedules for deaths occurring the twelve months prior to the federal census.
16. Look for county histories, look under the township or post office listed in the federal or state census records, or look at tax records.
17. Search nationwide census indexes at websites mentioned under #7 above.
18. Search city directories if in a bigger town or city to see approximate year of moving in and out.
19. Search military records - Civil War *State Indexes*, if ancestor was a male, born 1838 to 1852. If you find his name there, order pension/bounty land records.
20. Military records - War of 1812 *State Indexes*, if ancestor was a male, born 1787 to 1795. If you find his name there, order pension/bounty land records.

Illustration 8-2   Guide to Sources for Extending Your Pedigree

6. List *all of the sources that you search*, whether the results are negative or positive.

7. Determine *what other researchers have already discovered.* Avoid duplication of effort by making a **preliminary survey**.

8. Finally, write down *on a planner* the sources you will search next. And do not confuse a log with a **Research Planner**. The Research Log only records what was searched. The planner or calendar records not only what you found, what you did not find, where you searched, and when you made a search, but also what records *should eventually* be searched. Since using a calendar or planner is such an important step in the research process, we will study it in more detail after looking at the ways in which you can find additional information about an ancestor.

TIPS FOR EFFECTIVE USE OF THE RESEARCH PLANNER

One of the greatest aids to you as a genealogist is the Research Planner. It helps to focus your attention on the current research you are doing and reminds you to apply the eight techniques for researching the sources listed in the above chart.

Step 1 of the research cycle, and the first step in the effective use of your Research Planner, is to set specific goals. Those goals are arrived at through an analysis of existing family records. While it is the task of your genealogy computer program to organize the family records so that you can conduct an analysis, *it is the task of the Research Planner to help you, the researcher, go about your research in an orderly fashion.*

Terms to Understand

pre·lim·i·nar·y sur·vey - A comprehensive search of compiled sources and databases to prevent the repetition of previous research performed on a particular family or goal.

Terms to Understand

re·search plan·ner - A list of records to be searched for a particular goal, a list of records actually searched for a particular goal, call numbers of sources searched and the results of those searches, including the extract numbers for extractions which pertain to that research.

YOUR TURN

Step 1: Goal Setting

In order to make good use of the ideas you jotted down as you did your initial data

entry, here are examples of the kinds of questions a good researcher should ask that

could become goals.

1. What do you really know about your grandfather, John Morten, born 1898. You were

told he was born in Pennsylvania, but in what town? Turn this question into a goal.

2. Who in my family would have information on this family? Look at the Family Group

Records for your aunts and uncles, great-aunts and -uncles, cousins, and grandparents.

Keep in mind that youngest daughters often received the family Bible, which would place

the Bible in the hands of a different surname line, if the daughter married. Turn this

question into a goal.

Previously, you learned that if certain information is missing, that information could become a goal in itself; you also learned that reaching this goal could enable you to go further in your research. You may also have set some goals on your own while you were data entering your information, since the act of organizing that information in the genealogy computer program, and into timelines, often helps to reveal missing or questionable areas. These very questions can be listed on your Research Planner. Just be sure to use a separate planner for each goal, as most goals will need to be broken down into smaller objectives. For example, your goal may be to locate the father of Timothy Hundley, born 1847.

Begin by writing the goal at the top of your research calendar; then, smaller objectives can be written in the space labeled "object of search." This is a sample goal.

Goal: *Locate the father of Timothy Hundley born 1847 in Virginia*

Step 2: As you learn more about the research process, what sources are available, and where they may be obtained, you will be able to set better goals. In the goal to locate the father of Timothy Hundley, born 1847, a will which mentions Timothy as the son of a Mr. Hundley would be proof. Also, a census with a child of the same age as Timothy, listed with his parents, would provide evidence to solve the problem. You're just beginning your search, so you do not as yet have the name of a repository (a library, an archive, or a special collection) where this source might be found. Nor do you know the title of a book, a film number, or a full description of a source. That can be filled in later. Now you can see why these are called "planners"! In essence, you are "planning" work to be done later. Once you learn the whereabouts of a nearby Regional Records Services Facility which has census films, you will be able to proceed. Or you may learn that a local Family History Center has the **probate** records for which you are searching on **microfilm**.

Since you know the approximate time period, you can fill in the "Time Period Column." In the "Note" column, you can write the MRIN for the Family Group Record, in order to use it as a reference, later, as you data enter the information into your program. If you apply these techniques, your Research Planner will look similar to Illustration 8-3.

Terms to Understand

pro·bate - The process of legally establishing the validity of a will; or, all of the legal processes carried out at the death of an individual in order to establish ownership of, or the heir, to the deceased's goods.

Terms to Understand

mi·cro·film - A reproduction of printed or handwritten materials, photographed and stored on film at greatly reduced size in order to save space in libraries and archives.

Goal *Locate the father of Timothy Hundley born 1847 in Virginia*

SURNAME/SUBJECT *Hundley Family*

RESEARCHER *Your Name Goes Here* AREA *Virginia*

Repository Call #	Date	Description of Source	Ind Con	Object of Search	Time Period, Search	Note	Ext #
		Will records		*All Hundley*	*1848–1900*	*Mrin #123*	
		Virginia 1850 Census Index		*Timothy Hundley with father*	*1850*	*Mrin #123*	

Illustration 8-3   Research Planner Showing Step 2

Terms to Understand

ex·tract num·ber - The number assigned to an extraction made from a document which is listed on a research log or planner.

YOUR TURN

Step 2: Guide to Sources

Using the information in Illustration 8-2, select the goal in the left hand column which applies to finding a death date. Now assume that the individual died between 1880 and 1910. Which records should you look at to find this ancestor's death date according to the guide?

Step 3: Next, you learn that the numbers for the microfilms you want are available from the Internet card catalog for a particular repository, so now you can fill in the columns headed "Repository" (name of the library, archive or collection) and "Call #" (call number).

When you plan to visit a repository such as the Family History Center and the National Archives, you will be able to view photo-duplications of original documents on film. When you locate your families, you can also make copies of the filmed documents, which can then become a permanent part of your records. You can also make a "table of contents" for the sources you have searched that day by using the "Ext #" (Extract Document Number) field on your Research Planner.

In the upper right-hand corner of each set of records you have photocopied, write a code number representing the family, such as "H" for Hundley, and an **extract number** starting with the number "1." Therefore the first photocopy or set of photocopies indicating "Hundley family extract item 1," would be "H-1." Also, record that number under the heading "Ext #" on the Research Planner. Later, as you review the many documents and notes you have taken on your research trip, it will be very easy to determine which sources on your Research Planner matches which of the documents you have brought home. See Illustration 8-4

Goal _Locate the father of Timothy Hundley born 1847 in Virginia_

SURNAME/SUBJECT _Hundley Family_

RESEARCHER _Your Name Goes Here_   AREA _Virginia_

Repository / Call #	Date	Description of Source	Ind / Con	Object of Search	Time Period, Search	Note	Ext #
FHC #1245634		Will records, Henry County, Virginia		All Hundley	1848-1900	Main #123	
San Bruno Federal Archives Roll 125		Virginia 1850 Census Index		Timothy Hundley with father	1850	Main #123	H-1

Illustration 8-4   Research Planner Showing Step 3

YOUR TURN

Step 3: Keeping track of your documents

Assume you found the census record, a county history, and a probate record for John Smith which you needed in the previous "Your Turn" assignment. Provide an extract number for each one of them.

Step 4: When you searched the will records for Henry County, Virginia, you found nothing that related to the Hundley family. But you did discover that the Hs in the index were filed in error after the letter "I," so you made a note of that under the "Con" ("Condition" heading in the Research Planner), in case you ever need to search that file again. And you found that you ran out of space in a couple of columns, so you simply turned the Planner over and wrote additional notes on the back.

Since you didn't want to waste time reading a roll of census film that had already been indexed, you checked the card catalog for a notation indicating whether it had been indexed or not, and you marked this information on your Research Planner in the "Ind" (Indexed) box. You also noted the indexes you searched on your Research Planner. And when you found the census index for Virginia, you discovered that Timothy Hundley's father lived in Pittsylvania County, Virginia, next door to Henry County. Aha! That's probably why you hadn't found him in the Henry County probate records. But as you packed up to leave at the end of this very successful repository visit, you not only felt pleased that you had tracked down the elusive Mr. Hundley, but you had the satisfaction of seeing that your Research Planner looked like Illustration 8-5, with the name of another county to be searched for the will, at a later date. Now you are ready for the next step in the process.

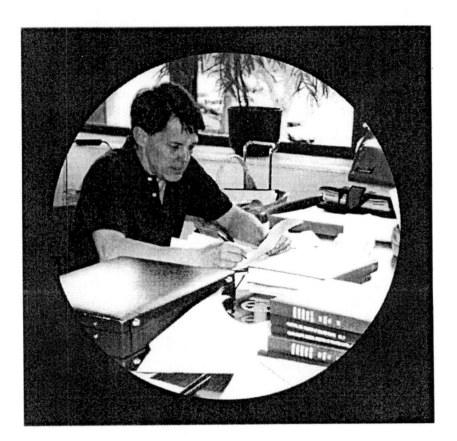

Goal _Locate the father of Timothy Hundley born 1847 in Virginia_ _____

SURNAME/SUBJECT _Hundley Family_ _____

RESEARCHER _Your Name Goes Here_ _____ AREA _Virginia_ _____

Repository / Call #	Date	Description of Source	Ind / Con	Object of Search	Time Period, Search	Note	Ext #
FHC #1245634		Will Index, Henry County, Virginia ** (all H's in index after I)	**	All Hundley	1848-1900	Mrin #123	Ø
San Bruno Federal Archives Roll 125		Virginia 1850 Census Index		Timothy Hundley with father	1850	Mrin #123	H-1
San Bruno Federal Archives Roll 127		Virginia 1850 Census Pittsylvania County		"	" pg. 243	"	H-2
FHC #1245689		Will Index, Pittsylvania County, Virginia		"	"	"	copied over

Illustration 8-5   Research Planner Showing Step 4

YOUR TURN

Step 4: Recording Indexes

1. Look at Illustration 8-2 under the goal to find a birth date between 1790 and 1850. Which record groups have indexes? List them.

2. How would you indicate on your Research Planner that there is an index to those records?

Step 5: Now that you're back home, you can't wait to enter the new information into your computer genealogy program. But you remember from class that there's a method for this, as well. You begin by using the ID numbers which you had listed under the "Note" column (the RIN or MRIN numbers). Then you look to the right of the "Note" column to the extract fields, pick up the document, and enter the information you located on that original document or any notes you transcribed on the back of your Research Planner.

Once the information has been entered, you mark lightly in pencil the MRIN number in the upper right-hand corner of the document, circling the number lightly to indicate that you have entered the document fully into your computer. That way, if you are interrupted and must return to the data entry later, you will know it hasn't been completed because the number has not been circled. When all of the data entry is complete, you file the Planners away in the section of your Family History binder titled "Research Planners." Thus, your Planners provide the bibliographic notations that you need for your family history's documentation, and they remind you of all of the sources you have searched, and for whom you were searching.

Research Planner

Remember to have only *one goal* per Research Planner.

Goal _____

_____

Surname/Subject _____   Researcher _____

Area _____   Client _____

Source Location		Description of Source	Object	Time	Remarks		
Date source searched	Library or repository & call #	(State, county, type of record, and time period of record)	(Person's name or what is sought)	(Person's age or date of event)	Comment or ID # of family	Index	File

Genealogy Research Associates, Inc. www.GRAonline.com

Illustration 8-6   Blank Research Planner

YOUR TURN

Timelines and Sources

Using the timeline in Illustration 8-7 and one of the

blank Research Planner in Illustration 8-6, list some

sources which might exist to cover some of the events

illustrated between 1864 and 1865.

One blank Research Planner will be found as Illustration 8-6. Others will be found in the Appendix. Be sure to put a return address stamp or label in the upper corner, so that they will be returned to you if they are misplaced or left behind after a visit to a library or repository.

THE RESEARCH PROCESS
1. Go from known to unknown.
   2. Don't skip sources.
      3. Get all of same surname.
         4. Check if this is the proper place.
            5. Do a locality analysis.
               6. List all sources + and -.
                  7. Do a preliminary survey.
                     8. Keep a Research Planner.

780　　　　　　　NORTH AMERICA

charters, state bank notes were driven out of existence by a tax of 10% (1865).

June 20. West Virginia (the loyal part of Virginia) admitted to the union as the thirty-fifth state.

1864, Nov. 8. Re-election of Lincoln. Andrew Johnson, vice-president.

1865, Feb. 1. Resolution in Congress to submit to the states the **thirteenth amendment** to the constitution, prohibiting slavery within the United States. The amendment was ratified by two-thirds of the states by Dec. 18.

1865-1873. Serious and recurring **epidemics** of smallpox, typhus, typhoid, cholera, scarlet fever, and yellow fever in Philadelphia, New York, Boston, Baltimore, Washington, Memphis, and New Orleans led to the realization of the need for improved sanitation. In 1866 a municipal **board of health** was created in New York and in 1869 a state board of health was established in Massachusetts.

1861-1868. New territories. In the years just before the war the discovery of precious metals in the Pike's Peak country and in the Washoe Mountains led to mining rushes to those regions, with the result that the territories of **Colorado** and **Nevada** were organized in 1861. Mining rushes elsewhere in the years of the war resulted in the organization of the territories of **Arizona** (1863), **Idaho** (1863), and **Montana** (1864). **Wyoming** was made a territory in 1868.

1862-1886. Taming of the Plains Indians. The constant pressure of white population, combined with broken promises, led to continued outbreaks of the Indians. The Homestead Act (1862) played a prominent part in the settlement of the west. The Morrill Act (1862), providing for grants of land to states in order to aid the establishment of agricultural colleges, opened up more areas. In 1862 the **Union and Central Pacific Railways** were chartered by Congress and given a large grant of land. They formed the first transcontinental railway (completed May 10, 1869).

In 1862 the **Sioux Indians** of Minnesota were defeated by Gen. Sibley at **Wood Lake.** In 1864 the **Cheyenne** went on the warpath, with the aid of the Arapahoe, Apache, Comanche, and Kiowa tribes. Troops under Col. Chivington staged a massacre of Indians at **Sand Creek,** Colo. (Nov. 1864). Efforts of troops to build an emigrant road from Fort Laramie along the Powder River to the mines of Montana and Idaho led to war with the **Plains Sioux** (1866). A commission authorized by Congress persuaded the Apache, Comanche, and Kiowa tribes to locate in **Indian Territory,** and secured the removal of other tribes from the Plains to more remote regions. In 1869 Congress created the **Board of Indian Commissioners** to supervise all government expenditures for the Indians. Meanwhile the advance of white settlers, slaughter of the buffalo, and the gold rush to the Black Hills caused an outbreak of the Plains Sioux (1876) under **Sitting Bull,** which resulted in the **massacre of Custer** and his men at the **Little Big Horn** (June 25). **Nez Percé Indians** under **Chief Joseph** were defeated (Oct. 1877) and removed to Indian Territory. The last important Indian uprising came in the years 1882-1886, when the **Apaches** in Arizona and New Mexico, under Victorio and **Geronimo,** resisted efforts to confine them to reservations. By 1886 the Indians had all been removed to Indian Territory or to reservations.

c. THE UNITED STATES, 1865-1917

1865, Apr. 14. ASSASSINATION OF LINCOLN; death Apr. 15. Andrew Johnson, vice-president, succeeded.

Cost of the war. National debt in 1860, $64,842,287; in 1866, $2,773,236,173, which great increase was in addition to the debts incurred by the states and municipalities.

May 29. President Johnson issued a **proclamation of amnesty,** granting pardon to all ordinary persons who had participated in the rebellion on taking an oath of allegiance.

Dec. **Joint Committee of Fifteen on Reconstruction** appointed by Congress.

Dec. 18. **Ratification of the thirteenth amendment,** abolishing slavery.

1866, Feb. Johnson vetoed a measure extending the life of the **Freedmen's Bureau,** thereby increasing tension between himself and Congress.

April. Congress passed over Johnson's veto the **Civil Rights Bill,** declaring all persons born in the United States to be citizens of the United States and entitled to equality of treatment before the law. This was designed to guarantee equal treatment to Negroes in southern states.

June 13. **FOURTEENTH AMENDMENT** sent to states for ratification. Declared ratified July 28, 1868. It incorporated in the constitution the principle of the Civil Rights Act; gave the southern states the choice of Negro enfranchisement or reduced representation in the lower House of Congress; barred from

Illustration 8-7 From An Encyclopedia of World History, compiled by William L. Langer

CONCLUSION

There are two ways to absorb the research techniques you have learned in this chapter.

1. You read through the rules once, apply the two or three you remember, and ignore the others. (Eventually, you'll learn the other rules, but only after you have had to repeat hours, days, weeks, months or years of research, redoing the steps you missed. In fact, the step you forgot and had to repeat, belatedly, will probably be the one you'll lecture your own students about when you become a genealogy teacher. Personal mistakes are great teachers, but they are soooo time-consuming.)

2. A better method is to learn from the mistakes of others and follow the steps in the research process. Try to memorize and absorb each step, and use the bookplate, on the bottom of page 8-14, to help you memorize these techniques. Cut them out, carry them with you, and learn these eight techiques.

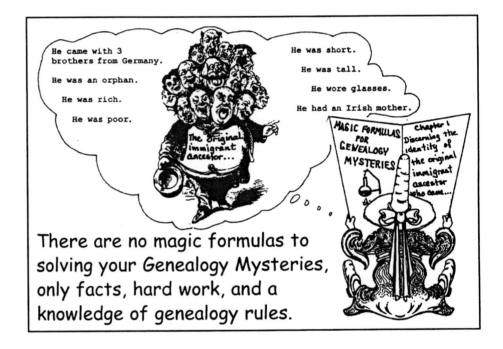

ASSIGNMENT 8: RESOLVING CONFLICT

1. What do you know about all of the people appearing on your Pedigree Chart? In other words, what has been substantiated in your family history? Make up a separate Research Planner for each unsubstantiated, questionable, or unknown event on your Pedigree Chart.

2. Write down a county (or county equivalent for a foreign country) for every locality on your Pedigree Chart.

3. Verify that the county (or county equivalent) actually existed at the time of the event of the person in question.

4. List which relatives might have information on the family you are researching.

YOUR TURN ANSWERS

Step 1: Goal Setting

1. In what town or county was John Morten's birth of 1898 in Pennsylvania?

2. Who would be a direct-line descendant of John Morten, born 1898 in Pennsylvania? Locate all of the spouses and children of the siblings of John Morten as well.

Step 2: Guide to Sources

Numbers 8, 14, 5, 9, which translates to looking for the ancestor on a census, if possible, and then searching for the ancestor in a county history if he or she lived in the Midwest; looking for church records; checking the probate index in the county of death where the person was last found on a census; locating obituaries in communities where the ancestor may have died.

Step 3: Keeping Track of Your Documents

Census record S-1
County history S-2
Probate record S-3

Step 4: Recording Indexes

1. 13, 16, 11, 20

2. Mark this information on your Research Planner in the "Ind" (Indexed) box.

Timelines and Sources

Tax records, territorial records for Colorado and Nevada; occupational or mining records for Arizona, Idaho, Montana, and Wyoming; homestead and other land and property records; Native American records; National Archives records involving Native Americans, military (specifically Civil War records), reconstruction, and Freedman's Bureau; census records, vital records.

COMPUTER CHECKLIST #8

Describe how to accomplish the following tasks in your genealogy computer program:

1. How do you correct a surname?

2. How do you correct a locality?

3. How do you unlink a child from a family without deleting the child and his/her notes?

4. How do you unlink a couple from one another?

5. How do you modify the general notes on an individual?

6. How do you modify the source notes on an individual?

WEB SITES

www.WhitePages.com
The White Pages for the Internet to search for phone numbers or e-mail addresses.

www.NationalAdoptionRegistry.com
Search International, Inc. is in the missing persons business primarily for missing heirs and beneficiaries, but also for their National Adoption Registry.

www.AdoptionRegistry.webs.com
Free online registries for adoption.

www.genealogy.com
Genealogy data online with over 500 million names from census records, marriage records, social security records, and submitted family trees. This is only an index, but for a subscription fee, you can see the submissions from others.

www.mytrees.com
Under the Resources tab, find links to living people, White Pages, free forms, and software. Also search for posted and compiled ancestries and extracted records. Look under Corporate for daily, monthly, or yearly subscription.

BIBLIOGRAPHY

Cerny, Johni and Wendy Elliott. *The Library: A Guide to the LDS Family History Library.* Salt Lake City: Ancestry, 1988.

_____. *The Handy Book for Genealogists.* 10th ed. Draper, Utah: Everton Publishers, 2002.

Greenwood, Val D. *The Researcher's Guide to American Genealogy.* 3rd ed. Baltimore: Genealogical Publishing Co., 2000.

Langer, William L. *An Encyclopedia of World History.* Boston: Houghton Mifflin Co., 1940.

Thorndale, William and William Dollarhide. *Map Guide to the U.S. Federal Censuses, 1790-1920.* Baltimore: Genealogical Publishing Co., 1987.

CHAPTER 9

State Vital Record Offices, Public Libraries, Courthouses and Local Repositories

"Let fame, that all hunt after in their lives,
Live register'd upon our brazen tombs."

—William Shakespeare

Now that you have been taught how to organize your materials, how to use a computer program to aid in that organization, how to enter sources properly, how your genealogy computer program may be used to record timelines to aid in research, how to analyze what is known, how to work backward in time with the aid of the "Guide to Sources for Extending Your Pedigree," and how to prepare and use a Research Planner, it is time to locate and obtain more original records.

ARMCHAIR GENEALOGY

Others in your family, or within the communities where your family lived, may have information to help you. Much of that information can be gathered through correspondence. A common term for research conducted through corre-spondence is *armchair genealogy*.

An **armchair genealogist** is one who does genealogy without having to leave home. That doesn't mean never going out, but it does mean doing as much as possible from home. The computer, with a simple word processing program, can be a great help here. A form letter (such as the one shown in Illustration 9-1) could be made up and used over and over again to write to relatives or friends of the family. In addition to the family, www.google.com can guide you to many others who might be of help to you:

Terms to Understand

Arm·chair ge·ne·al·o·gist - One who does genealogy through correspondence or the Internet, with-out leaving home.

1. Look up the ancestor's home town and county using www.google.com. Record contact information on the Chamber of Commerce, local historical societies, libraries, museums, and also how to obtain local area maps at those sites.
2. County and city clerks can be of great help. *The Handy Book for Genealogists* and the *County Courthouse Book* are two books you will want to own if you plan to do much research from your home. They include

addresses for every county in the United States and a list of the records available from the court house. The *Handy Book* also includes migration maps, railroad maps, and Web site addresses.

3. Larger cemeteries are often found online and can provide names of family members and burial dates, occupations, military service, church affiliation,

---

SAMPLE FORM LETTER

Date

Name
Address
City, State, Zip

Dear _____:

My (relationship) lived in your county in (year). This is what I know about (him/her):

Names
Birth date and place
Marriage date and place
Spouse name
Death date and Place
Names of children

Brief sources of information:

I am searching for (his/her) parents. Do you have (state a specific record series to search) which might give me the answer to my question?

I will be happy to pay for photocopies and would be more than happy to share information I have on this family.

Thank you so much for your time and consideration. If you are unable to help me, could you please write at the bottom of this letter the name and address of someone else who could help. Please find enclosed a self-addressed, stamped envelope for your convenience.

Sincerely,

Your name
Complete address
Phone number (optional)
E-mail address

Illustration 9-1 Sample Form Letter

citizenship, and place of birth. Good published finding aids include *The Source* with several addresses for cemetery associations. *The Researcher's Guide to American Genealogy* is very informative as well regarding back ground information and public libraries have directories for funeral homes and morticians.

4. Local historians might help you. In small towns the local postmaster might pass a letter on to a person he knows would have information.

5. Newspapers may help. State libraries can often send microfilm copies of

their state's old newspapers on interlibrary loan to your local library.

6. Military records are available by correspondence. These include service, pension and bounty land records, which can be ordered from the National Archives, or in some cases on the Internet from the U.S. government, or through a genealogy record look-up service (see *www.GRAonline.com*).

7. Several genealogical periodicals can be of help, including: *Everton's Genealogical Helper, Ancestry, Family Tree Magazine,* and similar magazines which are available in many public libraries. They are full of suggestions.

8. Genealogical and historical societies in each state are listed in a book called *The Genealogist's Address Book*. Genealogy societies can also be found on the Web at *www.fgs.org*. They could be contacted regarding information concerning publications or give an Internet link to the society itself.

9. Vital records repositories, where you can order birth, marriage and death records, are also listed in *The Genealogist's Address Book*.

10. Churches may be contacted. The Family History Library provides research guidance for free on the Internet at *www.FamilySearch.org*. This provides addresses for major religious repositories in the United States. *The Researcher's Guide to American Genealogy* describes the kind of records available and where these might be located.

11. Naturalization records and ships' passenger lists are available for loan or purchase on films through the National Archives and Records Service. Search *www.google.com* for the agency holding original naturalization records.

12. Employment and Social Security information is available. Addresses for obtaining the original Social Security application and the death record are available on the Social Security Death Index at *www.FamilySearch.org*.

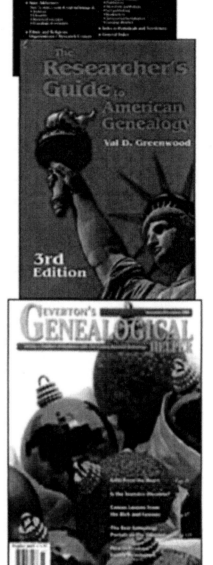

YOUR TURN

Indicate three organizations or agencies you could correspond with to resolve some of your family history questions.

1.

2.

3.

There is No Substitute for Original Records

Original records give an insight into problems that nothing short of speaking with the participants themselves could bring. Not only that, but the genealogist

Terms to Understand

cer·ti·fi·cates - An official document stating a fact or event, such as a birth certificate which states the birth date and place.

Terms to Understand

ap·pli·ca·tions - A form filled out in making a request.

Terms to Understand

banns - Official notification of a couple's intention to marry, usually given at a church service several weeks before the wedding.

Terms to Understand

bond - An official document created by a person, his heirs, an administrator, or an executor, promising a certain sum of money to cover expenses, usually in regard to a deceased's property and possessions and the execution or administration of that estate.

will find no substitute for searching original records to obtain the feel of the time and place of a particular problem.

The first primary records that family historians consult are vital records, including birth records, marriage records, and death records. Yet at least 50 percent of the dates and places given to me in research cases have been in error. Either dates, places, people, or events were scrambled over the years. Since vital records are the first pieces of primary evidence sought for by researchers, it is important to understand how to best use them and to realize that they, too, can contain erroneous information, as will be explained.

HOW TO SEARCH FOR VITAL RECORDS

It is a proven fact that searching the last event first will give clues to those which preceded it. Therefore, search death, then marriage, then birth records. By going after the later events first, you will save much time and expense, because you have more information to go on. CAUTION: Many informants on death records make errors regarding birth dates and parents' names of the deceased during their time of grief. Try to verify all information with other sources.

YOUR TURN

List the name of one individual for whom you should obtain a vital record?

Vital Records Have Many Names

In addition to the order in which vital records are searched, the item you are looking for may be listed under a variety of names. Birth records, for example, could be listed under a term which is set by the jurisdiction involved in its creation. For example, state offices call their records "Birth Records." Some religious denominations call their earliest records "Christening" or "Baptismal" records. Hospitals call their records **"Certificates,"** while municipal governments call their records "City Records."

Marriage records, on the other hand, could be listed under the headings **applications, banns,** proclamations, **bonds,** certificates, consent notices,

licenses, returns, register entries, marriage **contracts,** or **intentions.** As with birth records, these headings will vary between jurisdictions.

YOUR TURN

List four terms that refer to the birth of an individual.

1.

2.

3.

4.

YOUR TURN

1. List four terms that refer to the marriage of an individual or couple.

    a.

    b.

    c.

    d.

2. List two people in your family for whom you need a marriage record.

    a.

    b.

Terms to Understand

li·cense - A document indicating formal or legal permission to do something specific.

Terms to Understand

re·turns - Official document giving proof of an action performed that was ordered by the court or given by license.

Terms to Understand

reg·is·ters - Book kept by official authorities to record vital records or other official records.

Terms to Understand

con·tracts - A written or verbal agreement between two parties promising to do or not do something.

Terms to Understand

in·ten·tions - Giving notice to do something in relationship to marriage agreements.

When someone dies, several things happen. A death record in the hospital or a city certificate may be written up, an obituary may be entered in a newspaper, a mortician or coroner may be contacted, a cemetery may be located,

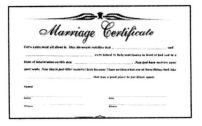

YOUR TURN

List three terms that also refer to the death of an individual.

1.

2.

3.

the local **sexton** may be contacted, a special church service may have been held, and relatives may have come to pay their respects.

Therefore, death information can be found through several sources. You can locate the names and addresses of morticians or funeral directors by using the *National Directory of Morticians.* Newspaper obituaries may be located by using the Web sites on page 9-28. For newspapers now found on-line, use the *Union Catalog of Newspapers* (available on **microfiche** through a Family History Center) to search for the paper's title; and then order the paper from the repository given via interlibrary loan through your college or public library.

Many vital records are found among church documents. The following sources help you locate U.S. church records: Kay Kirkham's *Survey of American Church Records;* Ancestry's *The Source; WPA Inventories of Church Records;* Kory Meyerink's *Printed Sources;* and using Internet search engines for the vital record office you seek. Many vital record events are also found among contemporary materials, including Bible records. Don't forget to look for death records on tombstones. Some are very interesting and humorous as well.

Vital statistics registration in the United States is a relatively modern phenomenon. There has never been a national registration, so it was left up to each state to determine how and what they would do. New Jersey was the first state to bring its vital records together on a statewide basis, beginning in 1848. Registrations are held in different jurisdictions than the state or county as well. In New England, the practice of registration began very early, on a town basis. In many large metropolitan cities and western states, registrations were not undertaken until the 20th century. A relatively new Web site for finding vital dates is *www.WorldVitalRecords.com* which uses all the traditional methods for finding dates and places and more unique sources as well. Kentucky even has it vital records index on line. Other sites are listed at the end of this chapter.

Birth Records

Early birth records are the rarest of the vital records. The heaviest concentration of early birth records is in New England. In most regions during the colonial period, church and Bible records serve as substitutes for missing birth records. By the mid 1800s, Virginia (and, therefore, West Virginia, which was not formed until 1862 out of Virginia counties) started keeping birth records.

Since vital records are relatively modern genealogically speaking, especially the recording of births and deaths, they often were not microfilmed. Illustration 9-2 shows the limited state-wide vital record indexes available in the Family History Library. Access the index through *www.familysearch.org* then click on Library Catalog. View microflms at the Family History Library, via loan films at a Family History Center, or by requesting a copy through a record look-up ser-

SAMPLE STATEWIDE VITAL RECORDS IN THE FAMILY HISTORY LIBRARY COLLECTION

STATE	BIRTH INDEX	BIRTH RECS	DEATH INDEX	DEATH RECS
Alabama	1917-1919		1908-1959	1908-1974
Arizona		1855-1926		1870-1951
Arkansas			1914-1948	
California				1905-1990
Connecticut				1949-1996
Delaware	1855-1955	1861-1923	ca. 1680 -- ca. 1934	1855-1955
District of Columbia	1874-1897	1874-1897	1855-1870	1855-1949
Florida			1877-1969	1877-1939
Georgia			1919-1999	1914, 1916-1927
Hawaii	1896-1949	1896-1925	1896-1949	1896-1925
Idaho			1911-1932	1911-1937
Illinois		1842, 1849-1872		1916-1945
Indiana * for 62 out of 92 counties			*1882-1920,	
Iowa	1880-1940	1870-1985	1880-1940	1921-1935
Kentucky	1911-1995		1911-1995	1911-1952
Louisiana			1850-75, 1900-54	1850-75, 1894-1954
Maine	1892-1922		1892-1922	
Massachusetts	1841-1910	1901-1905	1841-1971	1841-1905
Michigan		1867-1902	1867-1874	1867-1897
Minnesota				1900-1955
Missouri				1850-1909
Montana			pre 1954-2002	
New Hampshire	Early to 1900		Early to 1900	1901-1947
New Jersey		1848-1900		1848-1900
New Mexico			1889-1940	1889-1942, 1927-45
North Carolina			1906-74, 1968-94	1906-1994
Ohio	1888-1980	1869-79, 1888-1980	1888-1954, 1959-2002	1869-79, 1888-2001
Oregon			1903-2000	
Pennsylvania	1852-1908	1852-1908	1890-1905	1890-1905
Rhode Island	1846-1950		1846-1950	1900-43, 46-48, 51-53
South Carolina			1915-1944	1915-1944
Tennessee		1908-12, 1925-39	1914-1950	1908-12, 1914-53
Texas	1903-1953	1903-10, 1926-29	1941-1973	1890-1976
Utah			1898-1905	1904-1951
Vermont	Early to 1870, 71-1908	1909-1954	Early to 1870, 71-1908	1909-1954
Virginia	1853-1950	1853-1941		1853-1906
Washington	1907-1954	1907-1948	1970-1979	1907-1960
Wisconsin	1852-1907		pre 1907, 1959-1997	
West Virginia		1852-1930	1917-1991	1917-1973

Illustration 9-2   Sample Statewide Vital Records in the Family History Library Collection

NOTE: *Major cities like Chicago, New York City and its boroughs Philadephia, and counties surrounding major cities also have indexes.*

A RULE

Search the last event first (such as death records) for clues to those events which preceded it (e.g. birth records).

YOUR TURN

Search the list of vital records presented in Illustration 9-2, and indicate if any of these dates or localities cover one of your ancestors. Who is it, and which index is of interest?

vice at *www.GRAonline.com*.

Many other birth records after 1910 are available from local courthouses. They are very valuable, but many researchers fail to obtain them because they believe they already know most of the information. This reluctance to obtain these later vital records robs the researcher of vital clues.

Below is the information contained on a standard birth certificate in the 1900s.

Regarding the Child	Regarding the Mother	Regarding the Father
Name	Name, often maiden name	Name
Birthplace	Birthplace	Birthplace
Race	Race	Race
Date of Birth	Age	Age
Hospital or place of birth	Residence	Residence
Time of birth	Occupation	Occupation
Sex	Term of residence in the community	
	Marital status	
	Number of other living children	
	Number of other deceased children	
	Number of children born dead	

Illustration 9-3   Information Often Found on Modern Birth Records

Illustration 9-4 Example of a Certificate of Birth

Illustration 9-5 Example of a Newspaper Abstract of a Death and Birth in
Salinas, Monterey County, CA

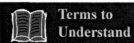

Terms to Understand

af·fi·da·vit - A written declaration made under oath before a notary public or other authorized officer.

YOUR TURN

After studying Illustration 9-3, indicate why you think it might be important to have this certificate for every member of your family including uncles and aunts.

Delayed Birth Certificate

Because birth records are often missing, and because the United States government legislated benefits (such as Social Security and civil service retirement) based on age, delayed birth certificates originated. A delayed birth certificate applicant had to fill out a petition to the county court stating his or her name, address, date and place of birth, parents' names, race, and evidence to support the information presented, such as a baptismal certificate, a school record, a census, or the **affidavit** of living people who witnessed the birth. Many of these records have been microfilmed throughout the United States.

Information Often Found on Modern Marriage Records		
Regarding the Event	**Regarding the Bride**	**Regarding the Groom**
Name of officiator	Name, including maiden name if widow	Name
Title of officiator	Birthplace	Birthplace
Date of license	Race	Race
Date of marriage	Age	Age
Place of marriage	Residence	Residence
Witness to marriage	Occupation	Occupation
Residence of witnesses	Marital status	Marital status
	Name of father	Name of father
	Name of mother, maiden name	Name of mother, maiden name

Illustration 9-6   Information Often Found on Modern Marriage Records

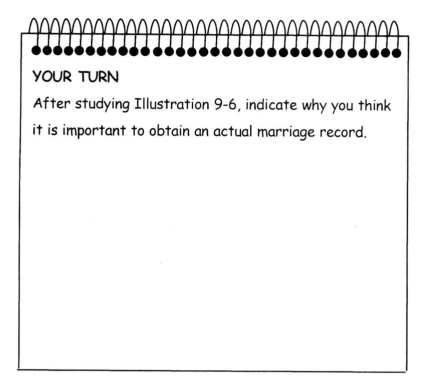

YOUR TURN

After studying Illustration 9-6, indicate why you think it is important to obtain an actual marriage record.

When a birth certificate cannot be located, a Social Security original application form SS-5 can be obtained by writing to the Freedom of Information Officer in Washington, D. C. These applications provide the individual's birth date and place, and by using the application people can apply for a delayed certificate or in the case of your deceased relative, you can see the date and place of birth on that application form

Marriage Records

Marriages were usually maintained from the time a U.S. county was formed, and that is the way they will need to be obtained—through county jurisdictions or towns in New England, either on microform, or by correspondence. Marriage records from the late 1800s to the present time contain wonderful information for the family historian, as shown in Illustration 9-6.

New FamilySearch posted first the beginnings of its enormous vital records collection online. Those that are currently available can be seen at www.familysearch.org then click on SEARCH then click on PILOT SEARCH. The index links to original vital records that can be saved electronically or printed.

Death Records

Early death records were usually recorded in registers, and they provided little more than the name, possibly the age, and the date of death. Sometimes the cause of death was mentioned. Today's death records are much more detailed, as shown in Illustration 9-8. Again, they are available at PILOT SEARCH as explained above under Marriage Records.

Modern death records are not standardized, even within the same state. Different state legislative orders required different information be collected. Death certificates are sometimes the most fruitful records for the family historian because they guide the researcher to many other sources of information. In Illustration 9-8 there is a column on the left covering what was known about the death. Experienced researchers understand that this information is most likely to be accurate, while the other information may be in error. Following up on the first column, "Regarding the Event," is most likely to bring other rewards.

Illustration 9-7 Example of a Marriage License

Regarding the Event	Regarding the Deceased	Regarding the Spouse
Date & time of death	Complete name of deceased	Name
Place of death	Birthplace	
Cause of death	Race and sex	
Informant's name	Age at time of death	
Informant's address	Residence at time of death	
Doctor's name	Occupation	
Doctor's address	Marital status	
Funeral Director	Name of father	
Funeral Home address	Name of mother, maiden name	
Informant's relationship	Birthplace of father	
Place of burial	Birthplace of mother	
Address of burial	In armed forces, yes or no	
Hospital or institution	Social Security Number	
	Usual place of residence	
	How long in the state	

Illustration 9-8   Information Often Found on Modern Death Records

YOUR TURN

After studying Illustration 9-8, indicate why you think
it is important to obtain death certificates.

Illustration 9-9 Example of a Death Certificate

For example, when using the information in this death certificate, the researcher should try to track down the **informant** and see if he or she is still alive. The researcher could also contact the funeral home and ask for its records. They could try to locate the cemetery and obtain the cemetery records. If the deceased was in the armed forces, military records could be obtained. If the deceased had a social security number, the official Form SS-5 Social Security Application could be obtained. And with an exact date of death, provided by the death certificate, you are more likely to locate newspaper obituaries. Today most of this follow-up work can be done online.

So you see, it is very important to obtain death certificates. They are rich in genealogical information and may clarify discrepancies in your family records. Remember: *look for an individual's vital records by obtaining the latest event first: death, then marriage, then the birth record.*

How to Locate Vital Records

In 1967, there were no publications to help you order vital records. Today we have several avenues to take, but there are several unique features to obtaining vital records in the United States which need to be understood first.

The Exceptions

1. Louisiana has "parishes," not counties.
2. There are special "recording districts" in Alaska and Hawaii.
3. There are multiple recording offices in Alabama, Arkansas, Iowa, Kentucky, Maine, Massachusetts, Mississippi, and Tennessee.
4. There are independent cities with their own vital records offices in Virginia.
5. Vital records are at the municipal (town) level in Connecticut, Rhode Island and Vermont.

In addition, other problems exist due to separate county recording offices, similarly or identically named localities, and other kinds of jurisdictional entities. For example:

ALABAMA: Four counties contain two separate recording offices: Barbour, Coffee, Jefferson, and St. Clair.

ALASKA: Alaskan counties are called "boroughs." There are 23 of them. However, land records are recorded in 34 "recording districts," which have different jurisdictions, so all the boroughs and districts overlap. You would need to know in which recording district any given town or city is located.

ARKANSAS: The counties of Arkansas, Carroll, Clay, Craighead, Franklin, Logan, Mississippi, Prairie, Sebastian, and Yell have two separate recording offices each.

HAWAII: One central office records all districts.

IOWA: Lee County has two recording offices.

LOUISIANA: The parish of St. Martin has two non-contiguous segments.

MAINE: Aroostook and Oxford counties each have two separate recording offices.

MARYLAND: The city of Baltimore has its own separate recording office.

MASSACHUSETTS: Berkshire and Bristol counties each have three recording

Terms to Understand

in·for·mant - An individual who provides information concerning a life event, such as a death. This individual could be a spouse, a son or daughter, or a next door neighbor.

A RULE OF THUMB

The county courts and recording offices usually have the public vital records.

offices. Essex, Middlesex and Worcester counties each have two recording offices.

MISSISSIPPI: Ten counties have two separate recording offices each: Bolivar, Carroll, Chickasaw, Harrison, Hinds, Jasper, Jones, Panola, Tallahatachie, and Yalobusha.

MISSOURI: The city of St. Louis has its own recording office.

NEVADA: Carson City has its own recording office.

PENNSYLVANIA: Although there is a statewide office, Pittsburgh and Philadelphia have their own recording offices.

TENNESSEE: Sullivan county has two separate recording offices.

VIRGINIA: There are forty-one independent cities in Virginia, but only twenty-seven have separate recording offices. The following fourteen share their recording offices with the surrounding county:

Bedford-Bedford County
Covington-Alleghany County
Emporia-Greenville County
Fairfax-Fairfax County
Falls Church-Arlington or Fairfax County
Franklin-Southhampton County
Galax-Carroll County
Harrisonburg-Rockingham County
Lexington-Rockbridge County
Manassas-Prince William County
Manassas Park-Prince William County
Norton-Wise County
Poquoson-York County
Williamsburg-James City County

States of Confusion

Those states which do not record vital records by county, such as the New England states, have other problems. With all recording being done at a city or town level, people may attempt to find documents in counties which are actually towns (or vice versa). Sometimes they are misfiled, as in the case of the Connecticut towns of Fairfield, Hartford, Litchfield, New Haven, New London, Tolland, and Windham, each having a corresponding Connecticut county by the same name.

In New Hampshire, the counties confused are Carroll, Grafton, Hillsborough, Merrimack, Strafford, and Sullivan.

In Rhode Island, this confusion takes place with Bristol, Newport, and Providence.

In Massachusetts (which does have a statewide vital records office), this also occurs with cities or towns having the names of the following counties: Barnstable, Essex, Franklin, Hampden, Nantucket, Norfolk, Plymouth, and Worcester.

Vermont has similar problems with Addison, Bennington, Chittenden, Essex, Franklin, Grand Isle, Orange, Rutland, Washington, Windham, and Windsor. There are also places in Vermont that have both a city and a town with the names of: Barre, Newport, Rutland, and St. Albans. So, even if you are given the place of birth, is it a town, a city, or a county?

Internet Access to State Offices

Today, most state offices can be reached via the Internet, and most state government offices are accessed on the Internet with a common **URL.** Examples are given below:

www.state.ak.us/   *www.state.al.us/*   *www.state.ar.us/*
www.state.az.us/   *www.state.ca.us/*   *www.state.co.us/*
www.state.hi.us/   *www.state.id.us/*   *www.state.in.us/*
www.state.il.us/   *www.state.ks.us/*   *www.state.ky.us/*
www.state.la.us/   *www.state.me.us/*   *www.state.va.us/*

You can also reach most state offices at their .gov websites, when you type out the state name, such as www.delaware.gov. A few exceptions of this are Massachusetts (www.mass.gov), Connecticut (www.ct.gov), and New Hampshire (www.nh.gov).

Also try:

Vital Records Information United States   *http://vitalrec.com*
VitalChek Network   *http://www.vitalchek.com/*

But for years genealogists have relied on a truly handy book, *The Handy Book for Genealogists,* to provide them with quick information to vital record offices. Genealogists can also consult *The Genealogist's Address Book* and *Ancestry's Red Book,* which provide similar information. These resources are most helpful for the genealogist. There are also links from vital record indexes at *Ancestry.com* to many vital record offices.

> **Terms to Understand**
>
> **URL** - Universal Record Locator or Internet address.

> **Terms to Understand**
>
> **tran·scribe** - To make a written or typewritten copy of a document, notes, etc.

YOUR TURN

After studying the previous materials, are there any family members for whom a birth, marriage or death record might need to be ordered? If so, name them.

Problems with Vital Records

Besides some of the obvious problems such as those shown above, as researchers we must be wary of:

1. Inaccurate information provided by informants.
2. Legibility and misreading of records.
3. The variety of spellings for names, which may cause records to be misfiled, difficult to find in indexes, or ignored (e.g., McPhail, MacPhaill, or McFail).
4. **Transcribed** indexes may contain errors in typing such as the transcriber reading an "L" for an "S" or a "T" for an "F". Try to determine all possibilities.

5. Sometimes records are severely restricted, or at least require a few hoops to be jumped through before going any further. For example, in some states you need to submit a copy of your birth certificate, drivers license, and a pedigree chart showing your relationship to the person on the record you are requesting.

Summary

Vital records offices are very valuable repositories. Duplicate copies of records held in smaller jurisdictions are often found at the county level as well, and they often have a better feel for the spelling of names found. If one set of records is lost or incomplete, try another place. And remember; there are many, many other sources for vital record information. See the bibliography at the end of this chapter for more sources to help you. Now, let's turn our attention to another location for obtaining genealogical sources--the public library.

PUBLIC LIBRARIES

Public libraries are important, and they exist to serve an entire community with a variety of needs. They are usually close to everyone, free of charge, and offer inter-library loan services to aid in obtaining other materials. However, because most of its sources are secondary sources, most *primary* genealogical research cannot be conducted in a public library. It often has a primary focus which caters to the needs of their users and contributors and not all are interested in genealogy.

While it is unlikely for every neighborhood library to have a major genealogy collection, it is not unlikely to find genealogical materials in every public library. Your next step after organizing your family information will be to ascertain what research has already been conducted by others, or who has already compiled a record on your family. This is part of a preliminary survey, the goal being to prevent duplication of effort. Much of this work can be accomplished through a public library. The problem for the beginning researcher lies in locating the materials he or she wants, because libraries use various cataloging systems.

Understanding the various identification systems will aid in locating materials wherever you go. If you look in the front of most new books you will find one or all of the following: the International Standard Book Number, the Dewey Decimal Classification, or the Library of Congress Classification.

A very wise teacher once said to me:
IT IS NOT SO IMPORTANT HOW MUCH YOU KNOW AND REMEMBER
as to know
WHERE TO FIND WHAT YOU NEED TO KNOW.

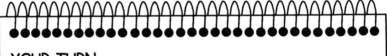

YOUR TURN

Write the name of a local public library you use.

International Standard Book Number

This is a group of ten numbers identifying a book and its publisher. International Standard Book Numbers, or ISBNs, simplify book ordering and, therefore, aid booksellers, librarians, and publishers. They have been used in the United States since 1969.

An ISBN has four parts separated by hyphens or spaces. The first group is called the "group identifier" and represents the geographical or language group of a book. For example, the English language is represented by the number "0".

The second group of numbers is the publisher prefix and represents the publisher of a book. The third represents the book title and is called the title prefix. The last number is called the "check digit" and is a number under 10 or X. As the ISBN goes through a computer, the check digit indicates errors that may have been made when the number was written.

SAMPLE

ISBN 0-016489-48-5

This is the ISBN number for the book *The Library of Congress: A Guide to Genealogical and Historical Research.*

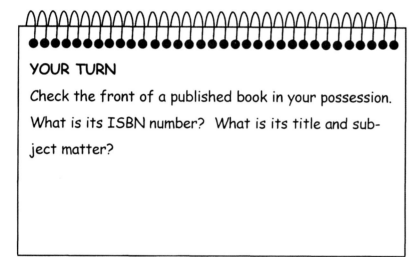

YOUR TURN

Check the front of a published book in your possession.

What is its ISBN number? What is its title and subject matter?

Dewey Decimal Classification

The Dewey Decimal Classification system was named for Melvil Dewey, who developed it in 1876. This system numbers books by dividing them into ten main groups, each represented by figures as demonstrated below:

000-099	Generalities (encyclopedias, bibliographies, periodicals, journalism)
100-199	Philosophy and Related Disciplines (philosophy, psychology, logic)
200-299	Religion
300-399	Social Science (economics, sociology, civics, law, education, vocations, customs)
400-499	Language (language, dictionaries, grammar)
500-599	Pure Sciences (mathematics, astronomy, physics, chemistry, geology, paleontology, biology, zoology, botany)
600-699	Technology (medicine, engineering, agriculture, home economics, business, radio, television, aviation)
700-799	The Arts (architecture, sculpture, painting, music, photography, recreation)

800-899   Literature (novels, poetry, plays, criticism)
900-999   General Geography and History

Each of these ten main classes are divided further into specialized fields. When the classification becomes very exact, the decimal is used. Specialists add or modify about 6,000 classification numbers yearly to account for current events and new knowledge.

The Family History Library in Salt Lake City, Utah, uses a modified version of the Dewey system in order to aid in browsing. However, browsing is not the best way to approach a library, since it might prevent a search of the true primary sources (those in *microform*). The library catalog should always be consulted.

Library of Congress Classification

This method of organizing and filing materials is found in many large research and university libraries because it provides greater precision in most fields and more room for expansion than the Dewey Decimal Classification system. While in 1900 only one library in the United States, the Library of Congress, had over a million items, by the 1980s, over 150 libraries in the United States had collections of over a million items.

The classification is broken down by a series of letters and numbers. The first letter in the set indicates one of twenty-one major areas of knowledge:

A=General Works	H=Social Science	Q=Science
B=Philosophy, Religion	J=Political Science	R=Medicine, Psychology
C=History	K=Law	S=Agriculture
D=History	L=Education	T=Technology
E=History	M=Music	U=Military Science
F=History	N=Fine Arts	V=Naval Science
G=Geography, Anthropology	P=Language, Recreation, Literature	Z=Bibliography, Library Science

The second letter stands for a subclassification. The numbers represent a specific topic. Many genealogy books start with "C" and "F" because of their historical background. F443 R5 W4 is the *History of Roane County, Tennessee* at the Sutro Library.

Approaching the Unfamiliar Library

Most genealogists are interested in similar areas: local histories, newspapers, maps, gazetteers, local biographies, old pictures, censuses, inventories of collections, and directories, to name a few. These materials are easy to find in a Family History Center because a FHC caters to genealogists. But what do you do when you enter a public library, a law library or other specialty library?

First: Have a Goal in Mind

You need to come prepared with specific questions you want answered.

Second: Always Use the Library Catalog

A library catalog is the easiest and fastest way to locate information in a library no matter what form of filing classification they use, because once you have found an item, the librarians can help you by using their knowledge of their own filing system.

First, look at the outside of the catalog, if it is in card form. Is it set up by locality, by subject, or by author-title? If it is on computer, look at the instructions in order to see if it is set up by locality, subject or author-title.

What is it you are trying to find? A county history under a "subject" catalog might be listed under the "history" category, or under the name of the county in the "locality" or "title" category. In summary, you need to understand the cataloging system used in the particular library you are using.

Second: Talk to the Reference Librarian

The local reference librarian could answer questions such as: Do you have newspapers on microfilm? Where are your maps and gazetteers? Do you have any "loose files" or "clip and save" drawers where biographical sketches of local people might be kept? Is there an old picture collection in this library? Do you have an inventory list of your collection?

The reference librarian also has information on interlibrary loan materials and other libraries or societies in the area that could help you. Often the local genealogical or historical society shares facilities with the local library, and it is possible that the librarian could put you in touch with others interested in genealogy.

Third: When All Else Fails, Browse

Although not the best way to locate information quickly, browsing the shelves and hideaways of libraries has been very fruitful over the years for this researcher when time was not of importance. And as you consider the history surrounding an individual's life, other sources may come to you. Perhaps those sources will lead you to a county courthouse.

COURTHOUSES

Courthouses often contain vital records, wills, and tax and land records. If the records have not been microfilmed, you might be required to visit a courthouse, or arrange for an agent to visit the courthouse, to obtain copies of records for you. Or you could write to the courthouse.

Courthouse

YOUR TURN

Indicate one individual and his or her birth and death dates. In which ways might visiting a courthouse help you obtain the information about the person you are seeking?

The *County Courthouse Book* (Genealogical Publishing Company) is an excellent source for information on courthouses you are interested in. It describes not only the locations, phone numbers, and e-mails, but also the cost of individual copies of records.

A word of caution. The public officials may be very overworked and under-paid in those departments dealing with the records you are searching. If at all possible, try to locate your court records on microfilm or fiche, if you are not close enough for a quick visit. This way, you have all the time you need to look carefully over the records, and the copies are much less expensive. I have found American courthouses very busy, and often the records are no longer in their care. The *County Courthouse Book* helps remedy much of the problem.

Courthouses are most important to search when people have lived in the 20th century. Many of their records are too recent to have been microfilmed and cataloged. There are excellent chapters on court records in both *The Source* and *The Researcher's Guide to American Genealogy*. Records from the past are often sent off to state archives or libraries. Except for records of the past hundred years, try the Family History Library first for the records you need.

HISTORICAL SOCIETIES

Historical Society

Throughout America, historical societies are involved in areas which touch the subjects dealt with by genealogists. They are cataloging memorabilia including diaries and vital records which could be of value to you. Often historical and genealogical societies are combined into one organization in a county. Sources in the bibliography for this chapter give suggestions for locating societies in the areas in which you may have an interest. Because of time limitations, they may not be able to do searches for you, but most can recommend someone who will.

I have always found some type of success visiting these wonderful places. Remember to search Mary Wheeler's *Directory of Historical Organizations in the United States and Canada.*

CONCLUSION

While we have only covered four basic repositories in this chapter, vital record offices, public libraries, local repositories such as genealogical societies and historical societies, and courthouses, more will be described in subsequent chapters. While you are learning which repository to use to solve which problem in your research, a "Repository Guide for Local Genealogists" has been prepared to help you (Illustration 9-10) determine where you might obtain a particular record in person, through correspondence, or on a loan basis.

REPOSITORY GUIDE FOR LOCAL GENEALOGISTS

FHC=Family History Center

RECORD	IN PERSON	BY CORRESPONDENCE	ON A LOAN BASIS
FEDERAL CENSUS	National Archives or its branch facility Libraries with census on film FHCs Purchase copies on CD	Hire record look-up assistance	Public library Heritage Quest loan program On loan at FHC Archival loan
STATE CENSUS	State Library	Hire record look-up assistance	"
VITAL RECORDS AFTER 1902	Courthouse in county of event	Write to state vital records repository	N/A
VITAL RECORDS BEFORE 1902	Courthouse in county of event State Library	Write to county of event; *Handy Book*; hire record look-up assistance	On loan at FHC Some on interlibrary loan
LAND & PROPERTY RECORDS	"	Write to county in question Hire record look-up assistance	On loan at FHC; indexes for others at FHC; some published in libraries
PROBATE RECORDS	"	Write to county in question Hire record look-up assistance	"
COMPILED FAMILY HISTORIES	Major libraries	Write societies; Hire record look-up assistance	On loan at FHC Heritage Quest loan program Major library interlibrary loan NEHGS loan; NGS loan
REVOLUTIONARY WAR & INDEXES	National Archives and field branches FHL	Order from National Archives Hire record look-up assistance	On loan at FHC Heritage Quest loan program Major library interlibrary loan
CIVIL WAR & 1812 SERVICE BOUNTY LAND* & PROBATE*	National Archives & some field branches; State Libraries have Confederate copies	State Adjutant General Hire record look-up assistance	On loan at FHC Some Heritage Quest Some interlibrary loan
COMPILED CENSUS INDEXES/1790-1920	National Archives & field branches & FHL	FHL photoduplication order, hire searcher	Some at local FHC such as AIS 1790-1850
FAMILY VITAL RECORDS	Family, periodicals, historical societies	Historical & lineage societies	On loan at FHC Some Heritage Quest
COURT RECORDS	Local courthouse	Hire record look-up assistance	On loan at FHC
CHURCH RECORDS	Local church or regional center	Hire record look-up assistance Local church or records center	On loan at FHC Some interlibrary
IMMIGRATION	Courthouse of jurisdiction	Hire searcher to visit courthouse	On loan at FHC
CEMETERY/BURIAL	Visit cemetery	Write to sexton	On loan at FHC

Illustration 9-10   Repository Guide for Local Genealogists

REPOSITORY GUIDE FOR GENERAL BACKGROUND

RECORD	IN PERSON	BY CORRESPONDENCE	ON A LOAN BASIS
FOREIGN & HISTORICAL	Public Libraries FHC	Hire record look-up assistance Historical & ethnic Societies Periodicals	Public library Heritage Quest On loan at FHC Archival loan
MAPS	State Library Public Libraries	Hire record look-up assistance Write to county Map sellers Historical societies	On loan at FHC Public Library
JURISDICTIONS AND COUNTY FORMATION	*Handy Book, Map Guide* County histories from public libraries	Write to county in question	Histories from FHL On loan at FHC Heritage Quest loan services

Illustration 9-11 Repository Guide for General Background

ASSIGNMENT 9: DETERMINING THE BEST REPOSITORY

1. Look over your pedigree. What records do you need to solve your current family history mystery?

2. Using the Repository Guide for Local Genealogists (pages 9-23 and 9-24), determine the most economical and most easily available repositories for solving your research problems.

3. Read a chapter in one of the books suggested in this chapter on repositories. List the chapter's title.

4. Write a sample form letter (on a separate piece of paper) which could be used for most correspondence to a genealogical or historical society. Keep in mind the following suggestions from your assigned reading: Limit your request to one or two items; make your request easy to answer; make copies of your letter; express appreciation; offer a fair exchange; and provide for return postage on a self-addressed, stamped envelope (SASE).

5. Visit your public library. Locate four of the following:
    a. A gazetteer (preferably the oldest one possible).
    b. An atlas of the area in which you are doing research.
    c. A history of your county.
    d. Newspapers or an index to them.
    e. The history of the state or country you are interested in researching.

6. Does your public library have a major genealogy collection? Could the reference librarian tell you where to go for more genealogical information in the area?

7. Select someone from your own research. Notice where he/she was born, married and died. Use some of the sources mentioned thus far in this book; *The Almanac of American History* by Arthur M. Schlesinger, Jr.; an area research guide for the states in which these events took place; an encyclopedia from a public library; or a history book of the place in question. Indicate an event which took place in the state in question during the years your ancestor lived there. Fill in the form below to help you get started thinking chronologically. Now try to locate some resources in your public library to understand these events.

Ancestor's Name: _____

Year of Birth: _____ Place of Birth: _____

What Happened That Year in This State: _____

_____
_____
_____
_____
_____
_____
_____

Marriage Year: _____ Marriage Place: _____

What Happened That Year in This State: _____

_____
_____
_____
_____
_____
_____
_____

Year of Death: _____ Place of Death: _____

What Happened That Year in This State: _____

_____
_____
_____
_____
_____

List Other Sources Which Might Now Be Searched:

_____
_____
_____
_____
_____
_____
_____
_____
_____
_____

YOUR TURN ANSWERS

Organizations or Agencies

A chamber of commerce in an ancestor's home town, county and city clerks, a local cemetery and its records, a local published history or historians, local postmasters, newspaper offices, state libraries, the National Archives, a genealogy record look-up service, genealogical and historical societies in each state, vital record repositories, churches, employment and Social Security offices are all possibilities.

Record Terms Providing Birth Information

Christenings, baptisms, hospital certificates, city records of births.

Record Terms Providing Marriage Information

Applications, banns, proclamations, bonds, certificates, licenses, returns, register entries, consent notices, marriage contracts, or intentions.

Record Terms Providing Death Information

Hospital death records, city death certificates, obituaries, mortician or coroner records, cemetery records, sexton records, church records of death.

General Value of Certificate of Vital Events

These could verify maiden name of mother, birthplaces of both parents, places of residence at various times, parents' occupations, if other children were born the descendants were unaware of, and the ages and location of birth, marriage and death for each person.

COMPUTER CHECKLIST #9

1. How does your program record repository addresses?

2. How do you link sources to their repository addresses in your program?

WEB SITES

Vital Records

Vital Records Information United States *http://vitalrec.com*
A comprehensive resource for obtaining vital records.

http://www.vitalchek.com/
Commercial site for ordering vital records online.

http://www.worldvitalrecords.com/
Commercial site where subscribers have access to United States and international vital records online. It was started by Paul Allen in 2006. Over 5,000 online databases with users in over 219 countries. After trying a search, you can look at their records for their low monthly or yearly subscription rates.

http://www.rootsweb.com/
Free site hosted by Ancestry.com that contains instructions on how to do genealogy in different parts of the world, abstracted and extracted information from vital records around the world, and user-supported pedigrees often with links to original sources. All genealogists should become familiar with this site.

Newspaper Archives

NOTE: Before subscribing, check the sites to see if your state is covered.

http://www.GenealogyBank.com
Newspapers from 1690-1977, obituaries from 1977-current, and other documents.

http://www.NewspaperArchive.com
Contains over one billion newspaper articles from 1759-present.

Tombstones
http://www.NamesInStone.com
This is a site that records cemetery tombstones in context with a GPS mapping system, and allows users to enter information on deceased persons. You can search the site for free, but membership allows you other options.

BIBLIOGRAPHY

Bentley, Elizabeth Petty. *County Courthouse Book.* 2nd ed. Baltimore: Genealogical Publishing Co., 1996

Bentley, Elizabeth Petty. *The Genealogist's Address Book.* 4th ed. Baltimore: Genealogical Publishing Co., 1998

Carter, Fran. *W.P.A., Works Progress Administration: Surveys, Guides, Inventories, City Town-County-States-National, Depositories-Unpublished-Published, Private Collections, Printed Church Surveys.* Galveston, TX: Frontier Press, c1990.

Eichholz, Alice, ed. *Ancestry's Red Book.* Rev. ed. Salt Lake City: Ancestry, 1992.

Ernst, Carl R. and Michael L. Sankey, eds. *Public Records Online: The National Guide to Private & Government Online Sources of Public Records.* 2nd ed. Facts on Demand Press, 1999.

_____. *The Handy Book for Genealogists.* 10th ed. Draper, Utah: Everton Publishers, 2002.

Greenwood, Val D. *The Researcher's Guide to American Genealogy.* 3rd ed. Baltimore: Genealogical Publishing Co., 2000.

Kemp, Thomas Jay. *International Vital Records Handbook.* 4th ed. Baltimore: Genealogical Publishing Co., 2000.

Kemp, Thomas Jay. *Virtual Roots: A Guide to Genealogy and Local History on the World Wide Web.* Wilmington, DE: Scholarly Resources, 1997.

Kirkham, E. Kay. *Survey of American Church Records.* 3rd ed. Logan, Utah: Everton, 1971.

Kot, James Douglas and Elizabeth Gorrell Kot. *United States Cemetery Address Book.* Vallejo, CA: Indices Publishing, c1994.

The National Directory of Morticians. Youngstown, Ohio: National Directory of Morticians, 1950—Irregular.

Neagles, James C. and Mark C. Neagles. *The Library of Congress: A Guide to Genealogical and Historical Research.* Salt Lake City: Ancestry, 1990.

The Sourcebook of Public Record Providers: The National Guide to Companies that Furnish Automated Public Record Information, Search Services, and Investigative Services. 2nd ed. Tempe, AZ: BRB Publications, c1994.

Schlesinger, Arthur M., Jr. ed. *Almanac of American History.* New York: Putnam, 1983.

Sperry, Kip. *New England Genealogical Research: A Guide to Sources.* Bowie, MD: Heritage Books, c1988.

Szucs, Loretto Dennis and Sandra Hargreaves Luebking. *The Source: A Guidebook of American Genealogy.* 3rd ed. Provo: MyFamily.com, Inc., 2006.

Wheeler, Mary Bray, ed. *Directory of Historical Organizations in the United States and Canada.* Nashville, TN: American Association for State and Local History Press, c1990.

U.S. Newspaper Program National Union List. 4th ed. Dublin, OH: Online Computer Library Center, 1993.

Magazines of a General Nature

Everton's Genealogical Helper. 1947-. Published by The Everton Publishers, P.O. Box 368, Logan, UT 84323-0368.

Ancestry. 1994-. Published by The Generations Network, Inc., 360 W. 4800 N., Provo, UT 84604.

Family Tree Magazine. 2000-. Published by Family Tree Magazine, Box 420235, Palm Coast, FL 32142.

CHAPTER 10

Resources of the Family History Library

"A library is thought in cold storage."
—Lord Samuel

The next major repository you should become familiar with is the Family History Library (FHL) in Salt Lake City, Utah, the largest genealogical library in the world. In addition, there are thousands of local Family History Centers around the world, which are "branch" libraries of this huge repository. Information on how to access and use a Family History Center will be given in Chapter 12.

In 1894, the Genealogical Society of Utah was organized for the purpose of collecting and making available all the genealogical information possible to interested persons who wanted to search out their ancestral lines. Over the years, the society tried to keep pace with the upsurge in genealogical needs, all the way from negotiating with nations for permission to microfilm their records to actually microfilming the vital records of the world.

By the late 1950s, computer technology was added, and in 1958 a shattering blast detonated a canyon wall southeast of Salt Lake City beginning what would take eight more years to complete—the Granite Mountain Records Vault. This vault was made to protect the library's precious resources, with 700 feet of solid granite overhead and three electronically operated, solid steel doors, each weighing over nine tons and all beveled inward so that any pressure or force, even from an atomic blast, would only seal them more tightly. Here, thousands of rolls of film are processed weekly and shared with anyone in the world who wishes to find his or her ancestors.

Then in June of 1999, the largest Internet site in the world for genealogists was introduced, making it possible for The Church of Jesus Christ of Latter-day Saints to share their computer databases of vital information freely with the world. The LDS site began to receive a half-million hits per day. I can but stand in awe!

But in order to benefit from these riches, you must become familiar with the *Family History Library Catalog (FHLC)*, so that you can access the non-electronic holdings. And to access the electronic databases of this repository, you will need to use the Internet.

Granite Mountain Records Vault

www.familysearch.org

Terms to Understand

e•lec•tron•ic re•sources - Refers to materials published or maintained in a computer or Internet format.

Terms to Understand

ser•ver - A computer with enough memory and ability to provide support to several other computers.

YOUR TURN

List one or more places you would like to learn more about at the *FamilySearch Wiki*.

YOUR TURN

List one place an ancestor lived, to see if the Family History Library has books, films, or fiche available covering that area:

FamilySearch, historically known as the Genealogical Society of Utah, is dedicated to the discovery and preservation of a record of the family of mankind, introducing individuals to their ancestors through the widespread access of records, and collaborating with others who share this vision. In 2008 the non-profit service known as *FamilySearch.org*, sponsored by The Church of Jesus Christ of Latter-day Saints, launched many new portions of its genealogical Web site. The launching of new services has been continuing as *FamilySearch* makes publically available in electronic format over one hundred years of collected materials formerly available in book, fiche, and film formats.

This chapter will cover the book, microfiche, and microfilm collections of the library and its Internet catalog, while the next chapter will cover **electronic resources**. Since it will be years before all data is available on the Internet, it is important to understand how to obtain these materials at a repository near you while the conversion to Internet availability is taking place. The basic purpose of the Internet catalog is to provide access to genealogical data and to assist individuals with their research processes from their home.

The *Family History Library Catalog*, the current name of the on-line catalog, was shortened to just *Library Catalog*, in the beta test of the new *FamilySearch*. It is used to locate the library's original and compiled resources. Using an enormous array of **servers**, new *FamilySearch* is built to facilitate collaboration between individuals, families, affiliates, and other repositories world-wide.

It was recognized that beginning genealogists would need research guidance in the use of specific records during specific time periods in different localities. A medium was sought that could be a friendly guide to the major surname histories, original vital records, and historical sources for each locality. This guide would be able to include sources available in the Family History Library as well as in other repositories. This resource was to be freely available to anyone having Internet access; accessable in a variety of languages, and able to contain millions of pages of printable instructions, maps, word lists, or images.

The original research assistance features were incorporated into a stand-alone program in 2008 called the *FamilySearch Wiki*. In 2010 it was pulled into regular *FamilySearch*. As stated on the front page it is "Free family history research advice for the community, by the community." Using a similar program that produced *Wikipedia* (a free encyclopedia with millions of articles contributed collaboratively using Wiki software, in dozens of languages), FamilySearch Wiki also uses meta Wiki but focuses on items of interest to family historians.

Users can enter a word search for a specific locations or subjects, or just browse the *FamilySearch Wiki*. Everyone is welcome to share information they have on areas where they have expertise; and genealogy societies are encouraged to post information about their resources and links to their society web pages. Current genealogy events are also listed under specific localities.

If you want to be kept abreast of articles in a specific locality at the *Wiki*, you can create an account and mark a page to be watched. If you contribute something, you are asked to post a biography of yourself and a place you can be reached. This is a wonderful resource for not only beginning genealogists, but also those more advanced.

USING THE FAMILY HISTORY LIBRARY CATALOG (FHLC)

The newest beta version of the FHLC made its debute in August 2010. It becomes better with input from its users. The catalog is the treasure map for locating the jewels in your family history. Let's review the old and new versions.

The new *Library Catalog* starts with two fields. The first is labeled **Search** with a dropdown list to select: **Place names, Last names,Titles, Author information, Subjects, Call numbers, Film numbers,** and **Keywords**. The second field is labeled **For** with a check box to click if you want "Exact" (e.g., spelling).

1. PLACE SEARCH: In the existing catalog *place search* is probably used the most. People want to know what films, fiche, books, or maps, for example, are available in the locality where their ancestor lived. Researchers obtain information from the most specific (a town or city) to the least specific locality (a county, state, region, and country). Within each level (city, county, state, or country), records are broken down further by subject categories. In this manner, a potential source of information on a family was not overlooked.

The beta version allows the locality entered in any way. When the locality is found, the catalog immediately displays **all** records of the FHL on that locality. The user may then narrow the selection by using new selection tools in the left margin labeled: **Place, Year, Category, Availability,** and **Language**. The **Place** search might include Europe or North America. **Year** might include centuries, e.g. 1600, 1700, 1800, 1900, according to what is listed; and when 1700 is clicked, for example, years are listed by decade so that sources are now arranged by records falling within those time periods. **Category** would list the record groups available in the currently displayed list. **Availability** would indicate sources at the FHL, as Digital Images, or at local Family History Centers. **Language** will sort all features by the language of the resource. This is particularly helpful on a surname search where text might be in Dutch, English, French, German, and Russian.

Illustration 10-1
Microfiche Sample

New York - Bibliographies
New York - Law and Legislation
New York - Military, Civil War
==========================
  New York, Allegany - Church Records
  New York, Allegany - Land andProperty
  New York, Allegany - Military - Civil War
================================
    New York, Albany, Berne - History
    New York, Albany, Albany - Census
    New York, Albany, Albany - Maps

Illustration 10-2
FHLC Place Search
with state and categories,
then state, county, and cate-
gories, then state, county,
town and categories.

Knowledgeable researchers used the "Place Search" feature as a helpful gazetteer-like section to know where to look when dealing with an unfamiliar locality. If you want to know what the FHL has available for Hastings, Nebraska, you could data enter "Hastings" in the top line of the PLACE SEARCH field. If you did not enter Nebraska in the other field, and there is something in the catalog involving this specific small locality anywhere, the results screen will provide all options. If you wanted the Nebraska listing, you would click on the hypertext link for Hastings, Adams, Nebraska. At this point, you would also know that there is at least one or more records specifically for the town of Hastings, in **Adams County**, Nebraska, at the county-wide level. In the new *Library Catalog*, all the sources appear at once so the above is not necessary.

This gazetteer-like feature is particularly helpful if you are looking for information on a foreign town and do not know how it is listed in the catalog, or if there is anything listed for that area. Many place names were recorded by recorders as they heard them, rather than the exact proper spelling for our immigrants. Names of places (towns, counties, and countries) can change over time. On the current version there is a browse feature to aid in locating a town or area with an unfamiliar name. You could, for example, enter the name of the country in the first place field box. Then click on the "Search button." Give the program time to find all options. Once the hypertext link to the country comes up, click on it. You will see a button "View Related Places" that when clicked, lists the next level of record jurisdictions. Browsing through those names and trying to pronounce them often gives you the correct spelling.

Knowing the larger area in the country such as a province worked as well. Click on the "View Related Places when viewing the Province. Look for a spelling similar to the one recorded in family, church or government records.

Terms to Understand

browse - While using the *Family History Library Catalog*, the ability to casually inspect various localities when, for example, an exact spelling in a locality is unknown.

Once you have located the place you seek, you need to be aware of the FHLC *category terms*, as shown on page 10-5. Category headings differ by locality.

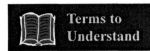

Terms to Understand

Eth•nol•o•gy - A study of human cultures including nationalities, races and their origins, viz., Huguenots, Cherokees, etc.

You might be seeking birth, marriage, or death records, but when you look at the FHLC Category Headings for the current catalog on the next page, those topics cannot be found. This is because the category term for them is *Vital Records*. This *Vital Records* heading may also include a whole variety of other records that would provide birth, marriage or death information, including ministers' returns, coffin maker's notes, or sexton's records.

Another category that gives beginning researchers problems is ship passenger lists that would be listed under the term *Emigration and Immigration*. The new *Library Catalog* beta includes three topics together: *Emigration, Immigration, and Citizenship*. The goal is to more easily guide users to records that would provide the same information.

Information listed under the largest jurisdictional area of a country would naturally contain more sources than smaller areas. But smaller localities may contain more specific information. Both catalog versions list the categories alphabetically. This would include federal census records listed under the locality of the *United States* and also under each state using the category heading "Census." That same category could be searched under the state, county, or town, and would usually contain different entries. Under the state, it might give the same film reel as under the United States, or it might give a state-wide index to the census. Under the county, it might give a county-wide transcript of the census. The first listings in the catalog for Nebraska will be references to information that pertain to the whole state listed alphabetically by category, such as Autobiographies, Biographies, Cemetery Records, Church Records, **Ethnology**, Histories, Land Records, Probate Records, Vital Records, etc. This will be repeated for categories at the county, and then town level.

2. SURNAME OR LAST NAME SEARCH: This section in both catalogs references family histories, biographies, personal journals, and other related information. Individual surnames are searched using key words to focus on those records most likely to contain the correct information.

In the current catalog these entries are arranged alphabetically in surname order, regardless of the country of origin or residence of the individual. By using the new FamilySearch catalog being beta tested now, you can arrange the records using new tools on the left margin. Either way (old or new) using this section of the catalog helps you to determine if there is already a published history for your family from which you can gain additional information and save much duplication of effort.

Each entry is also cross-referenced according to the other major names listed in the history. Every name mentioned in the history will not have an entry, but the major ones will. Because of former time and space limitations, only the surnames mentioned on the title page or introduction of a work were listed. The current version searches by all names in the catalog file and locates many more references.

Using the sorting tools in the left margin, allows greater ease in the new *Library Catalog* to sort a list of sources by year of coverage for example If the name of the history is *The Clark Anderson family, including the Surnames of Jones, Adams, Clark and Jackson*, references will also be found under the surnames of Jones, Adams, Clark, and Jackson, in addition to Anderson. Clicking on the title brings up a description of what is contained in the resource such as a locality, when the people mentioned in the book came to the U.S.A., and other unique identifying information to help you determine if these could be your relative. The other sorting tools help you to determine which repository might contain a record you could use such as a local Family History Center, or another research repository.

FHLC Category Headings

Almanacs	Medical Records
Archives and Libraries	Merchant Marine
Bible Records	Migration, Internal
Bibliography	Military History
Buddhist Directories	Military Records
Business Records and	Minorities
Commerce	Names, Geographical
Cemeteries	Names, Personal
Census	Native Races
Centennial Celebrations, etc.	Naturalization and Citizenship
Chronology	Newspapers
Church Directories	Nobility
Church History	Notarial Records
Church Records	Obituaries
Civil Registration	Occupations
Colonization	Officials and Employees
Correctional Institutions	Orphans and Orphanages
Court Records	Pensions
Description and Travel	Periodicals
Directories	Politics and Government
Dwellings	Poor Houses, Poor Law, etc.
Emigration and Immigration	Population
Encyclopedias and Dictionaries	Postal and Shipping Guides
Ethnology *3	Probate Records*
Folklore	Public Records
Gazetteers	Religion and Religious Life
Genealogy *1, 2	Schools
Guardian and Ward	Shinto Directories
Handwriting	Shinto Records
Heraldry	Slavery and Bondage
Historical Geography	Social Life and Customs
History	Societies
Islamic Directories	Sources
Islamic Records	Statistics
Jewish History	Taxation
Jewish Records	Town Records
Land and Property	Visitations, Heraldic
Language and Languages	Vital Records
Law and Legislation	Voting Registers
Manors	Yearbooks
Maps	

* Includes Wills
*1 Family Histories - Genealogy
*2 Research Aids - Genealogy, How To
*3 Studies of groups, nationalities, races and their origins, viz.,
   Huguenots, Cherokees, etc.

Illustration 10-3   FHLC Category Headings

3. KEYWORD SEARCH: Try using a word that would explain what you seek. This search can also be used to limit common surname histories that could be linked to yours. Keywords can be part of a title, a place, an author, note about a collection or series, and subjects. Type a word or phrase that describes what you want to find. This works for combined subjects such as "Finnish Immigration", which brought up 41 titles in numerous localities and time periods.

4. TITLE SEARCH: If you were given the name of a book as a source within a published family history or in the bibliography of a genealogy lecture, you could find that source fastest by using the Title Search. You also do not need to know the order of the words in the title for this option to work.

5. FILM/FICHE SEARCH: In a microfilm or fiche search, you should type the numbers only. Do not type punctuation, such as commas or hyphens. And you do not need to type zeros at the beginning of the number. This is very helpful if you find a film number as a citation in a periodical or published resource in traditional or electronic format.

6. AUTHOR SEARCH: If you were given the abbreviated name of a book in a bibliography, such as Mills Citation, you would find that information fastest by using the Author Search "Mills, Elizabeth Shown." Perhaps you heard of the Andrea Collection on South Carolina research. Look up "Andrea" and you could learn what this collection contains.

7. SUBJECT SEARCH: This section contains entries about particular subjects of a general nature that might cover more than one locality, such as LDS Church Records, Native Americans, Heraldry, or Quaker Records. This index will lead you to books, microfilms, microfiche, CD-Roms, and other resources available on those subjects.

8. CALL NUMBER SEARCH: This search is very useful when you have written down a call number on a research log, but have forgotten what the title was.

USING THE RESULTS FROM THE FHLC

Now that the eight search options to the existing and new catalog have been explained, here are some tips for using the results. Notice on this surname search results list that there were 35 matching titles that could be ordered by title or by the author.

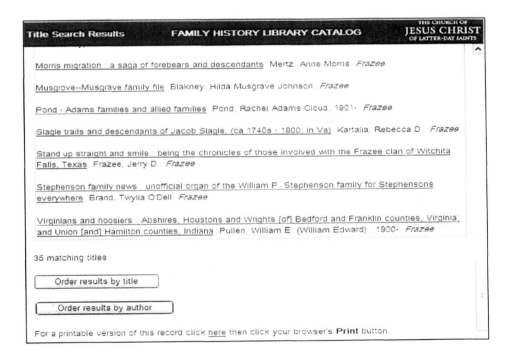

Clicking on the word <u>here</u> (shown at the bottom of the previous page) would give you a copy of this list, but it is better to click on the underlined (hyperlinked) entries themselves first for a full description. Below is an example of what is found when you click on the link for the last item on page 10-6.

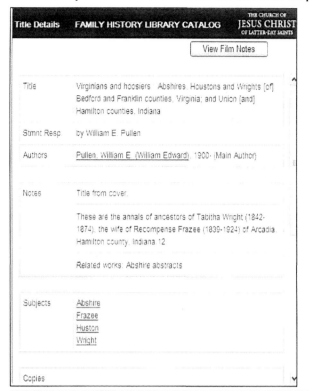

If the resource is also found on a microfilm, that film can be ordered to your local Family History Center (FHC). These FHC facilities will be covered in a subsequent chapter. This means that you can have access to much of the printed materials you seek at a local FHC if it is also on microfilm or fiche, even if it is not yet on the Internet. They can be rented for a nominal fee to pay for postage and handling. The book on the left is available on film if you look at the rest of the entry in the next illustration.

By clicking on the printable version option at

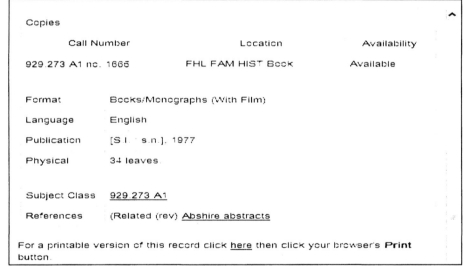

the bottom of the page, you can copy and paste the main words from the citation above into notepad in **text** or in **ASCII** format. This printable version option removes the **html** coding before pasting the text into your citation. Copy and paste can prevent typographical errors in call numbers from creeping into your citations, resulting in greater accuracy and saving time as you make proper citations for your genealogy computer program and your Research Planners. Citing a source for the death date of Recompense Frazee from the book is given below.

1924 DEATH: IN, Hamilton Co., Arcadia, Virginians and Hoosiers: Abshires, Houstons, and Wrights [of] Bedford and Franklin Counties, Virginia; and Union [and] Hamilton Counties, Indiana by William E. Pullen. FHL FAM HIST Book 929.273 A1 no. 1665, page 3:

Recompense Frazee died 23 Jan 1924 in Arcadia, Indiana.

Terms to Understand

Home page - In an Internet program, it is the main page of a particular Web site from which other pages branch.

Terms to Understand

Nav•i•ga•tion bar - On an Internet screen, a menu of options which take you somewhere else within the program.

But if you want to keep more information about the resource, you can keep a more detailed citation as follows by copying more information.

Authors: Pullen, William E. (William Edward), 1900- (Main Author)

Notes: Title from cover. These are the annals of ancestors of Tabitha Wright (1842-1874), the wife of Recompense Frazee (1839-1924) of Arcadia, Hamilton county, Indiana.

Subjects: Abshire, Frazee, Huston, Wright

Copies Call Number - Location - Status
929.273 A1 no. 1665 - FHL FAMHIST Book - Available

Format Books Monographs (With Film)
Language English; Publication [S.l. : s.n.], 1977; Physical 34 leaves.
Subject Class 929.273 A1; References (Related (rev) Abshire abstracts
Film Notes Note - Location [Film]: Also on microfilm. Salt Lake City : Filmed by the Genealogical Society of Utah, 1977, on 1 microfilm reel ; 35 mm. - FHL US CAN Film 982318 Item 5.

This ability to print items (to paper or to file) from the catalog is available through all eight searches. It is particularly helpful when searching probate, land and property, and military records where hundreds of reels of film might be found under one listing. You can save a lot of printing expenses by learning to use these copy and paste features into your word processing program.

NAVIGATING *FAMILYSEARCH.ORG*

Once you arrive at the **home page** of *FamilySearch.org*, you will have the option to immediately search for an ancestor using a very powerful search engine that searches several data bases at once. However, until you have more experience understanding record variations, this step might be unsuccessful for you, and you might decide this is not a good site. With experimentation and practice it can be one of the most powerful sites you will ever use. Current *FamilySearch* has a **navigation bar** across the top of the home page listing:

1. The SEARCH RECORDS tab.
2. The INDEX RECORDS tab.
3. The SHARE tab.
4. The RESEARCH HELPS tab.
5. The LIBRARY tab.

The SEARCH RECORDS tab includes an:
1. *Advanced Search* where you could search just the *Ancestral File*, the federal census record indexes made by the volunteers for the FHL that link to original census records, the *International Genealogical Index*, the *Pedigree Resource File*, the *US Social Security Death Index*, or the *Vital Records Index* (all of which will be covered in the next chapter).
2. Or you could select the *Record Search Pilot* option. Here is where the results of indexes being linked to original records by 30,000 volunteers around the world, are making more free records available online. It is a "pilot" because as this book goes to press, there will be times when records will not be available as additional records and features are added to the system. This will go on for years as over two million films containing records world-wide are digitized, indexed, and linked together. Those who help with indexing are given the opportunity to use the records as they are being indexed, and they don't have to wait for them to be made available to the public. Anyone is welcome to help with indexing. More on this in Chapter 11.

3.   There is also a link under the SEARCH RECORDS tab to the *Family History Library Catalog* that we discussed above.

4.   There is also a drop-down option to go to *Historical Books.* These are digitized books that can be used immediately online. There are over 17,500 of them currently online. The files in this collection are displayed using *Adobe Reader.* You can download a copy of *Adobe Reader* from this page.

5.   There is a link to *Websites* at the SEARCH RECORDS tab that provides information on genealogy topics that have been itemized using categories introduced in this chapter. There are also links to other research tools and support.

The **INDEX RECORDS** tab currently has only one link.

It leads you to the volunteer area of *FamilySearch* if you want to help speed up the availability of online records. Here you may sign up as a volunteer to help create <u>free</u> public access to new, as well as existing records.

The **SHARE** tab currently has one link as well.

Here is where you go once you have done your best to source and record the information on your family, and you are ready to share with others the records you have gathered. This is done by making a submission to the *Pedigree Resource File.* More on this option in later chapters because we are still working on locating, recording, filing, and sourcing our own information.

Click the **RESEARCH HELPS** tab if you want to:
1.   Find excellent genealogical articles: choose ARTICLES.
2.   Find research guides, such as a Latin Word list: choose GUIDANCE
3.   Learn about the record groups in South Carolina. You can print out a list of instructions under the hundreds listed at the: WIKI.
4.   Ask a specific question: select ASK A QUESTION
5.   Learn how to do German research: select ATTEND AN ONLINE CLASS, search the topics on this page and those offered in the left tool bar.

The **LIBRARY** tab was introduced above, but it has more options:
1.   Family History Library: select this option for these questions:
        A.   A current listing of the hours and holidays of the library.
        B.   Services, such as classes taught in the Family History Library each day given on a monthly calendar.
        C.   Find key resources of the library - see left tool bar.
        D.   Learn the rules covering the library, its floor plan, and how to prepare to visit the library, or bring a group to visit.
        E.   Learn about parking, and visiting Salt Lake City.
2.   Family History Centers
        A.   Find the addresses for a Family History Center in your area.
        B.   Find what is available at a local Family History Center.
3.   Education - Links to educational opportunities, such as independent study classes, genealogy courses, genealogy conferences, and institutes.
4.   Family History Library Catalog (this has been discussed above).

NAVIGATING NEW *FAMILYSEARCH.ORG*

When you arrive at the **home page** of new *FamilySearch.org*, you will have the option to click four options across the top: **Learn, FamilySearch Centers, Indexing** and **Blog**. The **Learn** option would take users to online training regarding genealogy research methodology given orally, by print or video.

FamilySearch Centers will be explored in Chapter 12. **Indexing** was explained on page 10-8. The **Blog** option is part of the new collaboration features. It leads to a link on *Facebook*, posts announcements regarding records recently discovered or made available, provides a place for news and press articles as well as instructing users on *FamilySearch Affiliates*.

Below the four options just reviewed, in the main window are the words "Search for an ancestor" with three other options: **Historical Records, Family Trees,** or **Library Catalog**. Fields are available to enter a **First and middle name(s), Last Name, Birth Year, Location, Death Year,** and **Location**. Once even a name is filled out the user can click one of two buttons: **Search** or **Advanced Search**. Depending on the option selected, either historical records, family trees, or published books regarding an individual will fill the screen.

Below the search fields, there is an option to "Browse by location." Users can either click on the world map, or select from **Africa; Asia and Middle East; Australia and New Zealand; South America; Europe; Pacific Islands**; or **USA, Canada, and Mexico**. This then brings up a list of new sources (currently in FamilySearch Pilot) that are indexed and linked to sources, or in the processing of being completed. Users may use the search template above to access these records. Clicking on **Historical Records** while using the search template, brings up all the resources in all the sources of FamilySearch for an individual. Selecting **Trees** brings up an individual sought in the search template in all the pedigree-linked databases. It identifies the contributors and their contact information. Selecting **Library Catalog** has been explained in previous pages and it focuses on performing a surname search for an individual.

In the right margin, users can click the words, **Getting Started, How to,** and **FamilySearch Centers**. These links have various sublinks depending on the area in which a person would like to focus.

CONCLUSION

As explained, the current and new *FamilySearch* features are powerful guidance tools to performing research anywhere in the world, to understanding the collection of the Family History Library itself, and to work with others to put together an accurate, well-sourced, family history. Mastering the use of these tools will bring you years of enjoyment.

Chapter 11 will cover the electronic resources of the Family History Library. Most beginners are unaware that millions of records from foreign countries have been extracted from their original format in a foreign language and indexed to

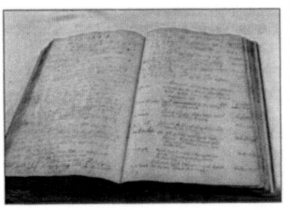

make them easier for you to find your particular ancestor. Others have been translated or transcribed to make foreign research easier to do. In addition, millions of U.S. records have been indexed and linked to original images which can greatly speed up a users abilities to find evidence on their families.

ASSIGNMENT 10: USING THE FHLC

1. Using either the *FamilySearch Wiki* or the RESEARCH HELP tab at *FamilySearch.org*, become familiar with the records of one state where your ancestors lived by locating that state and printing out the guide to its records. Then write a paragraph about some new things you learned about this state.

2. Use the *Library Catalog (or previous FHLC)* to search for a published history on one of your family surnames which you selected in the "Your Turn" assignments in Chapter 10. Record below what you discovered.

3. Use the *Library Catalog (or previous FHLC)* to search for the locality you selected in the "Your Turn" assignments in Chapter 10. Record below what you learned.

YOUR TURN ANSWERS

See Assignment 10 above for an application of this chapter's Your Turn Assignments.

COMPUTER CHECKLIST #10 Saving Time with Sources

Researchers often use the same information in different formats for different reasons. For example, they take the information from an online library catalog to prepare a list of materials to be searched when they can take advantage of the resources of that particular library. The information is recorded on a research planner if done in advance. If the information is recorded as the researcher is in the library and finds information in a resource, it is usually recorded on a research log.

When the researcher finds the evidence for a life event (such as a birth date, a marriage, a residence, or a migration clue) in a library source, the facts about the source are recorded as a citation in the general notes field of the researcher's genealogy computer program.

When the researcher writes a client report or a report for personal analysis of data, the same information used to locate the record or cite a source in the genealogy computer program would now be formatted to use as a footnote, end-note, or bibliography. Knowing how to quickly copy and record the information in online catalogs to save time and provide accuracy in source documentation, is an important skill to develop.

1. Explain how you could use the online *Library Catalog* of the Family History Library to obtain the complete information needed to form a research citation to be used in your research planner or research log.

2. Explain the process for locating the information, and then copying and pasting the necessary facts into a word processing program (such as Word, Notepad, or WordPerfect).

3. Then use this one source documentation entry in four unique formats, such as in:

    A.   A research planner or research log entry;

    B.   The general notes field of your genealogy computer program to provide evidence of a particular event;

    C.   In a report footnote;

    D.   In a report bibliography.

WEB SITE

http:/www.familysearch.org
Introduced May 24, 1999, it is the most user friendly, and largest genealogy site in the world. New information is constantly being added. Information scanned and indexed by *FamilySearch* is free to users worldwide, but some indexes found at this site may take users to sites where copies of original documents may need to be purchased from other owners who have paid to digitize images. Billions of indexes and images are available for the United States, Western Europe, Scandinavia, and Mexico, with other countries being added. All geneal-ogists should be aware of this key website.

BIBLIOGRAPHY

The Church of Jesus Christ of Latter-day Saints. Family History Library Catalog. Salt Lake City: The Church of Jesus Christ of Latter-day Saints, July 2010. www.familysearch.org>Click on the LIBRARY tab>Select the LIBRARY CATA-LOG option>Watch the online video>**The Family History Library Catalog Overview** then give feedback on the overview.

The Church of Jesus Christ of Latter-day Saints. Family History Library Catalog. Salt Lake City: The Church of Jesus Christ of Latter-day Saints, July 2010. www.familysearch.org>Click on the LIBRARY tab>Select the LIBRARY CATA-LOG option>Click on "Take a look at the beta FamilySearch Catalog," the give feedback on your opinion.

Major Databases of the Family History Library

"It is a capital mistake to theorize before one has data."
–Sir Arthur Conan Doyle

Learning to use specific resources in specific repositories is part of the success of a family history researcher. Databases have been developed for users of the Family History Library by taking facts from several record groups of particular value to genealogists and sorting the information by surname, dates, or events. These databases prove very helpful to beginning as well as advanced genealogists because they often lead to primary sources. Primary sources are critically important for accurate research.

FAMILY HISTORY LIBRARY DABABASE EXAMPLES

Below are listed some of the key database collections available through the Family History Library. Each has its own function. There are those that:

- Provide access to original national or international church records, as they also provide clues to relationships (*IGI*).
- Link continous generations, based on the submissions of many individuals (*Ancestral File*, unsourced; or *Pedigree Resource File*, sourced).
- Provide death and residence information for those deceased in the U.S. since the 1940s (*Social Security Death Index*).
- Provide the death date for those who died in some of America's wars (*Military Index*).
- Act as a finding aid to the millions of individuals who were enumerated in the United States census records (such as the *1880 United States Federal Census Index and Abstracts*).
- Act as a finding aid to the millions of individuals who were enumerated in Canada, England, Wales, Scotland, and Ireland in 1881 (such as the *1881 Canadian and 1881 British Census Indexes and Abstracts*).
- Index the christening and marriage records of the established church of Scotland up to 1855 (*Scottish Parochial Index*).
- Act as a finding aid to the vital records of Australia, North America, and several other countries. (Vital Record CDs).

Terms to Understand

International Genealogical Index (IGI) - Started in 1969, this index now contains over one billion names located under the SEARCH tab at www.familysearch.org. It is arranged by surname, date, and locality. Millions of names have been "extracted" by volunteers who copy data from original birth, christening, marriage, death, or probate records. Prior to 1942, names now in the IGI were submitted by various individuals using home sources or family knowledge. Using this index can help researchers locate elusive ancestors, find others searching your lines, locate primary sources, and pinpoint localities throughout the world where unique surnames are found.

Terms to Understand

ex•trac•ting - The process of copying specific pieces of essential information from an original record. The original source, if searched, often contains more valuable information that was not extracted.

Terms to Understand

sub•mit•ter - One who provides information to a database or other collection from their personal research.

Some of the above databases are found online at *www.familysearch.org*, and others are located at the Family History Library or its branch Family History Centers. Some indexes are available in CD format for purchase at the Web site. Often CDs have more search options than what can be done online.

Index	Family History Library	Family History Center	FamilySearch Internet	Available to Purchase
IGI	***	***	***	
Ancestral File	***	***	***	
SSDI	***	***	***	
Military Index	***	***		
Vital Record CDs	***	***		**
1880 U.S. Census	***	***	***	**
1881 British Census	***	***	***	**
Scottish Parochial Index	***	***		
Pedigree Resource File	***	***	Index only	**

Illustration 11-1 Some Indexes of the Family History Library
(*** Available at the locality in the column heading)
(**Available at www.FamilySearch.org)

WHAT IS THE IGI?

The ***International Genealogical Index (IGI)*** is an index to names found in the computerized files of The Church of Jesus Christ of Latter-day Saints (LDS). As of 2008, it contained over one billion names, and it continues to grow through the efforts of volunteers involved in a worldwide vital records **extraction** program of the LDS Church and other submitters.

The *IGI* contains ***names of deceased persons only***, so don't use it for locating **living** relatives. Most of the names are of persons living from the early 1500s to about 1900, although some are from more recent times. In the late 1990s, the information linking the IGI to records submitted by LDS Church members was separated from the IGI and placed into a file known as the *LDS Ordinance Index*, to make it easier to work with the two files. You must sign in as an LDS member to access the *Ordinance Index* at *www.familysearch.org*.

The IGI is literally the largest database of its kind in the world. It contains church records of almost every denomination, extracted and indexed for the vital information the records contain. It is a tremendous tool for genealogists internationally, since in many areas of the world church records provide the birth, marriage, and death information genealogists seek to establish their relationships.

Many entries in the IGI are duplicated or contain some, but not all, of the correct information. Duplication came about for several reasons. In some cases, those who submitted a birth date, for example, obtained that date from a family Bible and no locality was entered. Sometimes the submitter entered the family's last known residence as the birth place. Years later, another relative submitted the family information using a birth date found on a death certificate, and the date was wrong but the place might have been correct or partially correct. Usually, it is a good idea, to study all of the entries for the person you seek, and be aware of the sources provided. A great clue can be the name of the submitter. Learning about that submitter could give evidence of a relationship to a family and a cousin with whom to compare research.

The *IGI* Lists Individuals, Not Families

While the *IGI* does link one individual to another, such as a child to a parent, or a husband to a wife, it does not continue to link an entire family to show family relationships. For each record, the *IGI* includes the following:

1. Name of an individual.
2. Name of the parents OR the name of a spouse.
3. Sex of the individual if listed in the original record.
4. Type of event (birth, christening, marriage, etc.).
5. Date of event.
6. Place of event.
7. A film, fiche, or file from which the source of the original entry came.

The *IGI* is an index. If you find an ancestor's name in the index of a book, wouldn't you go to the original page and see what more could be learned? The same goes for the *IGI*. It does not necessarily include all the genealogical information known about a person even if that information was in the original record from which the index was extracted. Since millions of entries in the IGI are extracted from vital records created by governments or churches, and are, therefore, not limited to names of LDS Church members or their ancestors, this is a very important source for all genealogists. But the greatest value comes when the original source is studied. So, find your ancestor, or your ancestor's siblings in the index, and then trace back the information to the original record.

Searching the *IGI* requires some practice. In fact, in some geographical areas, an understanding of the names in general for that country is helpful. For example, in Norway, Finland, Sweden, Iceland, Wales, Scotland, and Monmouthshire, England, entries are arranged alphabetically by GIVEN name, as well as by SURNAME. This is because in those countries, historically, the surname changes in accordance with a **patronymic** naming system.

However, even in countries where a patronymic naming system is not used, name variations often occur because of the pronunciation of a word that might result in subtle naming variations. Johan in Sweden could be Jon or John in other countries. At the *FamilySearch.org* Web site, training is available for using the *IGI* under various circumstances.

IGI Sources of Information

The *IGI* was the first attempt to put LDS church data, as it related to temple work, into electronic format. Prior to 1942 members took names of their deceased relatives to the temple when they went. Each temple kept its own separate ledger of baptisms, endowments, and sealings that were kept in chronological order as they were performed. The information was cross indexed on little cards known as the *TIB*, or *Temple Index Bureau.*

 Terms to Understand

liv • ing - In many genealogical databases, including the *Pedigree Resource File* and the *Ancestral File* this term is used in place of an individual's name, if he or she was born in the last 95 years and no death date was listed. In the *IGI*, this term refers to individuals who do not have a known death date or whose birth date is less than 110 years prior to publication of the index.

 Terms to Understand

pat • ro • nym • ics Of, relating to, or derived from the name of one's father or a paternal ancestor. If Lisa was the daughter of Johan, her full name would be Lisa Johansdotter. If Michael were the son of Erik, his full name would be Michael Eriksson. If this Michael had a son Erik, that son would be called Erik Michaelsson.

Terms to Understand

pa•tron sub•mit•ted - Sometimes called "unverified information", from an individual's genealogy files or personal research. However, this would depend upon which year the information was submitted. While pre-1942 information was unsourced, later periods of time required more and more documentation. This term really means information submitted by a patron of the LDS Church into the IGI or other LDS files.

In the mid 1960s, the *TIB* was the only way to tell if someone had already submitted your ancestor's name. But even during the few days it took for the card to be pulled, and a letter written to inform you of the results of the *TIB* search, someone else could have performed the same work. Thus much duplication appeared at this time.

Today most of the names from the old temple record books are in the *IGI*. When you find someone in the *IGI*, you can look down at the bottom of the entry at *www.familysearch.org*, and see a reference to the source. If all you find is that this was submitted years ago and no other source is available, then you won't need to search further.

Between 1942 and 1969, names could be submitted on family group sheets. This tied a whole family together more easily, and a series of records known as the *Family Group Records Archives (FGRA)* was assembled. Some sources were provided and often errors occurred when information was transcribed by hand. Over the years these records have been microfilmed, and several were indexed by individuals and organizations in New England because so many of the early LDS converts came from that area. If you consult the film number on one of these IGI entries, you will see the group of names submitted by the LDS patron at this time and will probably be given a link to the *FGRA*.

Between 1969 and 1990 the LDS Church started using computers to aid **patron submitted** entries of family information. If an entry was submitted in 1972, it would be part of batch 72, followed by 3 numbers referencing the day of the year of the submission so those next 3 numbers would be lower than 365. Then the last 2 numbers would reference the batch number for that one day so this would be a number from 0-99, and then a two digit sheet number. So 7226414 15 translates to work submitted in 1972, on the 264th day, the 14th batch of names, sheet #15. This is helpful to know when the source references a batch number. Obtain the microfilm reel and scroll down to the number you want to see. The sources were given on these submissions, so seeing the submission form is very helpful for submissions during this time period.

Eventually, volunteers were used to extract births, christenings, and marriages from many countries to put into the *IGI*. The sources for these extracted items will indicate "extracted from" and give the name of the place and a film number. Often an entire roll of microfilm will contain extracts for one place. By ordering the microfilm for the computer output of those extracts (a second film number listed in the source on many extracted submissions), it is often easier to do research in a particular locality.

There is another reason to search this original record. Often there are records on the original film that were not put into the extraction batch. It might have been that the local government said that only records during specific years could go into the index being made. But now it is several years later, so you could find information on your ancestor who might be in the later record for the same locality. Don't assume your ancestor is not in the record, just because he or she was not indexed.

Between 1990 and the present time (2010), patrons were encouraged to submit genealogical information in electronic format called a GEDCOM file. This was used to submit information into the *Ancestral File* (however, the source information was not included), and currently the *Pedigree Resource File* (in which sources of information could be included and eventually they could link to original documents). However, temple work was submitted in its own program.

Extraction projects are continuing, and each extracted entry in the *IGI* has the original document cited and eventually linked to original sources. A new combined database including all submissions from the *Ancestral File*, the *IGI*, the thousands of extraction projects around the world, and other databases will soon link patrons directly to the sources of information from more and more indexes.

You can tell if an item was extracted by looking at the batch number as well. Extracted records are prefixed with a letter such as M, P, or C. Marriage extractions might be written M004161. These are very simplified instructions because New FamilySearch is involved in hundreds of new projects not released as this book goes to print. You might find it advantageous to use a Search Engine such as Google, and enter, "What's new at New FamilySearch?" and see what's new.

LIMITATIONS OF THE IGI

There are several limitations to the *IGI*, so study these in order to use this database most effectively:

1. It is an index only for those records entered into it.

   The *IGI* is not an index to ALL records for any place or time period. Nor is it an index to all records available at the Family History Library. Nor is it an index to all Temple information.

2. It may leave out names in the original record.

   As with any index, names found in the original records may be omitted, or a name may have been misinterpreted and indexed incorrectly. Even though the vital records of a place have been extracted, some names were illegible and so were not copied or entered into the *IGI*. Although every effort is made to assure correctness, some names are interpreted incorrectly. For example, Herfoot may be listed as Kerfoot, or Hubbins may be listed as Stubbins. Sometimes, due to rights of privacy, certain years were not included in an extracted grouping of records.

3. It does not list all the information on an individual.

   Because the *IGI* is an index, only the information sufficient to identify a person is given. But it does identify each person listed and provides a reference number for the source of the information. There may be additional information in the source document such as the names of a person's parents in a marriage record. Always search the original record the index references.

4. It does not cross-reference all events.

   There are millions of listings of events (birth, christenings, marriages, and some miscellaneous events) in the *IGI*, but there are no cross-references or links between those events. For example, a person might be listed in the *Social Security Death Index*, and in the *1880 United States Census* database but no link is currently automatically made between the two people.

   However, new custom searches are being built into *FamilySearch.org* that will allow greater sorting of information. If necessary, however, it is possible to download those that need greater sorting into an Excel database or into a new copy of your genealogy computer program to do some sorting.

   Remember, the *IGI* is arranged by the locality of the event. If you are looking in the wrong county in many countries, or in the wrong state in the United States, for example, you will not find the entry, although it may be elsewhere in the *IGI*. The Internet version does a broader search for you automatically (unless you specify the Exact Spelling option). You may want to try looking in additional localities leaving various spellings on as well. The locality is determined by where the event took place. If your ancestor was born in Vermont, married in Maine, and had children in Maine, New York, and New Hampshire, check all of those locations for possible entries.

5. Many *IGI* entries represent persons who died as infants.

In earlier generations, many children did not survive childhood. Deaths and burials were not generally extracted in the *IGI* so individual's birth record may have been extracted, but not his death as a child. As a general rule, the extractors did not index the burial records, and those burial records that were indexed were not matched against birth and christening records.

Therefore, many names in the *IGI* represent persons who died as infants, even though they may not be identified as such. If you find an entry in the *IGI* that appears to be for one of your ancestors, you should check the input source at the bottom of the page. If the individual died within a few years of birth (even though he or she had the same name and christening time period as your ancestor), this could not be your ancestor. You should also check the burial records for that area and time period to be sure that the individual lived to maturity.

6. The *IGI* is a secondary source.

The data in the *IGI* is only as accurate as the person who submitted it. It is always wise to verify information by checking original records. Many entries in the *IGI* were not checked for accuracy when submitted by patrons. Duplicate information may also have been entered due to typing errors or different spellings of localities.

While thousands of reels of microfilm have been extracted and indexed, thousands of other reels have not been extracted. If you don't find an entry in the *IGI*, search other records available for that area in the *Family History Library Catalog* and other sources. As mentioned previously it is always important to locate the sources others have used. You might interpret the information differently because of your background about the family or your knowledge of the time period or locality being studied.

To help you in your research, the computerized version of the *IGI* gives the source film with the entry that is hypertext-linked to that item in the *Family History Library Catalog*. There are several things to be gained by ordering a copy of the microfilmed entry forms, if the source is an individual entry:

- You will see a copy of the actual entry form as amended by the patron. (Now you know why you should be sure that your submissions are neat and legible!)

- You will note the name and address of another person who was working on your line at some time in the past. You could write to the address given and share information. If the address is very old, the submitter may not be living in the same place or may be deceased. However, it is something to check out.

- You will be able to see a reference to the source from which the submitter obtained the information. It could give you clues to the name of a book or the owner of a Bible of which you have never heard. This author has had some excellent experiences in finding elusive sources retained by family members unknown to the client, who had records in their possession that solved a case.

7. More hints about the *IGI*.

    In searching the *IGI*, you may find many entries for your family members with the same batch number but different serial/sheet numbers. This often indicates that the same individual submitted all the entries. If there are many entries, it would be to your advantage to order the film so that you could then look through the film and gain much insight into the sources being used by the other researcher. When the *IGI* became computerized, submitters were supposed to list a primary source for each major event in the individual's entry. Much could be learned by looking at the entry form. Unfortunately some submitters only recorded the words "family records" as their source of information. This should be a lesson to all of us to be more specific in recording our sources of information.

    However, you may find that there is only one, lone entry for your ancestor. It is still invaluable to go after the source of that information. You could find that this submission is totally incorrect, and that by adhering to its information you may be stopped from progressing further.

YOUR TURN
Choose the Internet version of the IGI by going to www.family search.org to search for your grandparents or great grandparents. At the home page, click on the "Search Records" tab and select "Advanced Search" from the drop-down list. Select the option in the left tool bar entitled "International Genealogical Index." Enter as much information in the fields that you are sure about, but if unsure, leave that box empty. Now select at the "Event" option the event you are wanting to find more information about: birth/christening, marriage, death/burial, other. What were the results?

If nothing was found, remove information from the fields you entered and try again. You may, for example, have entered the mother's maiden name; but this time, remove the maiden name, in case it wasn't given in the original record. You may find that by entering less information, you may find what you seek. Record what you discovered.

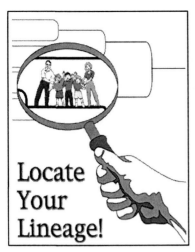

Locate
Your
Lineage!

WHAT IS THE *ANCESTRAL FILE*?

Simply put, the *Ancestral File* was the first lineage-linked, surname-indexed database. It contained all pedigrees and family group records submitted to *FamilySearch* since 1980 by researchers worldwide. In this first-of-its-kind database, submitters' names and addresses were provided for the purpose of sharing source materials. Due to limitations of file sizes in those days, source materials were not able to be shared. The basic names, dates, and localities data could be downloaded and added to an existing genealogy computer program and prevented the need to re-enter everything in your genealogy computer program if you were related to one of these lines.

The intent was that the users would contact other submitters and work together to complete their pedigrees. In reality, when it came to sharing, it was found that most people are basically shy, distrustful of information of others, or unknowledgeable about how to locate the submitters. In their excitement about finding a pedigree that extended beyond their own, and because The Church of Jesus Christ of Latter-day Saints had such a strong reputation for good records, novices accepted anything posted at *FamilySearch* as completely accurate. This resulted in thousands of files being downloaded and then later uploaded into other databases (many commercial) which further fueled the problem of unsourced research being spread abroad.

Then came the era of data experimentation in the use of "intelligent data manipulation". It was realized that hundreds of pedigrees in *Ancestral File* were related to each other. With the help of computer programmers, attempts were made to link these families together based not on individual sources for each person, but based on names, dates, and places of parents, children, and siblings. This resulted in more errors being introduced. It was decided to change direction, and allow researchers to post their own individual pedigrees with sources, and thus the *Pedigree Resource File* was developed around 1999.

The tendency for new users is to follow the impulse to download everything at *Ancestral File* and immediately bring several generations into their own genealogy computer files. **DON'T DO THAT.** You will also pull in incorrect linkages, conflicting dates and places, and missing children or siblings. Also **DO NOT IGNORE** the *Ancestral File.* It can provide clues as we build the foundation of a new personal family history. Just use the file wisely by removing the pests that plague it.

The easiest way to do this is to download the data and put it into a new genealogy computer program file. Then research original records to prove the relationship links from one generation to another and transcribe and cite those sources in this new database. Once you are satisfied that the information is correct, then pull it into your master genealogy computer program database. Doing it in this way allows you to save time in re-entering good information, but keeps the file small enough to allow for corrections as necessary.

YOUR TURN
Go to www.family search.org to search for your grandparents or great grandparents. At the home page, click on the "Search Records" tab and select "Advanced Search" from the drop-down list. Select the option in the left tool bar entitled "Ancestral File." Fill in the blanks and record what you find.

YOUR TURN

1. Did you find any erroneous information in the "Ancestral File" regarding your family? Record what you found below.

2. What evidence do you have that your information is more accurate than that submitted by others? Did you make a list of the submitters? Did you contact them? Record your sources below.

DOING A PRELIMINARY SURVEY

Generally follow the procedures below for performing a preliminary survey (as introduced on page 8-5) using several databases in *FamilySearch.org* that could contain the family you are studying.

1. Study the known pedigree. The main and maternal lines branching off the main line should be searched in the *IGI, Ancestral File,* and *Pedigree Resource File* to see if others have performed research on those families.

2. Download the information from these *FamilySearch* files and put them into a new genealogy computer program named after those surnames. Include the names and contact information of the submitters. Print copies of the pedigree charts and family group records located.

3. Prepare research planners using the chart on page 8-4 to find original sources to verify the names, dates, and places found.

YOUR TURN

1. List the main line you are following:

2. List the maternal lines that branch off the main line:

3. Indicate when research planners (page 8-13 & appendix) have been prepared for the main & maternal lines.

4. Locate the sources in the *Family History Library Catalog* that were indicated from chart 8-4 and entered on the research planner.

5. Determine if some of these sources are available either online at *FamilySearch*, at *www.ancestry.com*, at other online sites, or at a local Family History Center.

6. Make a plan to search the original sources by either going to a place that has access to them or using your own subscription to those services.

7. Search the original documents and make scanned images or photocopies.

8. Make good transciptions and citations of the information found in the original documents, and copy and paste that information into the genealogy computer program file you made for this surname.

9. Correct any erroneous names, dates, and places in the genealogy computer program.

10. Export the corrected information out of the temporary surname file using a GEDCOM file and import it into your master genealogy computer program file.

YOUR TURN

1. Did you locate sources in the FHLC? List some of them below.

2. Where are those sources available? List options below. If you don't know where to find the sources, ask others for help.

3. What plan have you made to obtain a copy of the sources you need? Did you ask others for help? Did you check nearby libraries?

YOUR TURN
After you have located, cited, and transcribed the documents that prove the connections or give evidence to the various events, it is time to correct any erroneous names, dates, and places in your genealogy computer program. Indicate new information you learned about one of your families by following these procedures.

CORRECTING ERRORS IN THE *ANCESTRAL FILE*

The *Ancestral File* is now archived and will no longer be changed. To make corrections or to find corrections made by others, use the *Pedigree Resource File.*

WHAT IS THE PEDIGREE RESOURCE FILE?

Like the *Ancestral File,* the *Pedigree Resource File* is a lineage-linked, surname-indexed database of pedigrees and family group records. However, this database (introduced in May 2000) includes the source notes if patron submitters entered their documentation. Also unlike the *Ancestral File,* the *Pedigree Resource File* makes no attempt to merge family files. Each submission stands alone as it was submitted. Submitters may submit as often as they would like to upgrade their information. For this reason, it is wise to look at the later submissions where upgrades to the family and their documentation are more likely given.

The index to the *Pedigree Resource File* is found at *www.familysearch.org* as soon as the information is ready for the file. The index points to the proper CD that contains the entire file.

CASE STUDY

At www.family search.org a search was performed for any submissions on Leander Holman Clifford. At the home page, the "Search Records" tab was clicked, and the "Advanced Search" option from the drop-down list was selected. In the left tool bar, the option entitled "Pedigree Resource File" was clicked. Then the box for an exact match was clicked and the name Leander Holman Clifford was entered. The first line of the results:

Leander Holman Clifford   Compact Disc #130   Pin #1691148   (AFN: 1869-LJ)

indicated that information or sources would be found on Compact Disk #130 Pin # 1691148 and that this person was originally in the Ancestral File as # 1869-LJ. A note on the bottom of the page indicated, "Each disc contains about 1.1 million names. With the publication of every five discs, a master index for those discs will be published and packaged with that set of discs. With the publication of every 25 discs, a master index for those discs will also be published and packaged with that volume of discs. Discs may be purchased as sets or volumes." To order copies of the CDs go to www.ldscatalog.com. There are 140 CDs at this time. The last set of 5 disks contained over 25 million entries.

YOUR TURN

It is now your turn to search for someone on your list. What did you learn from this experience?

WHAT IS THE VITAL RECORDS INDEX?

The *Vital Records Index* at *FamilySearch.org* at the beginning of 2010 included the records for Mexico and Scandinavia only. Several million births, christenings, and marriages were taken from various collections of records during several time periods and places. Most dates are prior to 1900. They are sourced, easy to use, and some may be purchased for use in your home. In addition to those online, there are four other sets available for sale at *www.ldscatalog.org*. Enter *Vital Records Index* in the search window.

The *Australian Vital Records Index* on CD covers New South Wales (1788-1888); Tasmania (1803-1899), Victoria (1803-1888), and Western Australia (1841-1905). Not included is information from Queensland, South Australia, and the Northern Territory. This index contains about 4.5 million records of births, christenings, marriages, and deaths. It includes the name, year, age, parents or spouse, date and place of the event, and an index reference that is used to obtain a certificate from the state civil registration office. Cost is $9.00.

The *North American Vital Records Index* contains 4.6 million entries that came from the extraction program of the LDS Church. It consists of christenings, births, and marriages that occurred in the United States and Canada from about 1700 to 1888. Cost is $8.50.

The *Western Europe Vital Records Index* of over 12 million entries of births, christenings, and marriages came from various records in Austria, Switzerland, Belgium, The Netherlands, Luxembourg, France, Germany (including Baden, Bayern [Bavaria], Hessen-Darmstadt, Lippe, Oldenburg, Pruessia, Turinga, Wuerttemburg), Italy, and Spain. Some names may also appear in the *IGI*. Cost for the CD is $27.00.

Middle America—Mexico Vital Records Index covers selected localities in Mexico only between the years 1659 to 1905 including both civil registrations and church records. About 1.9 million birth or christening records are included and 300,000 marriages are found on this CD. Cost is $7.25.

I wouldn't be surprised to see many of these vital record indexes and newer ones linked to their corresponding images and online by the end of 2010.

YOUR TURN
Study your pedigree chart and see if you would want to search any of the Vital Record Indexes. If so, check with a local Family History Center to see if they would be available at that locality for you to search. If you have many people from a specific area where these CDs originate, consider purchasing that CD set. Report on what you discovered below.

WHAT IS THE SOCIAL SECURITY DEATH INDEX (SSDI)?

The *Social Security Death Index* lists individuals who died between 1937 and the current year who had a social security number, and whose death was reported to the Social Security Administration. Although middle names are not given and many people are not listed, when your individual is located, information is available as to where to obtain a death certificate, if there are other living heirs, the date and place of birth, and the date and place of death.

With the listing from the index, you can order a copy of the individual's original Social Security Application Form SS-5, and/or Form OA-C790. Both forms basically contain the same information, including the name of the applicant, the date, town and country of birth, the names of the parents (usually the mother's maiden name), the home address, the occupation, and the personal signature of the individual recorded. The cost to order the form in 2010 was $27.00.

This is a very helpful index for the post-1937 period, but it mostly covers those who died after 1960. The first Social Security card was issued in 1936. The Social Security Administration began keeping records in electronic form in 1962, and the majority of birth dates in the *Social Security Death Master File* range from just after 1870 through 1987. Those individuals who died before 1962 may still be in the file, but a death certificate, obituary, and a social security number, if available, will be needed to prove to the SSA that it would be worthwhile for them to make a search.

The *Social Security Death Index* is available for free searching at *FamilySearch.org*. By clicking on the link "Tips on How to Search the Social Security Death Index" at *FamilySearch*, you will find a link for "Social Security Online" where you may print out a form and pay the $27.00 required by the government for a copy of the original application. You could spend days, months, or years searching for the maiden name of a mother, or pay $27.00 and find her listed on one of her children's SS-5 forms. The *Social Security Death Index* is also available at *www.Ancestry.com*, and other sites. The illustration below shows what the application Form SS-5 contains.

YOUR TURN
Study your genealogy records and see if you have any aunts, uncles, cousins, or grandparents who died after 1960 that you do not have an exact date or place of death in your records. Write their names below and search for them on the SSDI.

Illustration 11-2 Social Security Application Form SS-5

WHAT IS THE SCOTTISH OLD PAROCHIAL INDEX?

Prior to the establishment of Civil Registration in Scotland, the established Church of Scotland, the Presbyterian Church, maintained vital information on the citizens. Until this index was put together, if you did not know which parish your ancestor was from, you would have to search every parish in Scotland, one-by-one.

Since many Scottish ancestors came to the United States before the 1860s when parish names were not often recorded on ships' passenger lists or death records, this was nearly an impossible task. With this index, however, a name can be searched from throughout Scotland, and the birth and marriage dates located from the late 1600s to 1855. Of course, the more you know about your ancestor, such as other brothers and sisters, possible localities in Scotland, occupation, parents' names, etc., the more likely you are to find exactly who you are seeking in this index. Once found in the index, search the original record as well.

WHAT IS THE MILITARY RECORDS INDEX?

These are master indexes of those who died in the Vietnam and Korean Wars. They are found in master files in the Family History Library, and in some Family History Centers. In the Family History Library there are links to many other military databases. Online there is the Web Site link at the "Advanced Search" option at *www.FamilySearch.org*. You can find links by the name of the war in which the ancestor served.

WHAT IS THE 1881 BRITISH CENSUS INDEX?

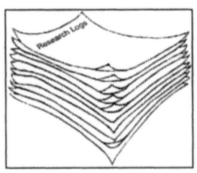

The *1881 British Census* is available at both *FamilySearch.org* and on purchasable CDs. The CDs are fully searchable indexes to the millions of individuals who were enumerated in England, Wales, Scotland, and Ireland in 1881. But in addition to being an index alone, the index links you immediately to an actual transcription of the information from the census, including full name, age, sex, color, birthplace, and relationships. You may also do a "neighbor search" and look for families on each side for possible collateral families. This comes on over thirty CDs, and again they are very reasonably priced and great to use on your home computer. The images are being scanned and will eventually be linked to the transcriptions. In the meantime, the original census records are available on microfilm from the Family History Library.

WHAT IS THE 1851 BRITISH CENSUS INDEX?

The *1851 British Census* is also more than an index. It includes transcriptions of the census records of Devon, Norfolk, and Warwick counties taken in England on 31 March 1851. It gives names, ages, relationships, occupations, and birthplaces. It is also purchasable on CD.

MORE INDEXES

When you select the SEARCH tab from the home page of *FamilySearch.org*, you will notice the *Record Search - Pilot Site* that launched in 2008. It is called a PILOT because it is still under development. Sometimes it will be off-line as information is added. But what you find here is awesome. Several state census records are now online here, including indexes for the following censuses: the 1855 and 1865 Massachusetts; the 1855, 1875, 1885, 1895, and 1905 Wisconsin;

the 1905 South Dakota; the 1935 and 1945 Florida state censuses. They link to the original records immediately online. Other collections are currently composed of images only until the indexes are linked to them.

New collections are added every few weeks. On December 29, 2008, a new image collection from the Czech Republic, Southern Bohemia, Trebon Archive Church Books 1650-1900 were added. Already posted are other sources for the Czech Republic, Argentina, Peru, Spain, France, Mexico, Canada, and scores for the United States including death, church, marriage, and tax records. You should take a look at this tab often. Sign up to be an index volunteer and you'll learn much in return, including: 1) how to read old handwriting better, 2) you understand the unique problems with indexes, and 3) you are given opportunities to use the newest records sooner. These records are free for public use.

WHAT IS THE HISTORICAL BOOKS SEARCH?

Over 17,500 historical books, published histories, and pamphlets have been digitized (as of August 2010) and are available immediately to search online, every-word-searchable through a joint project with several participating libraries, including:

- Harold B. Lee Library
- Allen County Public Library
- BYU Hawaii
- BYU Idaho
- LDS Business College
- Family History Library
- Church History Library
- Houston Public Library - Clayton Library Center for Genealogical Research, and
- Mid-Continent Public Library - Midwest Genealogy Center

This is an on-going project, so the number of books is constantly expanding. You can enter the surname you are seeking, and if you find something interesting, click on the title and the book is available for you to search online. You can print or save pages for reference to study later. Once again, there is no charge for using this file.

YOUR TURN
At the *FamilySearch.org* home page, select the SEARCH tab and then the "Historical Books" option. Search for those surnames you recorded previously from your main and maternal lines as part of your preliminary survey. Add the book titles that look promising to your research calendars.

WHAT IS THE GENERAL SEARCH OPTION?

So far this chapter has illustrated how to do individual searches in each record index collection at *FamilySearch.org*. You can also search all of the collections at once. Leave the default option as is to search "All Resources." The result of such a search is shown below. If you don't find what you seek, then do individual searches in specific record groups using specific locations where your ancestors may have lived. The next page will illustrate how to cite and transcribe such an entry into your genealogy computer program.

Nicknames can be such a pest.

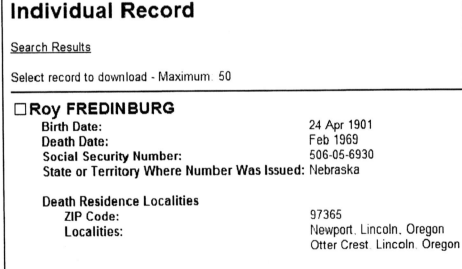

Individual Record

Search Results

Select record to download - Maximum: 50

□ **Roy FREDINBURG**

Birth Date:	24 Apr 1901
Death Date:	Feb 1969
Social Security Number:	506-05-6930
State or Territory Where Number Was Issued:	Nebraska

Death Residence Localities

ZIP Code:	97365
Localities:	Newport, Lincoln, Oregon
	Otter Crest, Lincoln, Oregon

Return to search results   Prepare selected r

Illustration 11-3 (Top) Results from FamilySearch "All Resources" option.
(Bottom) Results upon clicking on first SSDI option.

HOW TO CITE & TRANSCRIBE THAT SSDI SOURCE

1969 DEATH: OR, Lincoln Co., Newport and Otter Crest, Social Security Death Index at www.FamilySearch.org, version October 2006:

Roy FREDINBURG; Birth Date: 24 Apr 1901, Death Date: Feb 1969; Social Security Number: 506-05-6930; State or Territory Where Number Was Issued: Nebraska; Death Residence Localities ZIP Code: 97365 Localities: Newport, Lincoln, Oregon; Otter Crest, Lincoln, Oregon.

WHAT IS NEW *FAMILYSEARCH*?

New *FamilySearch* is beginning to roll out in segments across the world. It will incorporate new technology. As of August 2010 it is linking scanned images of original microfilmed records to indexes produced by over 30,000 volunteers and yet the scanning is far ahead of the indexing. There is an accelerated emphasis on making as much information available to homes where it can conveniently be studied by the user without charge. This naturally means there will be more information to analyze.

In order to keep informed as to what is available, volunteer to help index the records. A 30-minute weekly activity of indexing a batch of names will improve your ability to read the old handwriting, and keep your fingers limber for data entry work. The more each of us contributes to the indexing, the more information will be made available for us at little or no cost. Some original sources are available on paid subscription sites with the images at *FamilySearch*.

CONCLUSION

As this chapter has demonstrated, powerful databases have been developed for use in the Family History Library and at home by using the Internet. Think of *FamilySearch.org* as a mother ship guiding you to other resources on the Web.

These databases are most helpful to the genealogist who is prepared to use them. That preparation is visible through the preparation of research planners filled out to accomplish specific goals for each individual or family on the pedigree. While each database is a terrific finding aid, beginning genealogists should **never forget to include a line on your research planner underneath each index entry to record an entry to look up the original record.**

Finally, once the original record has been located, it should be studied carefully to see if it proved or disproved your research hypothesis. This may require a few paragraphs of researcher's evaluation, so that those important thoughts are not forgotten.

If your family is not found at *FamilySearch*, it is up to you to contribute information at this site or elsewhere where it will be maintained freely and updated constantly without your concern over whether you paid your server fees, or whether a potential computer crash happens.

And don't wait until you have written your first family history book to contribute. You can start with one family that you know most about. Post your information and see if others will contact you and share more.ion. One way to do that is to enter it first in your private genealogy computer program and then to share it at *www.familysearch.org*, or at *WeRelate* at the Allen County Public Library Web site.

> John Lee of Essex Co., born in the Town of Buxton, England, now of Faulkland Islands and the brig Hope, <u>George Farmer</u>, Master, of NY, bound on a sailing voyage. Shipmate Robert Robinson sole heir and executor of personal property. Witnesses John BAXTER, David Utt. butcher. and Jacob Hver.

One value of listing associates found in public records is the reward of finding the ancestor's parents.

More good databases are provided in this chapter's "Web Sites" listing, but remember, there are thousands of other links at *FamilySearch.org* under the SEARCH RECORDS tab and then WEBSITES.

The next chapter will guide you through the records of a typical Family History Center where you can use some original records, and receive one-on-one help becoming acquainted with their resources. But before your trip to a Family History Center (or watching a version of it online), take time to practice writing citations and transcriptions from things you have learned at *FamilySearch.org*. Below is a sample item found when using the "All Resources" option on page 11-16.

Without looking at the answer, experiment with writing your own citation and transcription of the sample below. Then compare your results with the answer on the next page. Then enter into the general notes field of your genealogy computer program all of those entries that you find on your own family.

Want to share what you have? Follow the guidelines on the next few pages to share and help others with their research.

Illustration 11-4 Results of clicking on the IGI #4 option as shown on page 11-16 (note the Source Film number 0883489 is hypertext linked to the Family History Library Catalog for convenience in finding the source).

HOW TO CITE & TRANSCRIBE THAT IGI SOURCE

1969 DEATH: From www.FamilySearch.org, IGI, version October 2006
Batch Number: T902480 Source Call No.: Film 0883489:

Roy Fredinburg born 24 APR 1901, Page, Iowa died 05 Feb 1969 Son of
Charles Fredinburg and Nancy Charlotte Chaney [No other information pro-
vided]

YOUR TURN
Cite & transcribe an entry
from *FamilySearch* where
you have found a refer-
ence about your family.

HOW TO SHARE USING THE PEDIGREE RESOURCE FILE

When you decide that you have a family you want to share on *www.family-search.org*, it is time to make a GEDCOM. Instructions for making a GED-COM are found on page 11-21.

When ready to SHARE, go to the homepage of the *FamilySearch* site and click on the tab labeled SHARE. You will need to register in order to upload information to the site. You will then be able to access any information you have submitted (via your own GEDCOMs) quickly in the future. Don't forget to write down your user name and password.

Once you have signed on, click once again on the SHARE tab. Here you can learn the value of protecting your information and learn that it is being pre-served in the Granite Mountain Records Vault located near Salt Lake City, Utah. If you click the option to understand "What is being done with the genealogies you submit," the full disclosure is presented. Information on how to submit your genealogy is also provided.

 Read through the information and see if your submission quali-fies. You must be **cautious** about submitting information on liv-ing persons without receiving their permission. Look carefully at your notes, because they may also contain information on living people.

Once you agree to the conditions for submission, an entry field is revealed where you will enter the path and file name of the GEDCOM file saved on your own computer. This is explained in the instructions on page 11-21. You can also give a brief description of your GEDCOM file to encourage others to read your source information.

If you have Web pages created from this GEDCOM file, and would like *FamilySearch* to link to those pages, indicate the URL of the root or index page. This is a great way to share much more material and be able to add to it at will.

At the end of a successful upload, a screen with your submission number will appear verifying that your GEDCOM file was received. You can check on the status of the submission in this SHARE area as well. Now you can continue to work on your other lines while *FamilySearch* works for you night and day, sharing your materials and helping to find others also interested in the same lines that interest you. At the same time you can be assured that your records are protected from fires, floods, and other disasters.

ASSIGNMENT 11: SEARCHING FHL DATABASES

1. Locate one individual in your family history on the *Social Security Death Index*. He or she would have died after 1937 and not been self-employed. Give the name of the individual and enter what was found below. If you found no one in your family, select anyone in the index to do the assignment.

2. Follow the link at the *U. S. Social Security Death Index* page on *FamilySearch.org* entitled "Tips on How to Search the Social Security Death Index." Select the option, "For More Information Visit Social Security Online" and select the link to go to Social Security Online. Print out the page on where to write for more information from the Social Security Administration and how to request a copy of Form SS-5 using Form SSA-711. Write the address below of where you would request form SS-5.

3. Go to www.familysearch.org>Search Records>Record Search Pilot. Search for the death or marriage of an individual you seek. If you find the name in the index, click to the right and find the link to the original record. Save a copy of the original record to a file on your computer and make a link to your genealogy computer program. If not found at Record Search Pilot, do a *Google* search to find the state vital record office where the ancestor died. Record the fees and address for requesting the death certificate. If possible order the certificate.

4. Do a preliminary survey as demonstrated in Chapter 11 for each of the main and collateral maternal lines on your existing pedigree. If you have no one on your pedigree in the United Stated upon which to perform this assignment, go to www.genealogylessons.com and look at the supplemental information provided for Chapter 11. Include the preparation of research planners that cover a search of the *Ancestral File*, the *IGI*, the *Pedigree Resource File*, the *Historical Books* collection, and the "Search Family History Web Links" option at *www.familysearch.org*. Selecting an individual who was born around the 1860s for this project will bring more results. It could be the parents or grandparents of the person found on the SSDI.

5. Use the *1880 United States Federal Census Index* and extracts to locate someone in your family who was born prior to 1880. If you do not have any one born prior to 1880 who lived in the United States during that year, determine if you have someone who lived in Canada in 1881 or in England, Wales, Scotland, or in Ireland in 1881 and search for them in the 1881 Census for the respective country. If you do not have anyone, go to www.genealogylessons.com and look at the supplemental information provided for Chapter 11.

YOUR TURN ANSWERS

Personal preferences are expected on all Chapter 11 responses.

COMPUTER CHECKLIST #11

1. Make a GEDCOM file using the free *Personal Ancestral File (PAF)* genealogy computer program (GCP) that you can download for free at the home page of *www.familysearch.org* by following the instructions below. If you used a different genealogy computer program, follow the instructions provided by that program.

EXPORTING A SINGLE FAMILY GEDCOM

Before making a GEDCOM file, make a backup of your existing Genealogy Computer Program (GCP) from which you are going to make the GEDCOM. If using *PAF* as your GCP, click on FILE from the top menu line of the PAF starting page. Select BACKUP from the drop down list. Save this file in an easy to find place with an understandable file name such as CoxFamPAF9Sep2010 saved on the desktop.

Locate in the Family view tab the family you want to export. If you just want to export this one family with the parents of the husband and wife do the following.

Select FILE from the top menu line of PAF.

Scroll down and select EXPORT.

In the Export screen, select PAF5 and under "Include," check all the appropriate boxes (such as Notes if you want your general notes to appear but NOT Living individuals if you are posting this export online).

Under the section entitled "Selected Individuals," click on the radio button that says "Partial" and click SELECT.

At the "Select Individuals" screen, the family you wish to export is highlighted if you highlighted that person when you started your export. If you didn't start with the head of the family, find the head in the list of individuals and click on him. Below where the head of the family was highlighted is an area entitled "Relationship Filter." If the word "Family" is not showing, click on the down arrowhead button and select "Family." Once "Family" is selected, click on the SELECT button right below the word "Family" and the number of people selected will show up at the bottom of that box and they will be marked on the list.

If you want to add another family, click on the name of another family head and continue the process. If you want to see just who those selected people were, look to the right at the "Filtered List" area and click on the option box "Show Results Only." Now you can see the people who will be exported. If satisfied, click on the OK button at the bottom of the "Select Individuals" screen.

You are returned to the "Export" window. You should see the number of individuals to the right of the Partial radio button. If you see the correct number, then click on the button that says "Export."

PAF will open in a window where you, or your computer, has set the preference to save .GED or GEDCOM files. If you like that folder, then just give your .GED file a name like CoxFamOnly.ged and click on the "Export" button in the "Export GEDCOM File As" window. If you don't like that folder, enter or browse for another place to store it. It is finished in less than a minute and ready to turn in as an assignment or to share online.

WEB SITES - Searchable Databases

It would take a thousand page book to list all the searchable databases related to genealogy online. Use a search engine like GOOGLE to find others but here are a few more that I have enjoyed:

http://www.cyberdriveillinois.com/departments/archives/data_lan.html
State of Illinois Public Domain Land Tract Sales, 1815-1880 and beyond.

http://thor.dafs.state.me.us/pls/archives/archdev.marriage_archive.search_form
Index to Maine Marriages 1892-1966 (more at Google search: Index to Maine Marriages)

http://www.andrews.edu/search/index.html
Seventh-day Adventist Periodical Index

WEB SITES - Searchable Databases (Cont.)

www.islandnet.com/ocfa/homepage.html
Ontario Cemetery Finding Aid for over 2 million interments from over 3,800 different cemeteries in Ontario, Canada.

www.islandnet.com/bccfa
The British Columbia Cemetery Finding Aid

http://feefhs.org/index/indexsur.html
Surname databases from the Federation of East European Family History Societies

www.usgenweb.com
Pick your state in the drop down list and/or select the record type in the drop down list under "Site Navigation." Try searching for transcribed federal and state census records, tax lists, or other items.

BIBLIOGRAPHY

FamilySearch An official Web site of The Church of Jesus Christ of Latter-day Saints, 2010. Salt Lake City, Family History Department. 1 Jan 2010 <http://www.familysearch.org/eng/default.asp>

CHAPTER 12

Using Local Family History Centers

"Madam, a circulating library in a town is as an evergreen tree of diabolical knowledge! It blossoms through the year! And depend on it, Mrs. Malaprop, that they who are so fond of handling the leaves, will long at last for the fruit."

—*Richard Brinsley Sheridan*

Because the Family History Library in Salt Lake City, Utah has as its major aim family history, you are very correct in assuming that they focus on primary sources. However, not everyone can travel to Utah to do research. Luckily, your local Family History Center (FHC) can provide you with a great many primary records, especially vital data and land, property, probate, church and military records.

YOUR LOCAL FAMILY HISTORY CENTER

Some Family History Centers have been in existence for nearly forty years, while others are only a few months old. Most centers have the *Family History Library Catalog* online, but since the computers at local Family History Centers are usually being used by others, it is a good idea to have an alternative method of locating sources. One strategy is to search the catalog on the Internet before you go to the center so that you have in mind what you wish to order when you arrive. First you need to know how to find a center.

Telephone Book

How to Locate a Center

1. Look in your telephone book under The Church of Jesus Christ of Latter-day Saints (Mormons).
2. Go to the home page of *www.familysearch.org* and click on the LIBRARY tab and select the option FAMILY HISTORY CENTERS.
3. Data enter the locality you wish to search for a center.

The address, phone number, and normal operating hours are given.

When Are They Open?

Most FHCs are open only certain days and hours of the week because they are manned by volunteers. Be sure to call ahead of time to find out the hours of the FHC nearest you. If you plan to look at specific computer files, you might ask if there is a sign-up list for the computers.

Orientation to a Family History Center

Family History Centers were started nearly forty years ago as branches of the Genealogical Society of Utah in Salt Lake City. They are operated by Mormon and non-Mormon volunteers who have various levels of expertise in family history research, but a common love for genealogy.

Volunteers are usually trained in the use of equipment, holdings, and basic techniques of research, but they are not expected to do research for patrons. They are, rather, like guides to lead patrons to the various source materials, rather than research assistants. However, often you will find very qualified research specialists volunteering at a local FHC, and you may have a difficult time keeping them from helping you if they know you are in need of help.

Most centers have microfiche and microfilm reader-printers, as well as standard copy machines, so you will be able to make copies of the materials you find. You will be charged for the price of the copies and enough to cover maintenance on the center's machines.

STEP-BY-STEP GUIDE TO THE FHC

Often, basic supplies are available, at cost, to help you organize your family. These may include Pedigree Charts, Family Group Records, census forms, correspondence forms, *IGI* forms, etc.

NOTE: The most common reason for not finding a record is looking in the wrong place.

Illustration 12-1 Basic Supplies You May Find at Your Family History Center

Also available are resources *on microfiche* of the most commonly-used reference materials such as historical atlases, maps, or gazetteers for various areas of the world. (Since centers are often short on space, they try to obtain as much information as possible on microfiche.)

RESEARCH STRATEGIES IN A FAMILY HISTORY CENTER

While Chapter 11 explained the various files of the Family History Library, this chapter may continue to explain when and why to search these files. The main reason for searching the databases of the Family History Library is to avoid duplication of research done by others by conducting a preliminary survey. Its purpose is to find sources which indicate that others have already researched and perhaps published information on your family.

Use the "Guide to the Family History Center" to begin your research (see page 12-13). It is a great do-it-yourself aid for the beginning genealogist. Copy it for your personal use, and fill in one guide sheet *for each line* you are researching. The end result will be a record of the major sources you have searched on an individual in that center. Chances are you may solve your problem by the time you have completed all the steps. Notice that you are asked to indicate the surname or locality you are searching. Sometimes you may want to do a locality or environmental study before you start on a surname, so you will have the proper name for the county or town in which the ancestor lived. The guide can be used for a locality survey as well.

Be sure to date the guide, put your name on the guide, and indicate the smaller localities where your ancestor lived, if you elect to do a surname search. The *Family History Library Catalog* (*FHLC*) at *www.familysearch.org* acts as a locating guide, but using the computer program *AniMap* (often available at FHCs) or gazetteers of a state are better. Refer back to what you were taught in Chapter 7 about gazetteers, maps, and atlases that are available at the center.

The guide encourages you to check off items you have accomplished. For example, it asks you to organize your family into Pedigree Charts and Family Group Records. Since you have already accomplished this task, remember to print out copies to bring with you to the center.

Start with the *Ancestral File* and the *Pedigree Resource File* even if you already experimented with them on the Internet. The center may have the CDs that contain the full information submitted. And if you need help learning how to download families onto a thumbdrive, there is usually someone there who can help you. These two databases are extremely valuable for pre-1900 families, for those having royal lines, and as a general reference for all families in the United States. They are two of the first sources searched in a preliminary survey.

Next, search the *FHLC* Surname File. You will find the computer's ability to filter common names such as Smith, Brown, and Green by combining your search with another name and using the Keyword Search option. Another way is to search the FHLC by locality and then search for Genealogies or Biographies in that locality, which is impressive as you determine if a published resource is available on your family. Detailed instructions are provided on pages 10-6 to 10-8 for using the FHLC.

If the computers are busy, see if your center has its own indexes, such as a surname index to their periodicals, or a collection of printed family histories that have been donated by their patrons. Next move on to the *International Genealogical Index* which is particularly valuable if your ancestors are from New England, Great Britain, or Mexico. The files are particularly strong in those areas, but no areas of the world are completely neglected.

Perhaps the center you are visiting has a local library source list of specific references, finding aids, or loan films and fiche. Perhaps your center has purchased other CDs or databases which are available for you to use. Many centers have their own Family History Center Catalog (FHCC) or a cataloging system on computer for keeping track of resources in their own center. Some also have a Patron Locality Surname File, which is an index to local patron genealogies or files for patrons to place copies of their research materials. In this way patrons can share their information with others. Go ahead and ask questions.

Terms to Understand

Pa·tron Locality Sur·name File - A file containing the names of Family History Center patrons, along with the surnames they are searching, their addresses, and phone numbers. This permits local patrons to contact each other regarding lines or names they have in common. You are invited to fill out a form as well. (This service is not available at every FHC.)

Many centers have copies of the published multi-volume set of indexes covering surname histories in the Library of Congress. If your center has such a set, that is also an item to check on your preliminary survey for the family you have selected. However, remember that it is far from complete.

Catalogs from Nearby or State Libraries

Often long-established centers will have catalog collections for nearby libraries. For example, at the Monterey, California, Family History Center, the card catalog for the California State Library, Sutro Branch, is available on microfiche. California's largest collection of family history materials *not related to California* is located at the Sutro Library just south of San Francisco. This repository is a two-hour drive from the center.

YOUR TURN

Check each of the following resources at your local Family History Center and report on your findings:

1. Does your center have a Patron Locality Surname File? Did you find anything in it?

2. Does your center have a Family History Center Catalog of their own local sources? What did you find in that?

3. Did the center you visited have a collection of printed family histories? Do they accept copies from others who wish to donate?

4. Does your center have a copy of the Library of Congress indexes for surname histories? Did you find anything?

Original Research

Once the preliminary survey phase of the Family History Center has been conducted on the family you are interested in, you can avail yourself of a variety of resources for pursuing original research, some of which are available at your FHC. Ask if they have any of the following resources.

Accelerated Indexing System (AIS)

The *AIS* is an alphabetically arranged surname index of town, tax, or census records in the United States on microfiche. It is nearly complete between 1690 and 1850, but it is incomplete beyond that date. Its value lies in its ease in use. If you don't know the location of your ancestor in a particular decade and you know only his or her name, this can help locate the county where he or she lived. County vital records can then be searched for further clues. Just be aware that there is a 20 percent error rate with this database, due to the difficult handwriting transcribers were faced with in these records.

Terms to Understand

FHLC Sur·name File – The Family History Library in Salt Lake City has a catalog of its holdings as well as .pdf images (see page 11-15) available through www.FamilySearch.org. The Surname portion of the catalog will lead you to published histories and collateral-line histories available through the Family History Center's loan system. Thousands of new items are accessed by the library each month, so as part of a preliminary survey, in order to avoid duplication, you should search the surname section in order to see if others have produced a book on your family lines.

YOUR TURN

Check your pedigree chart. Do you have a male who would be over the age of 21 in 1850? Try to find him on the *AIS* index or on the nationwide census index at *Ancestry.com.*

1. Did it tell you which state and county he lived in? If so, where was he living?

2. Before locating him on the *AIS*, where did you think he was living?

Census Records

Many Family History Centers have printed census indexes to the various states. Some centers have a subscription to *www.ancestry.com* or *Pro-Quest, Heritage Quest* online. These services have the index and links to the images for the entire or part of the U.S. When you don't know the state of residence for an individual, do a nation-wide search at *Ancestry.com.* Also many centers today have CD-ROM census indexes produced by Brøderbund, then *Genealogy.com*, and now sold by *Ancestry*, or *Heritage Quest.* The Family History Department produced an 1851 and 1881 every-name index to the British census, and several other valuable resources as well. Use those CDs which apply to the localities in which you are searching. Also search the card catalog of the local center to see if they have a census you are interested in on indefinite loan at their center already. You will learn more about census records in Chapter 14. Just be aware of their existence in your center.

Terms to Understand

in·de·fi·nite loan
- Films and micro-fiche are often kept at a local Family History Center for an indefinite period. They are usually not sent back unless the local center does not have the storage space to retain them.

Family History Library Catalog

The goals you have set for yourself should be aligned to the locations in which your ancestors resided during the time period of your goal. Now is the time to expand your knowledge of sources through the *FHLC*. At your center the *Family History Library Catalog* (*FHLC*) will be available on microfiche and on the computer, or perhaps through a catalog that covers items in the actual center.

Having determined the location of your ancestors, the *FHLC* should be searched for original records to assist in the research. If you have a film number or fiche number, ask the Family History Center staff if that film or fiche is on indefinite loan there. Happily, you may just find that it is already at your local center.

YOUR TURN

Look at your "Guide to the Family History Center," Illustration 12-3. What goal did you set for yourself?

1. What topic or individual could you search to find additional information on the *Family History Library Catalog*?

2. What locality (e.g., state, township, country, city, county) should you search in order to find reference materials on that topic or individual?

3. Did you check a reference book to see what year the county where your ancestor lived was organized?

4. Did you notice the county formation date as you searched the *FHLC* for its name?

5. What other information did it give you?

Ordering Films and Fiche

Once an item of interest is located, you may request a microfilm for a six-week or six-month loan to the center nearest you, but they may *not* be taken home. In addition, those already on loan at a local center may be used by anyone who uses the facility. Fees for rental of a film are very reasonable. Microfiche are always put on **indefinite loan**, and their cost is even less. Ask a librarian for a loan form. Films may take from 2 to 3 weeks to arrive, and you may be notified by phone or mail.

Terms to Understand

FHCC - The Family History Center Catalog contains information on the holdings available in the particular Family History Center you are visiting.

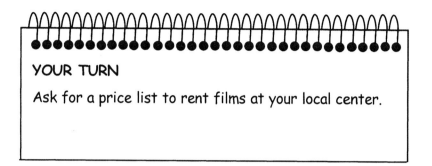

YOUR TURN

Ask for a price list to rent films at your local center.

Additional Research Guidance

Many Family History Centers sell copies of research guides for specific localities: individual "how-to guides" on research, in particular parts of the world. Prepared by the Family History Library staff, these Research Outlines are excellent references to the essential items to search in each geographical locality. They are available on the Internet at *www.familysearch.org* where they can be printed. Click on the tab RESEARCH HELPS and then select the state or country in which your are interested. Look for the title "[Place] Research Outline."

Also take the opportunity to study an unfamiliar location in your research online through the *FamilySearch Wiki* "Free family history research advice for the community, by the community." It was introduced on page 10-2. Here you can provide information about an area where you are an expert and receive help from those who are an expert in another area.

If you find yourself doing research in a foreign country about which you know very little, another set of reference materials that will help you are the *World Conferences on Records* reports. Two world conferences have been held in Salt Lake City under the auspices of the Family History Library: the first was in 1969, and the second was in 1980. International experts on genealogy and the preservation of historical or vital documents gathered to share their expertise in research, documentation, preservation, collection, and retention of the records of the world. The lectures were all translated into English and printed. This information covered topics and localities of varied interest, and it is available in book form or fiche at most Family History Centers. You can make photocopies of articles of interest.

Both world conference reports provide research aids for various areas of the world, as well as information on how to use special kinds of records. There is also information regarding the physical properties of records, their makeup and preservation, as well as much technical data that would be hard to find any other way. Remember, this was a *World Conference*, the *very best experts in all fields were there, so the reports contain a wealth of information* on a variety of subjects and material pertaining to genealogy.

Social Security Death Index

The *Social Security Death Index* is available through www.*FamilySearch.org* as covered on page 11-13. While you are at the Family History Center, try out this option. The original application for a social security number contains the date of birth, the original town in the foreign country if foreign born, and the parents of an individual.

Periodicals

Current genealogical periodicals are often available at FHCs. Ask for a list of their titles, or if an index is available. Also ask about any special indexes or catalogs for that particular library. The Monterey, California FHC has an extensive Library Periodical Surname Notebook and card catalog system, which indexes their collection of over 40 years of genealogical periodicals by major surnames and localities. Most centers have a copy of *PERSI* in microfiche or CD-ROM, or the printed version. *PERSI* stands for *Periodical Source Index*. It is a surname and locality index to nearly every genealogy periodical ever published since the 1830s. Once you locate an individual in that index, you can request a copy of the article from the Allen County Public Library in Fort Wayne, Indiana. Fees are very nominal.

Basic Genealogy Reference Books

Basic books for genealogy research may be available at your local Family History Center in printed format in addition to the "Most-Used Reference Books" collection on microfiche. Check this microfiche collection for over 500 histories, indexes, and finding aids which form the foundation of most FHC collections.

Local Interests

Many centers receive donations from local groups who have enjoyed using the center's services. I have seen large collections of Native American records, county sources, Portuguese research, Midwestern states resources, Pennsylvania German records, Germans from Russia information, and other items, such as CDs, all of which have been donated. (Some centers also index their local obituary notices.) These centers have grown with the needs and uses of their patrons, while at the same time keeping within their budgets.

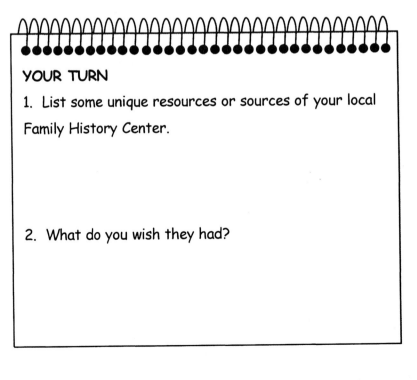

YOUR TURN

1. List some unique resources or sources of your local Family History Center.

2. What do you wish they had?

HELP FOR THE RESEARCHER

Check if the Family History Center you use has copies of any unique genealogy conference books, guides to other repositories nearby, computers or printers available for scanning images, a map collection or genealogy-how-to area.

Self-Help Resources

There are finding aids available in bound volumes, on microfiche and on film for use at some local centers. Some are listed below but may not be available in all centers.

Film Registers

Film registers are indexes to films available on a particular subject such as census, military, passenger and immigration, etc. They have been prepared to make the ordering faster and easier from the Family History Library in Salt Lake City and from other major film repositories.

A sampling of those at the Monterey, California, Family History Center is given below, but you may find similar ones at your own Family History Center.

F REG 1	AGLL Catalog: American Genealogical Lending Library
F REG 2	Four-Generation Family Group Records 1967-1976 (separate filmings)
F REG 3	Index to Civil Registrations of Births, Marriages, Deaths of England and Wales from 1837 forward.
F REG 4	Boyd's Marriage Index of England, 1st & 2nd Series, <u>1500-1837</u>
F REG 5	U.S. Census 1790-1880
F REG 6	U.S. Census 1900
F REG 7	U.S. Census 1910
F REG 8	Register of L.D.S. Church Records
F REG 9	Passenger Lists of Vessels Arriving in the U.S.
F REG 10	Federal Population Census, 1790-1880 (National Archives numbers)
F REG 11	Register for the Revolutionary War Pensions & Bounty Land Warrant Application Files (FHL numbers)
F REG 12	Federal Population Census, 1900 (National Archives numbers)
F REG 13	Federal Population Census, 1910 (National Archives numbers)
F REG 14	AGLL Canadian Census Listings, 1666-1891 (AGLL film numbers)
F REG 15	Canadian Marriage Index, Loiselle & Rivest Marriage Index
F REG 16	FHL Film Register of LDS Church Record Call Numbers, Vols. 1 & 2

Indexes to Local Collections

Each FHC may have guidebooks, instructions for using a particular collection, "clip and save" files, or donated local histories and biographies. Ask your local volunteer to show you around the center.

BRITISH CENSUS RECORDS

Since so many Americans have British roots, a brief introduction to some of their fundamental records will be given here. For excellent online instruction, use *http://www.genuki.org.uk/* which is a gold mine of information produced in England for those doing research in their country. Also use *www.freebmd.org.uk.* FreeBMD is an ongoing project, with its aim to transcribe the Civil Registration index of births, marriages and deaths for England and Wales.

Great Britain, England and Wales

The British census began in 1841 and continued *every ten years* thereafter. It is advantageous to learn the exact dates of these censuses so as to know if the ages listed were given BEFORE or AFTER the person's birthday. These are: 7 June 1841, 31 Mar 1851, 8 Apr 1861, 3 Apr 1871, 4 Apr 1881, and 5 Apr 1891.

Illustration 12-2 1851 British Census

As soon as 100 years have passed since the census was taken, it becomes available for genealogical research. The 1901 census was made available in 2001. The Family History Library has the censuses between 1841 and 1901 on loan films. These census films were not indexed by surname until the 1851 indexing project, which was mentioned in Chapter 11 (only three counties were included), and the 1881 index and transcripts which were released in 1999. Now, nearly all are indexed by *www.ancestry.com*, with several free if the indexing was done by LDS volunteers.

A place index to the census records is on microfiche and is available at many Family History Centers. The 1841 street index is on microfiche number 6026393, items 1 through 9; the 1851 index is on microfiche numbers 6054458 through 6054476; the 1861 index is on microfiche number 6026702, items 1 through 19; the 1871 index is on microfiche numbers 6054442 through 6054457; and the 1881 index is on microfiche number 6026715, items 1 to 44.

To locate the place of an ancestor for searching these census records, first locate a birth, marriage or death record of an ancestor whose birth, marriage or death occurred near one of the census years indicated above. This is done by:
1. Locating the individual's vital dates from home sources,
2. Locating the individual's birth year from federal census records in the United States,
3. Requesting a death certificate from a state in the U.S.,
4. Searching church records, or
5. Searching naturalization records.

Once the place has been located (England, Scotland, Ireland, or Wales), find the year of birth for the individual in these same records. Now search for your ancestor in the Civil Registration records. The indexes for these registrations are available on interlibrary loan at your local FHC, at the FreeBMD Internet site, and at *www.ancestry.com*. A copy of the Civil Birth Registration will indicate the place of the event, including the street address of the individual, the individual's parents, and where they were living at the time of the event. Now go to the street indexes listed above, if no printed surname index exists, and locate the family on the census. There you will find the brothers, sisters, and perhaps aunts, uncles and grandparents *with their parishes of birth provided.* Now you can search the parish records. Some parish registers are on microfilm and they are much less expensive than ordering copies of the original Civil Registrations. Sometimes, however, the Civil Registration is a bargain at any price when it gives the researcher solid information to begin a project.

The British censuses are, as a general rule, very well done. The 1841 census differs slightly from the other years in that the ages of a person over 15 years are estimated to the nearest 5 years below true age. All members of a family at home are shown, but no relationships are stated. The birthplace is not recorded but it will state if they were born in the county or not.

The 1851 and later censuses show EXACT declared age, relationships of all members of one household, the name of the *parish of birth* (or country if not in England) and occupation. A series of pamphlets known as "The McLaughlin Guides" provide easy-to-understand information on English records. These guides are available at many Family History Centers.

Many **Family History Societies** have indexed their own particular census records and may search them for you for a fee. Some are posted at *http://www.genuki.org.uk*. For example, the Nottinghamshire Family History Society has published surname indexes for the whole county for both 1851 and 1881. Other counties with indexing projects include: Derbyshire, Devon, Essex, Hampshire, Lancashire, Lincolnshire, Norfolk, Oxfordshire, Staffordshire, Warwickshire, Surrey and Yorkshire.

One great benefit of using the censuses is that it leads one to further research at the *parish level.* On the other hand, the great advantage of ordering a birth certificate is it will give you the address to find the correct census. It may be necessary to pay for the birth certificate of a sibling in order to locate a census address at the correct time for your own ancestor, but ultimately greater success on the entire family is achieved.

When the 1861 census was taken in England, people on board ships at sea and docked in English ports were also included. The FHL has microfilm copies of the census returns for these ships. A surname index on microfiche to the census records for ships at sea and in port is available on microfiche 6025598 and entitled *Surname Index to the 1861 Ships at Sea and in Port.* The ships which were enumerated are on microfiche 6025599, and the listing is called *Ships Enumerated During the 1861 British Census: A Companion List.* The microfilms themselves are located under:

ENGLAND - CENSUS
ENGLAND - MERCHANT MARINE

Scotland

Scotland censuses up to 1901 are open to the public and contain nearly the same information as Great Britain.

Ireland

Irish censuses of the nineteenth century are nearly non-existent. At least the parts you want never seem to be available. The National Archives of Ireland,

Terms to Understand

Fam·i·ly His·to·ry So·ci·e·ties - In England, Genealogical societies.

*www.genuki.org.uk
cover all these areas*

Bishop Street, Dublin 8, has a few. The 1901 and 1911 censuses are open to inspection, but they normally give only the county for birthplace. They do give religious affiliation which may be of help to those searching these records.

CONCLUSION

Family History Centers, conveniently located around the United States, provide access to major genealogical materials and instruction on computer usage, and are open to the public. They are one repository of which we should all take advantage as we pursue our family history research.

The only way you will learn of the great value of a Family History Center is to use it frequently. Remember to thank the volunteer staff whenever you visit the center. Perhaps they need more volunteer helpers, and you perhaps could give an hour or two. They do a marvelous job and receive no monetary compensation for their efforts.

```
                GUIDE TO THE FAMILY HISTORY CENTER
Surname or locality you are searching _____
Today's Date _____ GOAL_____

The family you are searching is thought to have lived in these coun-
ties or states: (Records are recorded by county name...locate the
county if you know the city or town by using a gazetteer)
_____  _____  _____

CHECK OFF WHEN ACCOMPLISHED

  1. I have organized family information onto a pedigree chart  _____
  2. I have put family information onto family group records    _____

I HAVE PERFORMED A PRELIMINARY SURVEY BY...

  3. Searching the Ancestral File                              (  )
  4. Searching the FHLC Surname File                           (  )
  5. Searching a Surname Index to Periodicals such as PERSI    (  )
  6. Searching printed Family Histories at the center          (  )
  7. Searching the IGI by county, state, surname               (  )
  8. Searching the Pedigree Resource File                      (  )
  9. Searching the Library of Congress Published Surname       (  )
     Histories
 10. Searching any other local library source lists if any     (  )
     such as www.ancestry.com Family Trees.

ORIGINAL RESEARCH...

 11. The federal census records of the county available        (  )
     at the FHC via electronic subscriptions or on CD
 12. The AIS: census indexes 1600-1850/60 by surname or        (  )
     Census films from FHL, Heritage Quest or Genealogy.com CDs
 13. FHLC Locality File for Vital Record Indexes/Extracts CDs   (  )
 14. The Locality file of any other major repository catalog    (  )
     available
 15. The Local FHC Card Catalog containing their holdings       (  )
 16. Area Research Outlines for specific help on localities     (  )
     or subjects or research guidance at FamilySearch wiki.
 17. THE HANDY BOOK FOR GENEALOGISTS for localities, or other   (  )
     basic books such as Ancestry's RED BOOK
 18. Social Security Death Index (abt. 1937-2009 by surname on  (  )
     FamilySearch)
 19. Research Papers by the experts in genealogy worldwide
     WORLD CONFERENCE ON RECORDS                               (  )
 20. Category/Surname/Title References in the FHC Card Catalog  (  )
 21. Loose Files for maps, miscellaneous information, pedigree  (  )
     charts
 22. Jacobus, PERSI, and other periodical indexes              (  )
 23. MAP GUIDE TO THE U.S. FEDERAL CENSUSES 1790-1920 or AniMAP (  )

    OTHER WAYS A LOCAL FAMILY HISTORY CENTER CAN HELP YOU...

 24. Information on entering your genealogy on a computer       (  )
     program
 25. Seminars and workshops on your personal area of interest  (  )
 26. Film Register Books as explained on pg. 12-9              (  )
 27. Forms, charts, photocopies of books,                      (  )
 28. Local CDs applying to your area of research               (  )
 29. Information on creating a GEDCOM to submit family data     (  )
 30. Unique items in this center:
```

Illustration 12-3 Guide to the Family History Center

ASSIGNMENT 12: VISIT A LOCAL FAMILY HISTORY CENTER

1. Plan a visit to a local Family History Center or major genealogical library. Using the "Guide to the Family History Center" (Illustration 12-3), become familiar with as many of the sources discussed as possible. What did you find?

2. If the guide is not usable at your nearest facility, make up a guide of your own to match your available resources.

3. Call up in advance to schedule the use of a computer at the local Family History Center, and experiment with the features available on the center computers that are not available on the Internet in *FamilySearch*.

4. Order a film or fiche on a surname you are researching.

ALTERNATIVE ASSIGNMENT:

1. If a Family History Center is not available to you, locate a historical or genealogical repository nearby. What were you able to find?

2. Try to get other relatives involved, if they live near a center. Perhaps they can help you to look through films.

YOUR TURN ANSWERS

Personal preferences are expected on all Chapter 12 responses.

COMPUTER CHECKLIST #12

1. Enter the repository name and address for your local center into the repository locality portion of your notes fields.

2. Cite one source in your notes that you searched at your local center or located from the Web site.

3. Explain how you would import a GEDCOM "download" from the *Ancestral File* into your own files.

WEB SITE

www.footnote.com
This site makes millions of original historical documents easy to access, annotate, and share. It includes Revoluationary War, Civil War, World War I, World War II, naturalizations, newspapers, and Continental Congress papers. It is a commercial site.

BIBLIOGRAPHY

Adkins, Wilma. "Periodical Source Index (PERSI)." *Genealogical Journal* 22, no. 1 (1994): 12 17.

Butler, Steven R. ""Finding Your Mexican War Veteran Ancestor." *Genealogical Journal* 22, no. 3 (1994): 73-77.

Cerny, Johni and Wendy Elliott. *The Library: A Guide to the LDS Family History Library.* Salt Lake City: Ancestry, 1988.

Chapman, Colin R. *Pre-1841 Censuses & Population Listings in the British Isles.* 3rd ed. England: Lochin Publishing, 1992.

Clifford, Karen. "California's Gem - The Sutro Library." *Genealogical Journal* 23, no. 1 (1995): 28-35.

Davenport, David Paul. "The State Censuses of New York, 1825-1875." *Genealogical Journal* 14, no. 4 (1985/1986): 172-197.

Davies, Ian and Chris Webb. Using Documents. *English Heritage,* 1996.

Deputy, Marilyn and Pat Barben, *Register of Federal United States Military Records: A Guide to Manuscript Sources Available at the Genealogy Library in Salt Lake City and the National Archives in Washington, D.C.* Bowie, Md.: Heritage Books, 1986.

Dilts, G. David. "Hamburg Passenger Lists 1850-1934: A Hometown Finder for Central and East European Emigrants." *Genealogical Journal* 22, no. 4 (1994): 100-108.

Foot, William. *Maps for Family History.* London: PRO Publications, 1994.

Galles, Duane L.C.M. "Using Life Insurance Policies in Genealogical Research." *Genealogical Journal* 20, no. 3 & 4 (1992): 156-171.

Gardner, David E. and Frank Smith. *Genealogical Research in England and Wales.* Vol 2, 12th printing. Salt Lake City: Bookcraft Publishers, 1976.

Gardner, David E. and Frank Smith. *Genealogical Research in England and Wales.* Vol. 1, 11th printing. Salt Lake City: Bookcraft Publishers, 1976.

Gay, Beth. "Dreams Do Come True-Odom Library." *Genealogical Journal* 23, no. 4 (1995): 186 188.

Green, Arnold H. "Baptismal Registers of the Coptic Orthodox Church." *Genealogical Journal* 19, no. 3 & 4 (1991): 123-137.

Hey, David. *Family History and Local History in England.* New York: Longman Inc., 1987.

Horan, Dorothy. "The Family History Library Nebraska Collection." *Genealogical Journal* 22, no. 1 (1994): 28-40.

Humphrey-Smith, Cecil. *The Phillimore Atlas and Index of Parish Registers.* 2nd ed. West Sussex: Phillimore & Co. Ltd., 1995.

Hunter, Dean J. "British Archives: England's Public Record Office." *Genealogical Journal* 26, no. 4 (1998): 172-181.

____. "Scottish Census Substitutes." *Genealogical Journal* 17, no. 3 & 4 (1990): 145-161.

Kartous, Peter. "Genealogical Research in Slovakia." *Genealogical Journal* 22, no.3 (1994): 59 64.

Kenyon, Sherrilyn. *The Writer's Guide to Everyday Life in the Middle Ages.* Cincinnati: Writer's Digest Books, 1995.

Kitzmiller II, John M. "British Military Ancestry: Part I." *Genealogical Journal* 20, no. 3 & 4 (1992): 134-155.

____. "British Military Ancestry: Part II." *Genealogical Journal* 21, no. 2 (1993): 26-55.

____. "British Military Ancestry: Part III" *Genealogical Journal* 21, no. 3 & 4 (1993): 109-125.

La Count, Louise. "Loyalists." *Genealogical Journal* 26, no. 1 (1998): 3-23.

McCleary, Linda C. "The Arizona State Genealogy Library." *Genealogical Journal* 21 no. 3 & 4 (1993): 95-97.

Mehr, Kahlile. "German-Russian Genealogical Records." *Genealogical Journal* 22, no. 1 (1994): 1-8.

____. "The International Genealogical Index (IGI), 1993." *Genealogical Journal* 22, no. 3 (1994): 45-58.

____. "The International Genealogical Index, 1992 Microfilm Edition. *Genealogical Journal* 20, no. 1 & 2 (1992): 5-15.

Parker, J. Carlyle. *Going to Salt Lake City to Do Family History Research.* 2nd ed. Turlock, California: Marietta Publishing Co., 1993.

Owens, Preston J. "The Use of Twentieth-Century Military Records: A Case Study." *Genealogical Journal* 26, no. 3 (1998): 65-70.

Rawlins, Bert J. "Records of the Established Church in Wales." *Genealogical Journal*, 17, no. 3 & 4 (1988-1989): 166-176.

Rencher, David E. "Tracing Your Irish Protestant Ancestor." *Genealogical Journal* 20, no. 2 (1993): 71-81.

Roberts, Jayare. "Ellis Island: Bibliography." *Genealogical Journal* 23, no. 4 (1995): 147-175.

____. "Ellis Island and The Making of America." *Genealogical Journal* 23, no. 2 & 3 (1995): 51 142.

____. "Ellis Island: Up Date." *Genealogical Journal* 23, no. 4 (1995): 176-185.

____. "Treasures of the Genealogical Library: Unites States Sources." *Genealogical Journal* 14, no. 4 (1985/1986): 135-171.

____. "Using U.S. Newspapers." *Genealogical Journal* 23, no. 1 (1995): 3-11.

Ryskamp, George R. "Basic Concepts of Archival Research: Lessons Learned in Southern European Archives." *Genealogical Journal* 26, no. 3 (1998): 71-86.

Slater-Putt, Dawne. "Where Did They Come From and Where Did They Go?" *Genealogical Journal* 26, no. 4 (1998): 163-171.

Smith, Clifford Neal. "Some Eighteenth-Century Emigrants to America from Durlach, Wuerttemberg-Baden, Germany." *Genealogical Journal* 14, no. 3 (1985): 99-104.

Starks, Wade C. "Norwegian Ecclesiastical Sources: Finding Your Ancestors in Norwegian Church Records." *Genealogical Journal* 21, no. 3 & 4 (1993): 56-64.

Suess, Jared H. "Some Notes on the Sound Changes of German and English." *Genealogical Journal* 13, no. 3 (1984): 96-99.

Triptow, Adelphia. "A Brief History of the Utah Genealogical Association." *Genealogical Journal* 18, no. 3 & 4 (1990): 101-107.

National Archives and Regional Records Services Facilities

"Knowledge is of two kinds. We know a subject ourselves, or we know where we can find information upon it."

—*Samuel Johnson*

The last major repository that we will cover in this volume is the National Archives and Records Administration (NARA), also referred to as the Federal Archives, which is most commonly known for three great sources of records: census, military, and passenger or **immigration** lists. However, there are many other records available through the National Archives or their Regional Records Services Facilities. In fact, there are so many records that it takes three volumes just to list the record groups and what they contain. Some of these include piracy, Native American, mobster, **mutiny**, bankruptcy, and **draft** records. However, since most beginners use National Archives field branches, or Regional Records Services Facilities, for census records, and since they form part of the basic structure of your primary research, the next chapter will discuss censuses more thoroughly.

THE REGIONAL RECORDS SERVICES FACILITIES

Before we discuss military records and ships' passenger lists, may I point out that you may have a service facility of the National Archives very close to you. They are located in the following cities:

- Atlanta, Georgia
- Pittsfield, Massachusetts
- Chicago, Illinois
- Denver, Colorado
- Kansas City, Missouri
- Fort Worth, Texas
- Dayton, Ohio

- Laguna Niguel, California
- New York, New York
- Philadelphia, Pennsylvania
- San Francisco, California
- Seattle, Washington
- Anchorage, Alaska

 Terms to Understand

im·mi·grate - To enter and settle in a country or region to which one is not native.

 Terms to Understand

mu·ti·ny - Open rebellion against constituted authority, especially rebellion of sailors against superior officers.

 Terms to Understand

draft - To select from a group for compulsory military service and to register them.

The address, telephone number, hours and holdings of your local Regional Records Services Facility may be located by reading Loretto Szucs and Sandra Luebking's *The Archives: A Guide to the National Archives Field Branches,* or by going on the *Internet to http://www.archives.gov.* More information is available by clicking on the genealogists/Family History link.

Regional archives branches have text, microfilm, and indexed materials that are common to all, or most, branches. The best way to know what is available at your favorite facility is simply by visiting, as things are constantly changing. In addition, there are text, microfilm, and indexed materials unique to each branch because of its specific location and the interest of its patrons. For example, the records of San Francisco ships' passengers to Angel Island are at the San Francisco branch and not in New York. The admiralty records for Key West are in Atlanta. The Atlanta Branch even has Admiralty Court records from the South Carolina colonies, 1716 to 1756, even though we were not yet a country.

YOUR TURN

Using www.archives.gov, the book *The Archives,* the military chapters in *The Researcher's Guide to American Genealogy,* or one of the books in the bibliography for this chapter, determine which records of the National Archives would be of value to you, and list them here.

1.

2.

3.

Summary

Since this is a beginner's book, I will not go into depth on the many records in the National Archives, but I will, hopefully, help you to gain a desire to search the records of these marvelous collections. Let's discuss the records which cover our immigrants during just one time period.

IMMIGRATION RECORDS

You learned in previous chapters about the Extraction Program of the FHL. Similarly, volunteer extractors are also working with records pertaining to the National Archives. Climbing the family tree today takes a lot less clawing with the help of these volunteers and the many organizations who are trying to make information available to the public.

One nonprofit foundation, the Statue of Liberty-Ellis Island Foundation in New York the same organization that gave Lady Liberty a face lift in 1986 without any public funding, raised $15 million to post **Ellis Island** immigration records on the Internet. When it launched in 2000, this project revolutionized genealogical research for many of the more than 113 million Americans who already actively pursue their family histories—many of which include immigrant ancestors.

At that time, it was estimated that more than 40 percent of Americans can trace their European ancestry back to Ellis Island. Their program will search more than twenty million records for a match and will be able to tolerate misspellings. If a match is found, the researcher can choose to print out a photo of the ship and a copy of the original **passenger manifest** that marked the immigrant's arrival.

The database catalogs those documents that were stored in microfilm format at the National Archives, and at the Immigration and **Naturalization** Service. This is a free service, but you must register with them and set up a user name and password. Be sure to keep the user name and password in a place you can find it later, as you may use this resource often. Just go to the Web site found at at *www.ellisisland.org* and start tracing your European immigrant ancestors now or after you have traced back to them!

Terms to Understand

`Ellis Island` - An island southwest of Manhattan, the chief immigration station of the United States from 1892 to 1943.

Terms to Understand

`pas·sen·ger man·i·fest` - Itemized list of passengers.

YOUR TURN

Do you have ancestors who came to this country during the period from the late 1800s to the mid 1900s? If so, go to the Web site at *www.ellisisland.org* and see if any of the records listed there could be of interest to you. List below the records or the names of the individuals whose records you hope to find:

1.

2.

3.

Terms to Understand

`nat·u·ral·ize` - To grant full citizenship to one of foreign birth, or to acquire citizenship in an adopted country.

MILITARY RECORDS

Military records have solved many family mysteries. Not only can they provide you with wonderful background material on your ancestors, they may also provide you with vital records that no longer exist in any other way. Since a soldier or his heirs had to prove their identity, their relationships, and their service in order to receive benefits, many vital documents may be found among these papers that are not strictly military.

Terms to Understand

boun·ty land - Public land given as a reward, inducement, or payment, especially one given by a government for acts deemed beneficial to the state, such as enlisting for military service.

Terms to Understand

pay vouch·er - An official written document which promises to give money in return for goods or services rendered.

Terms to Understand

war·rant - A voucher authorizing payment or receipt of money or land.

Military records kept prior to the Revolutionary War period contain mostly the names of individuals, their places of service, the conflicts their units served in, and, very occasionally, information on the soldier's origin. Records kept since the Revolution, however, contain facts relating to birth, marriage, death, relationships, migration movements, and other genealogical clues.

Categories of Military Records

There are three major categories of military records helpful to the family historian:

- Service Records
- Pension Records
- **Bounty Land Warrants**

Service Records

These contain very little in the way of vital data, but they provide excellent supplementary information. They include descriptions of events which happened to the soldier during his tour of duty, **pay vouchers**, records of enlistment, captivity, issuance of clothing allowance, and notices of separation or discharge.

There are eight series of service records in the National Archives:

- Revolutionary War, 1775-1783
- Post-Revolutionary War, 1784-1811
- War of 1812, 1812-1815
- Indian Wars, 1816-1860
- Mexican War, 1846-1848
- Civil War, 1861-1865 (Union/Confederate)
- Spanish-American War, 1898
- Philippine Insurrection, 1898-1901

Pension Records

Beginning with the Revolutionary War, regular payments, or pensions, were paid for injury or service rendered. The records which resulted may contain a treasure trove of information, such as marriage licenses, children's birth certificates, letters establishing relationships, family movements, names of family members, the health and occupation of the soldier, etc. Four types of pension records are usually available. A pension given for a soldier's disability is called an *invalid pension*. That given to a surviving widow at the death of her husband is called a *widow's pension*. That given to the minor children of a deceased father is called a *child's pension*. And that given to a mother who was solely supported by a son who died in the service is called a *mother's pension*.

Bounty Land Records

Land warrants were provided for wartime service rendered between 1775 and 1855. The information found in these records is similar to that in pension records, and they can contain many important clues and sources for the genealogist since the soldier (or his heirs) had to prove his identity in order to gain rights to bounty land. Generally, this required that the soldier mail his discharge papers to the Secretary of War. If everything was approved, he would receive a warrant (a certificate granting him land in the public domain). Once the soldier located the land he wanted, he mailed in his warrant, and received a **patent**. Most men sold their warrants. A man did not have to serve for years to receive a pension or bounty land. Often, service of only a few weeks was required.

How to Find Military Records

This will be a very simple overview because there are exceptions to nearly every statement made. In general, most of the federal service and pension records have survived and are available at Washington, D.C., in the National Archives. A major exception are the early Revolutionary War records (the majority of which were destroyed during the War of 1812). The indexes to the other service and pension records from about the 1870s back in time are available through the National Archives, the Family History Library (FHL), the Sutro Library, and other such major libraries on microfilm.

For each set of records, consult the indexes before trying to locate the actual records. Because of spelling inaccuracies, check all name variations for your ancestor. Various pension acts, beginning in 1776, gradually liberalized pension requirements and allowed **enlisted men's**, widows' and orphans' benefits. Congressional Acts, beginning in 1776 and continuing until 1885, granted bounty lands to veterans of the U.S. military and of state militia.

Indexes to the Revolutionary War, Indian Wars, the War of 1812, the Mexican War, and the Civil War (Union forces) are available on microfilm through the loan services of the National Archives, the FHL and its centers, and through some state and local libraries. The Confederate Army indexes and most of the Confederate service and pension records have been microfilmed by the states and are available through the FHL and its centers, as well as the state archives and libraries. The pension and bounty land records for the Revolutionary War are available at National Archives Regional Records Services Facilities, as well as the above cited repositories.

The pension and bounty land packets for the Old Wars (Indian Wars between the Revolutionary War and the War of 1812), the War of 1812, Indian Wars, the Mexican War and the Civil War are available by correspondence with the National Archives, a personal visit, or hired researcher. These records have not, as yet, been filmed. Be sure to request a complete packet if you desire every paper belonging to the soldier's case. Some packets contain hundreds of papers, but the staff will generally select ten of the most pertinent pages, so you could miss clues you need. Many early military records have been abstracted and indexed in printed form and are available at major genealogical and research libraries.

After the Treaty of 1783, both the United States and Great Britain provided a way for *Loyalists,* those who were loyal to Great Britain during the Revolutionary War, to be compensated for their property losses. These claims were preserved and are available on microfilm through the Family History Library loan service, the National Archives, and other repositories.

A Regular Army was permanently established in 1789 (as opposed to a **volunteer** Army), and the records relating to the personnel involved have also been preserved. Indexes are available through the sources previously cited. In the National Archives, Regular Army records are filed in two major groups: the period between 1789 and 1821, and those for the period between 1821 and 1912.

A majority of the existing records involving World Wars I and II were centralized at the Federal Records Center in St. Louis, Missouri. Due to a fire in the record facility many of the WWII records were lost. The FHL has the World Wars Draft Records linked to their images at *FamilySearch.org.* Many military records are available for a fee from various fee-based sites (see the chapter bibliography and Web sites, and pg. 12-15.).

Terms to Understand

pat·ent - A land grant made by a government.

Terms to Understand

en·list·ed man - Male member of the armed forces who ranks below a commissioned officer or warrant officer.

Terms to Understand

vol·un·teer - Somebody who has offered to serve in one of the armed services without being required to join by law.

Ordering Military Records

Army, Navy and Marine Corps service records were not compiled by the federal government. Therefore, check the archives of the state in which your ancestor served for regular military service records. Once you have identified the unit and a time period, check federal pension records.

To request a copy of the service, pension or bounty land packets prior to World War I, ask for a form entitled *ORDER FOR COPIES OF VETERANS RECORDS, NATF Form 80* which is found at their Web site. You may request: (1) the Pension Application; (2) the Bounty-Land Warrant Application; or (3) the Military (service) Record on this form. You must submit a separate form for each file you request, even when requesting this information for the same person, and you should allow a minimum of eight to ten weeks for processing. Requests for blank forms by snail-mail should specify how many forms are needed and should be addressed to:

General Reference Branch (NNRG)
National Archives and Records Administration
7th and Pennsylvania Avenue, NW
Washington, D.C. 20408

The forms are free, but there is a minimum fee for copying pages of the documents you request. Normally, the staff at the National Archives will copy those pages they feel are most representative of the information, but not the entire packet. If you wish the complete packet, write on the form that you wish to be informed of the cost of copying the entire packet, or you can charge it to your credit card. You will need the following information to request a copy of the military packet:

Name of soldier
State from which he served
Infantry, Cavalry, Artillery
Officer or Enlisted
Volunteer or Regular
Pension or Bounty Land File Number

All of this information will come from the indexes and the instructions which pertain to them. If you also know the date and place of birth and death, it will be helpful. To request information on World War I and World War II soldiers, write to the current address provided at *http://www.archives.gov* or to:

National Personnel Records Center
Military Personnel Records, NARA
9700 Page Boulevard
St. Louis, MO 63132-5100

YOUR TURN

Check your own family records. Do any of the individuals listed qualify to have served in one of the wars mentioned above? If so, write their names here:

1.

2.

3.

CONCLUSION

There are many other kinds of helpful military records in addition to these major categories, including **regimental histories** and Adjutant General Records. You can search the Internet at *http://www.archives.gov* for information you are seeking. In fact, there are so many sources available through the federal government that we must stay focused in order to obtain our desired results. Before we search immigration and military records, we need the very important information contained in the U.S. census records, so that will be the basis of our next chapter.

ASSIGNMENT 13: USING RECORDS OF THE NATIONAL ARCHIVES

1. Become familiar with the records of the federal government by reading the introduction to the book *The Archives* or to the *Guide to Genealogical Research in the National Archives,* or found at www.archives.gov. Describe the differences between the Regional Records Services Facilities and the National Archives.

2. Make a note on your Research Planner to search at least one set of records pertaining to the National Archives for one of your ancestors. Indicate what record you selected and where you hope to search that record.

YOUR TURN ANSWERS

Personal preferences are expected for all Chapter 13 responses.

COMPUTER CHECKLIST #13

Determine how you would enter military sources into the Notes field of your genealogy computer program.

WEB SITES

http://cwar.nps.gov/civilwar/
The National Park Service Civil War Web site built by volunteers across the nation orchestrated by the Federation of Genealogical Societies, the FHL, and the Federal Government. Originally called the Soldiers and Sailors System Web site it contains more than 230,000 soldiers' names who served during the Civil War.

http://www.arhives.gov
For links to the Federal records of the Adjutant General, enter these words: "Federal Records of Adjutant General" in the search field.

http://www.archives.gov/
For links to the National Personnel Records Center, enter these words in the search field: "National Personnel Records Center."

http://www.Cyndislist.com
Click on "M" and select Military Resources Worldwide.

http://jefferson.village.Virginia.EDU/vshadow2/contents.html
Excellent Web site for comparing the Civil War on to communits: Valley of the Shadow: The Civil War as Seen by Franklin County, Pennsylvania (Union), and Augusta County, Virginia (Confederate).

BIBLIOGRAPHY

Deputy, Marilyn and Pat Barben, *Register of Federal United States Military Records: A Guide to Manuscript Sources Available at the Genealogy Library in Salt Lake City and the National Archives in Washington, D.C.* Bowie, MD: Heritage Books, 1986.

Greenwood, Val D. *The Researcher's Guide to American Genealogy.* 3rd ed. Baltimore: Genealogical Publishing Co., 2000.

Guide to Genealogical Research in the National Archives. Rev. ed. Washington, D.C.: National Archives Trust Fund Board, 1985.

Heitman, Francis B. *Historical Register and Dictionary of the United States Army, from its Organization, September 29, 1789 to March 2, 1903.* Washington, D.C.: Government Printing Office, 1903.

Horowitz, Lois, A. *Bibliography of Military Name Lists from Pre-1675 to 1900: A Guide to Genealogical Research.* Metuchen, NJ: Scarecrow Press, 1990.

Military Service Records: A Select Catalog of National Archives Microfilm Publications. Washington, D.C.: National Archives and Records Service, 1985.

Neagles, James C. *U. S. Military Records: A Guide to Federal and State Sources, Colonial America to the Present.* Salt Lake City: Ancestry, 1994.

Neagles, James C. and Mark C. Neagles. *The Library of Congress: A Guide to Genealogical and Historical Research.* Salt Lake City: Ancestry, 1990.

Szucs, Loretto Dennis and Sandra Hargreaves Luebking. *The Archives: A Guide to the National Archives Field Branches.* Salt Lake City: Ancestry, 1988.

Excellent Printed Indexes to Military Records

White, Virgil D. *Genealogical Abstracts of Revolutionary War Pension Files.* 4 vols. Waynesboro, TN: National Historical Publishing Co., 1990-92.

White, Virgil D. *Index to Indian War Pension Files, 1892-1926.* Waynesboro, TN: National Historical Publishing Co., 1987.

White, Virgil D. *Index to Mexican War Pension Files.* Waynesboro, TN: National Historical Publishing Co., 1989.

White, Virgil D. *Index to the Old Wars Pension Files, 1815-1926.* 2 vols. Waynesboro, TN: National Historical Publishing Co., 1987.

White, Virgil D. *Index to Volunteer Soldiers in Indian Wars and Disturbances 1815-1858.* 2 vols. Waynesboro, TN : National Historical Publishing Co., 1994.

White, Virgil D. *Index to War of 1812 Pension Files.* Rev. ed. 2 vols. Waynesboro, TN: National Historical Publishing Co., 1990-92.

CHAPTER 14

Census Records Between 1850-1930

"Anything processed by memory is a fiction."

—*Michael Ratcliffe*

Oral histories and traditions can be in error. There are several records which can clear up some of these earlier discrepancies, but none as useful as federal census records. Census records are public records, and therefore they may be used free of charge at a federal public facility. If you use a loaned census film from another repository, however, you may have to pay a small fee. Because they are free, because they provide so much information on the family, and because they are generally quite accurate for the majority of the population, census records are among a genealogist's favorite sources.

Besides providing you with the obvious clues, such as the names of siblings, dates of birth, years of marriage, relationships, and nativity, census records provide other subtle clues. For example, a village name or post office is usually listed on a census page. This could lead you to an unindexed county history where information in the table of contents about the post office might bring you within pages of information on your direct family. Also, lists of neighbors could be followed, if your own family line disappears, in the hopes that they kept in contact and moved together to another area. At any rate, a good understanding of census records is very helpful.

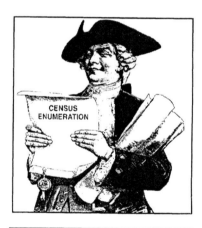

GENERAL GUIDELINES

Every item on the census can give you a clue. If it says that your ancestor could not read and write and you have found a handwritten document bearing his signature, you should think twice about its having been written by your ancestor. The document could have been written by someone with the same name. The occupation of your ancestor, the value of his real estate, his place of birth, the names of his children and his wife's name all help to identify this particular individual from others of the same name.

 Terms to Understand

o·ral his·to·ries - A transcribed or a tape-recorded history made from the memories and recollections of an individual who experienced the history or heard the history. Usually done through an interview.

Terms to Understand

pho·ne·tic spel·ling - Spelling based on the sounds of speech rather than an accepted orthography.

Terms to Understand

var·i·ant - Tending to differ; deviating from a standard, usually by only a slight difference. For example, variant name spellings indicate different ways to spell a name. The name Gahan can also be spelled Gahann, Gahagn, Gahen, Gaghan, Gaghann, or Gehan.

Copy Information Correctly

Copy *all* information given, *exactly* as it appears. Be sure to copy the information from the top of the page, as to the county, township, ED (Enumeration District), page or sheet number, etc. You need this for proper documentation of your information and research! Otherwise, you will ask yourself some day, "How do I know that?" "Where did I find that?" It is always easier to write it down the first time than to have to go back and do it all again.

While there are errors in the information in the census, it is amazing how often the information is correct and family tradition is incorrect. If you know that your ancestor was a school teacher, and the family in the census are all listed as unable to read and write, they may not be your family. You should look further. Remember: There were many people with the same names living in the same places.

Caution: Phonetic Spellings Abound

Because **phonetic spellings** were commonly used in the early decades of the census, *be sure to look at all variant name spellings.* Sometimes the information was given by a child or a neighbor, and sometimes your ancestors just gave wrong information. People who could not read and write could not always remember exactly when they were born, either. There is much of value to the census, but you should be prepared for some interesting surprises.

YOUR TURN

1. Write down a way an ancestor's surname could be spelled differently, i.e., Smith vs. Smyth, Thompson vs. Thomson:

2. Write down a way an ancestor's given name could be written differently, i.e., Mary vs. Polly, Jack vs. John, William vs. Bill:

Learn How Various Census Years Differ

Not all U.S. censuses were exactly alike, so it's important that you learn what particular information is available from each census year. Before 1850 only the head of the household was listed by name, while all other members were enumerated by age group: males and females. These censuses can still be valuable, as you can "track" a family by whether or not they have children of the same age and gender as the family you are seeking. Below are the key points about each of the census records we will study.

Illustration 14-1 United States 1850 Federal Census Transcription Form
(Larger versions of each of these Census Transcription Forms are located in the Appendix)

1850 Census. 1850 was the first year that all members of a household were listed by name, and that little fact makes 1850 a very important year to search. For the first time, you can see family members' names, ages, and where they were born. Since birth years are provided, you can determine the exact ages of family members; so if the wife is 24 and the oldest child is 18, you have a good idea that she is a second wife, and you know to look for other marriage records. In addition, you may find "lost" children and, generally, better identify the family that is yours. After 1850, each census has a little bit of information that is characteristic of that particular year, as will be shown. Looking at Illustration 14-1, which is a transcription form for the 1850 census, you will see the way the information is recorded.

Illustration 14-2 1850 Census Handwriting Example

GENEALOGY RESEARCH ASSOCIATES, INC.
1860 United States Federal Census Transcription

SCHEDULE 1.—Free Inhabitants in _Mt Hope_ in the County of _McLean_ State of _Ill_ enumerated by me, on the _2_ day of _June_ 1860. _H.S.Abbott_ Ass't Marshal

Post Office _McLean_

Street/ route name	Street/ route number	Dwelling in order of visit	Family in order of visit	Name of every person whose usual place of abode on 1 Jun 1860, was in this family	Age	Sex	Color	Occupation or trade of each male person over 15 years of age	Value of real estate owned	Value of personal estate	Place of birth, naming the state, territory or country	Married within the year	Attended school	Person over 20 who can't read/write	Deaf and dumb, blind, insane, idiot	Estimated birth

Head of Household _____ State _____ County _____ City/Township _____ Written page number _____

Printed page number _____ Enumeration District _____ Microfilm roll number _____ Call number _____ Repository _____

Illustration 14-3 United States 1860 Federal Census Transcription Form
(Larger versions of each of these Census Transcription Forms are located in the Appendix)

1860 Census. In the 1860 census, property value was listed for the first time. This information can lead you to further researches in tax, land, and probate records. The census information is shown in Illustration 14-3.

3	4	5	6	7
Edwin Salesbury	44	m		
Alfred Freeman	44	m		
Isaac Holloway	27	m		Contractor
Mary "	34	f		
Sarah "	13	f		

Illustration 14-4 1860 Census Handwriting Example

GENEALOGY RESEARCH ASSOCIATES, INC.
1870 United States Federal Census Transcription

Illustration 14-5 United States 1870 Federal Census Transcription Form
(Larger versions of each of these Census Transcription Forms are located in the Appendix)

1870 Census. In the 1870 census, parents of foreign birth were indicated. This can be the information you need to discover the immigrant generation. Black Americans were recorded with their own surname for the first time in the Southern States. The census information is shown in Illustration 14-5.

Illustration 14-6 1870 Census Handwriting Example

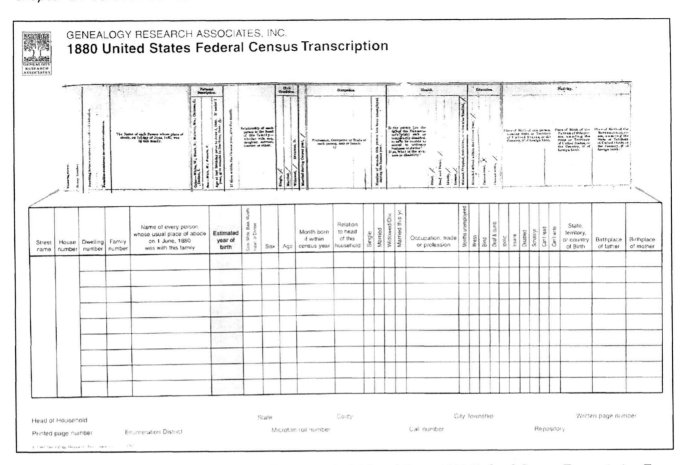

Illustration 14-7 United States 1880 Federal Census Transcription Form
(Larger versions of each of these Census Transcription Forms are located in the Appendix)

Terms to Understand

Sound·ex - A coded surname indexing system in which the vowels, as well as the silent letters, w, h, and y, are removed, and a progression of consonants rather than the alphabetical spelling of the surname is used; the name is phonetically "sounded" rather than spelled in the usual way. The Soundex system was adopted by the federal government for several indexing projects because of widespread misspelling on records that caused difficulties in locating individuals.

1880 Census. The 1880 census was the first to use a **Soundex** indexing system! More will be covered on this subject in the next few pages. The head of household's surname, however, was only indexed if there was a child 10 years of age or under living in the home. If your family was not in the Soundex, you would need to read the actual census film to find them. Today, thankfully, as indicated on page 11-1, the 1880 census has an every-name index and it links to images at *www.FamilySearch.org*. (If you are doing research in Utah for this period, be aware that there was some juggling of households due to polygamous families.) The census headers are shown in Illustration 14-7.

Illustration 14-8 1880 Census Handwriting Example

Illustration 14-9 United States 1890 Federal Census Example

1890 Census. The 1890 census is extremely fragmentary, as most of it was destroyed by fire. However, you should still check the census guides in case your family may be listed. It was indexed by Soundex, but with so few families left in the census, the printed indexes are faster to use. Illustration 14-9 shows what would be available on this census.

Illustration 14-10 United States 1900 Federal Census Transcription Form
(Larger versions of each of these Census Transcription Forms are located in the Appendix)

1900 Census. The 1900 census *included everyone in the Soundex.* Every state now has an every-name index linked to the original image at *www.ancestry.com* with *ProQuest* and *FamilySearch.org* working on indexes and links as well. The month as well as the year of birth, the year of immigration, the year the couple was married, and if a first or second marriage, the number of children born and the number living, whether naturalized or not, and information on the ownership or rental of land, are additional pieces of information enumerated in 1900. Here is evidence as to the total number of children and even the names of some you may not have known, including their birthplaces, and possibly a marriage place. See the transcription form Illustration 14-10.

Illustration 14-11 1900 Census Handwriting Example

GENEALOGY RESEARCH ASSOCIATES, INC.
1910 United States Federal Census Transcription

Street name	House number	Dwelling number	Family number	Name of every person whose usual place of abode on 15 April 1910 was with this family	Relation to head	Sex	Color	Age	Sng. Mar. Wid. or divorced	# of yrs. married	# of children	# of children liv.	Birthplace	Birthplace of father	Birthplace of mother	Year of Immigra.	Naturalized?	Speak eng. if not what lang.	Profession, occupation or business	General nature of industry business etc. such as cotton mill, dry goods store, farm etc.	Employer/ employee	Out of work 4/15/1910	# of weeks in 1909 unemploy.	Can read	Can write	In school	Own/rent	Free/Mortgage	Farm/house	Farm Schedule	Civil war	Blind	Deaf

Head of Household _____ State _____ County _____ City/Township _____ Written page number _____

Printed page number _____ Enumeration District _____ Microfilm roll number _____ Call number _____ Repository _____

Illustration 14-12 United States 1910 Federal Census Transcription Form
(Larger versions of each of these Census Transcription Forms are located in the Appendix)

1910 Census. In 1910, the federal government produced indexes for only twenty-one states, and many large cities had separate indexes from their state counterparts. Therefore, it was good to have street indexes to certain large cities available on FHL fiche # 6331480-1. Today we have an every-name index that is available for students at some colleges and universities who subscribe to the *Ancestry Library Edition*, from *ProQuest/Heritage Quest*. 1910 is an important census for immigrants from the Germanic countries because a more complete description of the place of birth was often recorded. Always check your public or school library to see if they subscribe. The information found on this census is shown in Illustration 14-12.

Illustration 14-13 1910 Census Handwriting Example

*Illustration 14-14 United States 1920 Federal Census Transcription Form
(Larger versions of each of these Census Transcription Forms are located in the Appendix)*

1920 Census. The 1920 census also has an every-name index linked to its images at *Ancestry.com*, *FamilySearch.org*, and *ProQuest.com*. This census should not be ignored. Often a date for immigration and naturalization is provided for your ancestors in this census if they were from the old country, or if one of their parents was living with them and listed this information. The information found on this census is shown in Illustration 14-14.

Illustration 14-15 1920 Census Handwriting Example

Illustration 14-16 United States 1930 Federal Census Transcription Form
(Larger versions of each of these Census Transcription Forms are located in the Appendix)

The 1930 United States Census called for the name of the street, avenue, road and house number which helps link people on the census with city directories which could provide other family information (see www.uscitydirectories.com). This census asked if the head of household rented or owned the home and if they owned a radio set. Two other items on this census were the age of each person at their *first* marriage and if they had attended school *or college* any time since September 1, 1929. If this is the first census you have looked at, be sure to transcribe all you find because there are so many clues such as the language spoken by the parents in the home prior to immigration. This can lead to a specific area of birth. If the person indicated they were not at work the day the enumerator came, the census included this person's line number on an unemployment schedule. The census also indicated if the person was a veteran of the U.S. military or navel force and, if yes, which war or expedition. The farm schedules have not survived for this year.

Illustration 14-17 1930 Census Handwriting Example

Terms to Understand

Mir·a·code - The Miracode indexing system is very similar to the Soundex system, using the same rules to code a surname. However, the Miracode card is a typewritten census card instead of a handwritten census card. The Miracode also indexes by family visitation number instead of sheet number. Miracode was used to index several states for the 1910 federal census.

RESEARCH AIDS

Until all census records are free and researchers do not need to use soundex codes, the following information is needed. There were several census aids developed to help locate an individual on a federal census:

1. Soundex or **Miracode** indexes on microfilm (1880-1930)
2. Printed statewide head-of-household indexes (1790-1870), followed later by CD-ROM indexes
3. Printed statewide every-name indexes, followed by electronic indexes linked to images
4. Printed countywide every-name, or head-of-household indexes found in numerous libraries and archives.
5. Accelerated Indexing System™ (AIS) nationwide computer indexes on fiche (see page 12-5), followed by database indexes online (such as at Ancestry.com available for a fee, or use in a library).
6. Map guides.

Soundex or Miracode Indexes on Microfilm (1880-1930)

Both the Soundex and Miracode indexing systems allow for *most* names that "sound the same" to be grouped together, regardless of the actual spelling. (There are problems such as Carr and Karr, Thompson and Thomson not being grouped together.) Your ancestor was not given the opportunity to write down his or her name, but was asked to give it orally. The person writing would then write it the way he heard it, "accent and all." It was also a fact that phonetic

1910 CENSUS SOUNDEX FORM

CODE	HEAD OF FAMILY OR INDIVIDUAL NAME		ED	SHEET
COLOR	AGE	BIRTHPLACE	VOL.	
COUNTY	CITY		STATE	

ENUMERATED WITH:			
NAME	RELATIONSHIP	AGE	BIRTHPLACE

Illustration 14-18 1910 Census Soundex Extraction Form

spelling was the norm until recent times. Therefore, you may find some rather interesting spellings of your own surnames.

Soundex and Miracode forms were designed for your use in extracting information from the index rolls, and their use could help you keep all of the information in proper order so that you could locate the original census record on microfilm. Above is a sample of a soundex form for 1910.

YOUR TURN

1. Which census records would be most valuable for finding information on one ancestor? List the ancestor and the census years below:

Ancestor   Census Year

2. In what states did this ancestor live during the years listed in #1?

3. Was the ancestor male or female?

4. If the ancestor was a female, was she married?   Yes   No   What would her last name have been during this census?

6. If the ancestor was a male, was he 21 years old or older? Yes   No
What was his age in each census year?

These are the kinds of questions you must ask yourself with each census you search.

```
        ST LOUIS CITY          ST LOUIS           111 0299 0174
  H300  HEADE            JOHN              H    W 74 IRE            MO
                         ELLEN                  W    73 IRE
                                 JOHN B        S    37 MISSOURI
                  SAVAGE         AGATHA        D    41 MISSOURI
                  ULNR           NELLIE B      D    34 MISSOURI


        ST LOUIS CITY          ST LOUIS           111 0302 0207
  H300  HATHAWAY         JOHN              H    W 25 MISSOURI    MO
                         HAZEL                  W    21 ILLINOIS


        ST LOUIS CITY          ST LOUIS           098 0387 0300
  H300  HOOD             JOHN              H    W 43 MISSOURI    MO
                         LIZZIE                 W    25 MISSOURI
                         WILLIAM O        S    08 MISSOURI
                         OWENS            S    06 MISSOURI
                         JOHN             S    02 MISSOURI
                  2 NON-RELATIVES
```

Illustration 14-19 1910 Census Miracode Example

1910 MIRACODE					
COUNTY	CITY	VOLUME	ED #	VISITATION	
CODE SURNAME	GIVEN NAME	RELATIONSHIP	RACE /AGE	BIRTH PLACE	RESIDENCE

SURNAME	GIVEN NAME	RELATIONSHIP	RACE/AGE	BIRTH PLACE

Illustration 14-20 1910 Federal Census Miracode Extraction Form

Miracode is essentially the same as Soundex in coding a name, but the typescript produced differs from the handwritten Soundex cards. Care had to be used in transcribing the information from the card so as not to confuse the Enumeration District on Soundex cards with the **Visitation Number** on Miracode cards. An Enumeration District is usually recorded on the actual census in the upper-right or left-hand corner, while the Visitation Number is the number found in the far left column of the actual census, beside the individual's

Only heads of household with children under 10 were indexed in 1880

YOUR TURN

1. Do you have the name of an ancestor who would have been the head of a household in 1910?

2. In which state would this ancestor have lived in 1910?

3. Does that state have a 1910 index?   Yes   No

Is there an online Ancestry Library Edition near you?

Look at it this way. . .
When you finish with census records, probate records will be a breeze.

name. See an illustration of the 1910 Miracode card in Illustration 14-19 and a sample of the Miracode Extraction Form in Illustration 14-20 so you can compare it with the Soundex Form shown in Illustration 14-18.

Miracode was used to index part of the twenty-one states in 1910, and Soundex was used in 1880, 1900, the rest of 1910, 1920, and 1930. The 1890 census was nearly all destroyed by fire, so it has only a printed index.

Since we previously broke down the census years individually, let us now look at 1880, 1900, 1910, 1920 and 1930 as a unit and determine with which one you should start. *It is always preferable to search records from the known to the unknown,* without skipping any ground in the middle. So we should normally begin with the latest one open to the public, which is both indexed and easy to use in 1930 if your ancestor were alive then.

Most of us are too young to remember what happened in the 1920s, so we should look at that record, *even if our family information already takes us a*

Are census records primary sources or *pry-Mary* sources? It depends on who gave the information.

1880 CENSUS SOUNDEX FORM

SOUNDEX NO:	YEAR:	STATE:		
HEAD OF FAMILY:			VOL:	ED:
			SHEET:	LINE:
COLOR: MONTH: AGE: BIRTHPLACE:		CITIZENSHIP:		
COUNTY:		MCD		
CITY:	STREET:		HOUSE #	

NAME	RELATION-SHIP	AGE	BIRTHPLACE	CITIZENSHIP

Illustration 14-21 1880 Census Soundex Extraction Form

1900 CENSUS SOUNDEX FORM

SOUNDEX NO:	YEAR:	STATE:			
HEAD OF FAMILY:				VOL: SHEET:	ED: LINE:
COLOR: MONTH: AGE: BIRTHPLACE:			CITIZENSHIP:		
COUNTY:			MCD		
CITY:	STREET:			HOUSE #	

NAME	RELA-TION-SHIP	BIRTH MONTH	BIRTH YEAR	AGE	BIRTHPLACE	CITIZENSHIP

Illustration 14-22 1900 Census Soundex Extraction Form

generation or more beyond that. You never know what clues may be found in these records.

Using the Soundex System

The Soundex was helpful if the county of residence was unknown but you knew the state, because all names from a given state are listed together in the Soundex. But remember, whether you use the soundex films in a local library or the electronic indexes online, when you read the index *you will not be reading the actual census.* The actual census indicates so much more than the Soundex card or electronic file.

If you do not find your direct-line ancestor on the 1880 Soundex, can you think of any aunts or uncles who may have had younger children and lived nearby? This might get you within pages of your own family, and then you can conduct a page-by-page search if the index has misindexed your person. If you know the county and township of your family, it is also possible to go directly to the census, but an index usually saves much time. Everyone should take part in the indexing project at *FamilySearch.org* so you can learn how records might be misinterpreted. Today *FamilySearch* has freely available and every-name index to the 1880 census. How easy it is for the letter *a* to look like an *o*, or just the reverse. Soundex search features still exist at all major genealogy sites to help you find names that sound alike.

On the Soundex or Miracode cards, you would see filmed rows of index cards that were either handwritten (Soundexed) or typed (Miracoded). The Soundex code would be in the upper left-hand corner of these cards. The surname would be given first, then the given name. When you get to your correct Soundex code, you would *look for the given name* next, and ignore the surname until you found the given names you were looking for.

The cards were alphabetized according to given name. Soundex was also used to index ship passenger lists and others records kept by the federal government. Other information on the card included the county, the city or township, the age and birthplace of head of household and then everyone who is listed in that household, with age, place of birth, etc. *But not even half of the information from the actual census is given.* So don't stop yet. You want to look at the actual census.

If you are looking for someone who was a child in the 1880 census and you do not know the father's or mother's name, the Soundex could still be very helpful. Locate the proper section of the Soundex according to the surname you are searching, then go through that section and watch for all possible spellings of your surname. When you find a family, see if they have a child with the same name and age as the person for whom you are looking. This takes longer, but it can often work to your advantage. Watch also for siblings of your person, as well.

The Soundex card will provide the actual location in the census where you can find the family that interests you. This information is listed by an *Enumeration District* (ED) number, but it is very important that you copy down the name of the county as well as the Enumeration District and *sheet number.* Extract forms for the various census records have been provided to aid you in

Terms to Understand

mixed codes - Instead of being in numerical order, these Soundex codes are inter-filed alphabetically by given names.

O H I O   1 8 8 0   C E N S U S   I N D E X

NAME	CODE	PAGE	NAME	CODE	PAGE	NAME	CODE	PAGE
REYMAN,HENRI	ERW5	334B	REYNOLDS,ANN	HKPE	121A	REYNOLDS,EDWD	CYW3	173D
REYMER,FRED	MTBU	004D	REYNOLDS,ANNA	MTW2	093A	REYNOLDS,EDWD.	LUW5	297B
REYMER,HENRY	LGPE	180D	REYNOLDS,ANNA	VNSW	159D	REYNOLDS,EDWIN	LREY	481B
REYMER,JOHN	LGPE	180D	REYNOLDS,ANNIE	JFW3	499D	REYNOLDS,ELI	VNMC	051D
REYMER,WALTER	EROX	141C	REYNOLDS,ARTHUR	SUW5	100D	REYNOLDS,ELISEBATH	HULY	099D
REYMILLER,HANNAH	MMSP	314D	REYNOLDS,ASHER	WYCR	516D	REYNOLDS,ELISHA	BUW3	410C
REYMOND,AUGUSTUS	HKLA	088B	REYNOLDS,BARNEY	GUJK	086A	REYNOLDS,ELIZ.	CHRU	337A
REYMOND,CHARLES	VWUN	275C	REYNOLDS,BARNEY	HMW4	428B	REYNOLDS,ELIZA	HMW5	041B
REYMONK,NETTE	CYSO	351A	REYNOLDS,BARNEY	MHSM	207C	REYNOLDS,ELIZA	LKPA	399B
REYNALD,SAMUEL	HLRL	379B	REYNOLDS,BASCOM H.	LGZA	286C	REYNOLDS,ELIZABETH	FUAM	049A
REYNALDS,JNO.	CKGE	053D	REYNOLDS,BELLE	HMW1	610B	REYNOLDS,ELIZABETH	HNJA	489B
REYNALDS,MARY	CMMM	159B	REYNOLDS,BELLE	MTW5	191A	REYNOLDS,ELIZABETH	JFW2	470D

Illustration 14-23 1880 State-wide Census Index from a Printed Register recording the necessary information from these indexes. (See Illustrations in this chapter.) Since several surnames would have the same code, the cards were arranged alphabetically by given name. In addition, there are usually divider cards to let you know that you have gone from one Soundex code into another. However, sometimes there are **mixed codes** in a given range. Instead of being in numerical order, they are inter-filed alphabetically by given names.

Since Soundex cards are filed by given name, not surname, when you get to your Soundex code, don't waste time looking for your surname. If you are looking for William Jason Brown, go directly to the *W*s. If he is not there, he may have been listed as *Jason, Jason W., W., W. J., J. W., J., Will, Bill, Wm.*, or another nickname, so check the first part of the *W*'s first, and then go to the Williams and look for your ancestor. This works with an electronic index as well. If you cannot find the surname, just enter the given name in a county as see if you can find how the person's surname may have been mis-indexed.

Summary

You will save yourself much time if you remember these details:

1. Look for the given name first (including possible variations).
2. Record the county, state, Enumeration District (or Visitation Number), and sheet or page number.

OTHER INDEXES

Statewide Head of Household Indexes (1790-1870)

Many statewide head of household indexes are available in book form (see sample page in Illustration 14-23). They can be found on the shelves of Family History Centers, National Archives branches, and major libraries, and nearly all printed census indexes are available at the Family History Library in Salt Lake City. If you are unable to find the one you need in a local FHC, you may request, through a photo duplication order form at the center, that certain names be copied from an index available in Salt Lake City.

ALPHABETICAL INDEX-JACKSON CO IN CENSUS								
OCCUPANT	**ACCT#**	**TWP**	**PGE#**	**HH**	**A**	**S**	**OCCUP**	**B/P**	**DTE**
Lee, Mary	00582	Hamilt	103		19	F		In	8/15
Lee, May	00325	Hamilt	100		31	F		Tn	8/9
Lee, Robert	00328	Hamilt	100		01	M		In	8/9
Lee, Samuel	00324	Hamilt	100	HH	32	M	Farmer	In	8/9
Lee, Symantha	01135	Hamilt	110		14	F		Ky	8/23
Lee, William	00581	Hamilt	103	HH	25	M	Cooper	Ky	8/15
Leeson, Benjamin	10808	Grassy Fork	232		08	M		In	9/19
Leeson, James	10807	Grassy Fork	232		10	M		In	9/19
Leeson, John	10804	Grassy Fork	232	HH	55	M	Laborer	Va	9/19
Leeson, John	10806	Grassy Fork	232		13	M		Va	9/19
Leeson, Nancy	10805	Grassy Fork	232		49	F		Va	9/19
Leeson, Nancy J	10809	Grassy Fork	232		04	F		In	9/19
Leeson, William	10814	Grassy Fork	233		20	M	Laborer	Ob	9/19
Lennor, Mary	06910	Driftwood	183		30	F		England	8/16
Lennox, Catharine	06912	Driftwood	183		16	F		Ky	8/16
Lennox, Isabella	06911	Driftwood	183		21	F		Pa	8/16
Leonard, Celestis	06810	Driftwood	181		06	F		In	8/15
Leonard, Ludice	06809	Driftwood	181		28	F		In	8/15
Leonard, Paschal	06808	Driftwood	181	HH	32	M	Farmer	Ky	8/15
Leonard, Sarah	08492	Owen	202		16	F		In	8/27

Illustration 14-24 1850 Jackson County, Indiana Census Index (compiled by Carol Stultz, FHL US/CAN 977.223 28s)

Statewide Every-Name Indexes

Although not as common, there are some printed census index books to every name in a state. Read the catalog entry carefully to see if the book you wish to search is an every-name index. It is sometimes helpful when you cannot find an ancestor's name using a fee-based search engine, and you have the printed index available, to scan through the names and see a possible name variation. The researcher could also try a search on a *given* name rather than the surname in a specific locality and time period. This may prove beneficial while using an online search engine.

Statewide every-name indexes are available on the Internet through fee-based services such as at *Ancestry, ProQuest's HeritageQuest* sites, and *Genealogy.com* (owned by Ancestry). *Ancestry.com* has scanned images of all the actual census pages and their indexes which they make available on line through a subscription service.

If you cannot afford your own subscription, try *FamilySearch.org* to see if they have indexed the locality and time period you seek as they have started to release in 2008 the census indexes linked to images. There is no charge for this service. See Chapters 11 and 12 for more information. Also, check your local colleges, archives, genealogy societies, and Family History Centers as they may subscribe to *ProQuest* and *Ancestry's Library Edition.*

All Internet services provide some form of printing capability or copying to a portable device. The technology each company has developed for users pro-

---

YOUR TURN

1. Look at your Pedigree Chart. Do you have any ancestors who would have been alive between 1850 and 1870? What were their names?

Choose one to study, and write his or her name.

2. In what state did he or she live in those years?

3. Check the *FHLC* at *www.familysearch.org* or a printed index at a library, or a fee-based service online and see if you can locate your ancestor. What did you find?

Terms to Understand

The Mor·tal·i·ty Sched·ule - Contains information on people who died within the twelve months prior to the census and was taken for the years 1850, 1860, 1870, 1880 and 1885. They exist prior to death records in most states and include the full name, cause of death, age, birth state, occupation, and in 1870 place of parent's birth was added. In 1880 how long the person lived in the area.

Terms to Understand

pre·pon·der·ance - Superiority in weight, force, importance, or influence.

Terms to Understand

mi·gra·tion path - A route traveled by a group of people while moving from one region and settling in another.

vides different possibilities for viewing and saving the images for your research. Most require some sort of downloaded program to save to your own computer.

Countywide Every-Name, or Head of Household Indexes

Using the online catalog of the Family History Library could lead you to other county-wide every-name census indexes. If you know the county, search by the STATE, COUNTY, CENSUS, INDEX in that order. Hundreds of these have been written. Illustration 14-24 is such a sample.

Accelerated Indexing System™ (AIS)

The *AIS* or *Accelerated Indexing System™* was introduced on page 12-5 as a resource often found in older Family History Centers. It is a compilation on microfiche of the published books that provided an index to the heads of households in the federal census records for the period 1790-1850. This means that only the father, husband, mother, widower, or single person would be listed. There are some years in some states that have been indexed for the years after 1850 on the fiche as well. The reason the *AIS* is important is that it is the equivalent of a "nationwide" search when you do not have access to an online nation-wide search.

The microfiche sections of the *AIS* are called "searches." A search, in this case, is a microfiche printout for a particular time period. For example, Search 1 covers Early Colonial Records and the U. S. 1600-1819. Searches 5 to 7A cover the 1850 census, with each sub-search in Search 5 covering a particular section of the country, and Search 7 covering the entire United States. Search 8 is the **Mortality Schedule**, which contains information on people who died within the year prior to the census. Very valuable as the schedule preceded death records.

The information recorded on the *AIS* (whether on microfiche or in a printed index) will be:

1. The name of the head of household.
2. The county of residence.
3. The page on the census upon which he or she appears.
4. The town or area in which he or she lived. Sometimes it will give a district number, sometimes it will list a city, sometimes "No Township Listed" will be indicated.

Additional Value of Every-Name Indexes

The *AIS* or a nation-wide index online can aid you in locating the county and state in which your ancestor lived, if you do not know this information. This is very important because vital records, land and property records, probate records, etc., are usually maintained at a county or town level. Other important records, such as military records or original land patents, might be at a statewide level. The more you find out about the locality of your individual, the easier it will be to pinpoint research sources.

Even if you do not locate a known relative in the *AIS* or the 1850-1930 nation-wide index at *Ancestry.com*, you can see what areas of the country had a **preponderance** of the name you are seeking. Or, if your family was on the move, you might see a **migration path** developing as you trace them from one place to another. If your ancestor's name suddenly disappears in New York and appears in Michigan, you have an idea of when he was traveling and can better track him that way.

YOUR TURN

1. Look at your family. Do you have an ancestor who stayed in the same state from 1850 to 1920, or for several decades in a particular state? What was his or her name?

2. Try to obtain one of the maps mentioned above and see if the boundaries for the county where your ancestor lived ever changed. What did you discover?

Once you have located your family in the index, go to the original record by either ordering the roll of film for that family, or clicking on the image online in order to retain a copy and verify the information. It is also a good idea to check the information in other printed statewide indexes if you are using that method- now that you know the state to search. Since many indexes have been made by different individuals and organizations, it could be that your ancestor was left off of one index but has been included in another.

Map Guides

One of the problems with locating early ancestral records is that county boundaries changed as the states became more settled. This idea was intro-duced in Chapter 7. What had been a particular county in 1850 may not even exist today, or it may be part of another county. While the *Map Guide to the U.S. Federal Censuses, 1790-1920,* by William Thorndale and William Dollarhide, is extremely helpful for locating county boundary changes during the exact year of the census, many events could have occurred in each of the ten years between census records.

YOUR TURN

Determine which repository is the best place for you to obtain copies of federal census records. Write the name here.

If your family says they lived in Buchanan County and you can't find them there, it doesn't mean that they have been telling you stories. Perhaps the boundaries changed for that county.

It is important, before searching for records, to look at a census maps for the proper year and see if the county was the same then as it is now. Perhaps they were exactly where they said they were, but the names have since changed. Or, perhaps that particular county doesn't even exist anymore. It's even possible that you have been looking in the wrong county (as we now know it). Each map in the *Map Guide* has the current counties in black and the counties as they were in that census year in white. You can see where perhaps one little corner belonged to another county during the time period you are searching, and that may give you just the clue you need to find the appropriate records. If you need a year-by-year view of boundary changes use an automated mapping program.

Animap™ is an automated mapping computer program that was introduced to you in Chapter 7. It provides the county boundary changes for every year from the colonial period forward and, therefore, goes beyond the printed map book in yearly ranges. When you find the maps you want, they can be "printed" to paper or to a computer file and brought into your own electronic records or filed in your Family History Archival Notebooks.

OBTAINING CENSUS FILMS

The actual census records may be obtained in many ways. Originals are found in archives, courthouses, and state libraries. Surviving census records up to 1930 are available on film; and most are available in scanned electronic format on the Internet freely at *www.familysearch.org* or through a fee-based subscription service at *www.Ancestry.com*. Many are available in public libraries who paid for a subscription to *ProQuest*. All provide some form of printing (either line by line or an entire page).

Microfilm versions of census records are available through:

1. FHC film orders through the Family History Library.
2. Film purchase through the National Archives.
3. Interlibrary loan at your local public library.
4. A personal visit to a National Archives or one of its Regional Record Service Facilities.
5. Record Look-up Services at *www.GRAonline.com* provides a copy of the census page in photocopy or scanned image formats for a fee.

Since the process for using census records varies at the different repositories, instructions will be given on how to use them at a National Archives branch. The techniques will need to be modified for other localities using other film numbers.

YOUR TURN

1. Write the surname code of the individual you are seeking, here _____.

2. Write the name of the state in which the person your are seeking lived, here _____ _____.

SOUNDEX CODING GUIDE

Code Key Letters and Equivalents

Code	Key Letters and Equivalents
1	b,p,f,v
2	c,s,k,g,j,q,x,z
3	d,t
4	l
5	m,n
6	r

Illustration 14-25 Soundex Coding Guide

COMPUTING THE SOUNDEX CODE

For Ancestors Living 1880-1930

Compute the Soundex code for any census films in 1880, 1900, 1910, 1920, or 1930 by following the instructions below, or by using a feature in your genealogy computer program that automatically computes the information.

1. The letters *a, e, i, o, u, w, h,* and *y* are NOT coded. (Just remember "WHY vowels," and you'll have an easy way to remember those letters which are *not* coded.)

2. The *first letter* of a surname is *not coded, but it is written* as the beginning of your Soundex Code. Therefore, Cook would be: C 200.

3. *Every Soundex Code must have a three-digit number.* If a name yields no code numbers, then zeroes would follow. Lee would be L 000. Kuhne would be K 500, Ebell would be E 140, and Ebelson is E 142 not E 1425.

4. When two key letters (see chart above) appear together, such as ll in Kelly, or when two or three letters combine to make a single sound, such as ck in Buerck, sch in Schaefer, or sck in Buscker, they are coded as one letter. Kelly would be K 400, Buerck would be B 620 and Buscker would be B 260. Schaefer would be S 160.

EXAMPLES: Eckhardt = E263; Jones = J520; Clifford = C416; Fritzenheimer = F632; Bauer = B600.

5. Prefixes such as "van", "Von", "Di", "du", etc., are sometimes disregarded, so be careful. Nuns were sometimes recorded as though Sister were their surname, and Indians may have shortened names.

Now, follow the steps in the "Step-by-Step Procedures" chart in Illustration 14-26.

Step-by-Step Procedures for Locating Your Ancestor on the 1880 to 1930 Census Rolls at the National Archives or Branch Archives

1. Go to the appropriate U.S. government-produced census booklet (1930, 1920, 1910, 1900, or 1790-1890) which contains the film numbers for the state Soundex you seek.
2. In the Soundex portion of the booklet, locate the state where your ancestor lived in the census year you are researching.
3. Now, look down the columns until you locate the Soundex code number within the range of numbers allowed.
4. Write down the "T" number (located beside the state name), which helps locate the drawer in which the films are located, and then write down the number of the film itself (located to the far left of the Soundex range). The "T" number is: _____. The film number is: _____.
5. Take the Soundex film from the drawer and place it onto the microfilm reader.
6. Roll the film forward until you locate the Soundex code number in the upper-right or left-hand corner. There are often several numbers on each roll, and they are usually in numerical order. Sometimes, however, the codes are mixed.
7. Now, search for the given name, not the surname, of the individual you seek. If it is William Thomas, look for: William, William Thomas, William T., W. T., Wm., Wm. T., Thomas, Tom, or Bill. Once you have found the given name under the particular Soundex code, look for the correct last name (or as close to correct as possible). The spelling is often incorrect.
8. Once you have found the right family, write down all of the information on the appropriate Soundex transcription card. Particularly important are the name of the county in which the family was living, the state, the ED (Enumeration District), the sheet number, and the line number. [To assist you, the appendix contains forms to help you in this step as you are learn ing to correctly copy raw material.]
9. Having now obtained the correct county and ED number, go to the appropriate booklet again. Look under the section which covers the actual census films. Go to the state in which you are interested and find the particular county given on the Soundex card. Sometimes there are so many Enumeration Districts in a particular county that you will need to check two rolls of film to cover your district. Write down the film number(s) to the far left of the county. The film number(s) is/are: _____.
10. Now, go to the film cabinet, find the film you want, and put it onto the machine. Often, you will see a list of the counties on that roll, so you can see how many counties you will need to roll through to get to your county.
11. Roll ahead until you find your county (the name is usually written in the far left corner).
12. Now, look at the far right-hand corner for the Enumeration District you are seeking.
13. Once you have found the Enumeration District, go to the sheet number (page).
14. Finally, go down the page to the line where the Soundex card indicated you would find your family.
15. Copy all of the information in every column (including that in the top part of the form, which will give the township, the post office, and the date the census was actually taken); better yet, have a photocopy made. Be sure to look back five or six pages before and after your ancestor to see if in-laws, cousins, brothers, sisters, aunts, uncles, parents, etc., are living close by, and photocopy those pages as well.

Illustration 14-26 1880-1930 Procedures

Step-by-Step Procedures for Locating Your Ancestor on the 1790 to 1870 Census Rolls at the National Archives or Branch Archives

1. Decide in what state the individual you are researching was living at the time of a census.
2. Check the book cases in the area for state-wide every-name, or head-of-household printed census indexes which are filed in alphabetical order, or check the *AIS*™, or search on-line indexes.
3. Locate the individual you seek in the index, and copy the county abbreviation and page number for the census.
4. Go to the appropriate federally printed booklet (1790-1880), and look under the year you are researching.
5. Find the state in which you are interested.
6. Go to the county indicated in the above printed index, locate the film number for that county and write it here:_____.
7. Locate the film in the drawer. NOTE: If you find a string of numbers in the printed index book, "0120423-12304" (the actual numbers will be different but there will be a long line of them), it indicates that the actual information on that census has already been transcribed. You might think it is not necessary to look at the original census, but when you do, you may find that the numbers were not transcribed correctly, you might find another locator clue such as a township name, military district number, or a riverway, and you might locate possible neighbors. Those numbers (0120423-12304) refer to family member ages (0 means no male 0 to 5 years, 1 means a male under 10, 2 indicates 2 males between 10-15, etc.). Having a copy of a Census Transcription Form available is very helpful. If you record these numbers in order on such an extract form, it will make the ages readily apparent and easier to transcribe into your genealogy computer program.
8. Place the film onto the viewer. Roll it to the correct county, then to the particular page number indicated in the index. This is often tricky, because some indexers used the printed numbers on the pages, which changed with every county, while other indexers used the hand-written numbers that ran through the entire film. Other films have stamped page numbers throughout. If you can first locate the correct county and township, the page will be easier to locate.
9. Transcribe all of the information on your census abstract forms. Be sure to look around at the neighbors on the surrounding pages. Very likely there are in-laws, cousins, brothers, sisters, aunts, parents, etc., living nearby.
10. Not all printed indexes are complete for 1870, but the census films are available. Try looking up the individual you just found in the same county and township ten years earlier, and go page by page through the area. You may very well locate him. You could also check county histories to see when the townships developed, and then go back to the census films to locate those new townships.

Illustration 14-27   1790-1870 Procedures

CONCLUSION

Federal census records are important primary sources of information for your family. Family research should include census records early in the research phase (usually immediately following the preliminary survey for those families alive in the 1790 to 1930 time periods). Census research should exhaust the information in all census records. This means that every census record in which the family might appear should be located, analyzed, and used to determine where to locate county records. This is easily done by building a time line of localities that corresponds to each census year.

ASSIGNMENT 14: CENSUS RECORDS

1. Obtain copies of the appropriate maps for the states in which an ancestor lived between 1850 and 1930. Highlight the area in which he or she lived, and note any boundary changes, or the option that the family could live over the border in another state or county.

2. Using the previous guidelines, locate an ancestor in each of the following years (or at least obtain a sample copy of a census record for each year) and record below the state, county, and the name of the individual located:

   a. 1930 census _____ (ancestor's name)

   b. 1920 census _____ (ancestor's name)

   c. 1910 census _____ (ancestor's name)

   d. 1900 census _____ (ancestor's name)

   e. 1880 census _____ (ancestor's name)

   f. 1870 census _____ (ancestor's name)

   g. 1860 census _____ (ancestor's name)

   h. 1850 census _____ (ancestor's name)

3. Compare the variety of information given on the census records by writing a statement of common elements and unique items that could appear on the census records between 1850 and 1930, and why you would want to know this information.

4. Compare the legibility and availability of these records for your personal use.

YOUR TURN ANSWERS

Personal preferences are expected on all Chapter 14 responses except #3:

Census records between 1880 and 1930 contain the name and relationship to head of household, as well as the birth place for each individual and that individual's parents. Starting in 1900 the year of immigration and whether naturalized was recorded, and whether the person could read or write.

Unique items in 1930 would be: value of home, if there was a radio set, the age of a person at his/her first marriage, if the males were veterans and of which war, and if not working they would be on the unemployed census.

Unique in 1920: the mother tongue for each person and their parents.

Unique in 1910: number of years married, mother of how many children and the number of children alive, who speaks speak English and if not what language, if out of work and for how many weeks, and if a Civil War Veteran.

Unique in 1900: Month and year of birth, number of years married, mother of how many children and the number of children alive, immigration year, naturalized, number of years in USA.

Unique in 1880: first year relationships given, first year parent's birth places asked, specific disabilities recorded, married during the year.

Unique in 1870: First census to record all Black individuals by name.

Unique in 1860: Value of personal property recorded for first time.

Unique in 1850: First census to record every person in the houshold, value of real estate, and those over 20 who cannot read or write.

COMPUTER CHECKLIST #14

1. Describe how you would enter census records for the following years into your genealogy computer program:

   a. 1880-1930

   b. 1850-1870

2. Transcribe all census records located regarding your family into your genealogy computer program.

3. Print out the results of what you entered.

WEB SITE

Soundex Conversion Program
www.gedpage.com/soundex.html
   or
http://www.jewishgen.org/JOS/jossound.htm

BIBLIOGRAPHY AND REFERENCE LIST

Adams, Enid Eleanor. "Who is 'XZLLY MZFGIN'?" *The American Genealogist* 59 (1983).

Brewer, Mary M. *Index to Census Schedules in Printed Form.* Huntsville, Alabama: Century Enterprises, 1969. Supplement, 1970-71.

Buckway, G. Eileen, et al. *U.S. 1910 Federal Census: Unindexed States: A Guide to Finding Census Enumeration Districts for Unindexed Cities, Towns, and Villages.* Salt Lake City: Family History Library, 1992.

_____ and Fred Adams, *U.S. State and Special Census Register: A Listing of Family History Library Microfilm Number.* Rev. ed. 2 vols. Salt Lake City: Family History Library, 1992.

Eakle, Arlene Haslam. "Census Records," in *The Source: A Guidebook of American Genealogy.* Edited by Loretto Dennis Szucs and Sandra Hargreaves Luebking. Rev. ed. Salt Lake City: Ancestry, 1997.

Lainhart, Ann S. *State Census Records.* Baltimore: Genealogical Publishing Co., 1992.

McMillon, Lynn C. "An Index Can Be A Roadblock." *Virginia Genealogist* 21 (1977): 205-06.

Records Indexed by AIS. Genealogical Library Reference Aids Series B, no. 11. Salt Lake City: Genealogical Society of Utah, 1984.

Saldana, Richard H. *A Practical Guide to the "Misteaks" Made in Census Indexes.* Salt Lake City, Utah: R.H. Saldana & Co., 1987.

Steuart, Bradley W. *The Soundex Reference Guide: Soundex Coded to Over 125,000 Surnames.* Bountiful, Utah: Precision Indexing, 1990.

Szucs, Loretto Dennis, and Mathew Wright. "Census Records," in *The Source: A Guidebook of American Genealogy.* Edited by Loretto Dennis Szucs and Sandra Hargreaves Luebking. Third Edition. Provo: Ancestry, 2006.

Thorndale, William and William Dollarhide. *Map Guide to the U.S. Federal Censuses, 1790-1920.* Baltimore: Genealogical Publishing Co., 1987.

Vallentine, John F. "Census records and Indexes." *Genealogical Journal* 2 (1973): 133-39.

CHAPTER 15

Analysis and Goal Setting

"Once more on my adventure brave and new."

—*Robert Browning*

Have you noticed the remarkable difference in your ability to set more realistic, meaningful goals, now that you have at least a partial understanding of basic research tools? The Research Planner, for example, keeps you focused on your target while it helps you make a plan. Without a plan, it's unlikely that the purposes you set out to accomplish will be achieved. Now that this book has guided you through the Research Cycle and the principles of good research, it is time to revisit our initial research process. Many researchers think of their research objective as the larger target such as extending the family line. They consider goals as smaller steps that help them reach the larger objective. In genealogy research, the majority of goals or objectives focus on:

Finding the parents' names
  Finding an individual's birth date or place
    Finding a marriage date or place
      Finding a death date or place
        Finding a spouse's name, or maiden name
          Finding the names of siblings
            Finding background information on the family.

Referring to these goals could make it easier to determine the next step in your research, and to practice using logical record sources to accomplish your goals. This leads us to the topic of organization.

ORGANIZATION

As we progress in our research skills, we must make a concerted effort to consistently put our materials in a format that will not leave any clue behind.

Terms to Understand

rel·e·vant - Having a bearing on or connection with the matter at hand.

Terms to Understand

re·cord type
Information about a group or class of records; i.e., military records, land records, or vital records.

Terms to Understand

pri·or·i·ty -
Precedence by order of importance or urgency.

Remember what a hard time you had finding what you wanted, because it was just *too much*! Now, the *principle of organization* has prepared you for greater future success, but it won't work unless it is practiced consistently. Beginners often come into a library with a suitcase full of old documents, notes, and letters. They spend most of the time in the library finding this or that piece of information. This can happen to seasoned genealogists if they find more evidence than they expected or they work on so many family lines that they forget to leave a trail behind of what they searched and what they found. They eventually determine that they will never leave a project without leaving a mini-report behind. You will have "Arrived!" when you can pick up a three month old project and know just what you were doing, what you need to do in the future, and in less than 30 minutes can take off on that old project.

Let's review what made that researcher so organized. Success in genealogical research requires *careful planning and successful recording of information*. All facts relating to the person being studied should be recorded in chronological order for that person. Previously completed research should be itemized in a brief, descriptive form, and as much information as possible should be obtained about the **relevant** events in question.

Once organized, the researcher is to seek out available record sources, and use them correctly and wisely to get the information needed to achieve the next goal. Each major **record type** should be studied for its general value to your research problem.

Sorting information by chronology and sorting goals by **priority** can be a tremendous help. We can get our thoughts about every individual lined up. We can then take stock of the priorities we have left, make a focused plan with the use of a good Research Planner, and begin a new phase of our project. When we do this, we feel better about ourselves, and our best efforts are given to those things that are most important.

DETERMINING WHAT IS MISSING

We next ask: "How do I get this information, and how do I search that source?" The research cycle first learned on page 1-4 repeats itself over and over again. And it always comes back to determining which goal to pursue to solve a problem in an existing family.

The easiest way to find a goal is to study your Pedigree or Ancestral Chart, Family Group Records, or the individual data fields on your genealogy computer program. Is anything missing or questionable? Could those missing items fall under one of the goals mentioned above?

Good goals record all the basic facts known at the time the quest is started. Obviously, this is **not a good goal**: "Find grandfather John". Here is a goal that is a bit better: **"Find the spouse of John Butterfield. John was born 26 June 1867 and died in 1921 according to his tombstone in San Jose, California. In 1910 he was found on a census record in Monterey, California as a widower, with an 18 year old daughter Lisa Marie".** But, what is missing from this goal?

If this person was found on the 1910 census, that census should have told where the daughter was born, and where her mother and father was born. It should have indicated the same information for John. Leaving out ANY of the important facts from previous research slows down the research progress. Everytime you find a new source, that source may add information to what you then know and the goal may need to be changed.

Basically, goal setting involves asking questions, recording basic facts, and listing sources. And while it's true that greater success involves applying good research techniques, the foundation of our success depends on focusing on the details of our goals from the very beginning. By the way, in the bolded longer goal above, what county was San Jose a part of in 1921? Was the 1910 census in the town of Monterey, or county of Monterey in the bolded goal mentioned above?

Once the details are fully recorded, we must put into practice those research techniques introduced previously to prevent researching the wrong family line? Let's review them for a minute.

Go from Known Information to Unknown Information

Part of setting a good goal is to separate fact from tradition, hypothesis from actuality. If someone on the Internet or in a published genealogy has extended your family line three generations, don't just accept it as fact and start going backwards from the end of the purported "new" third generation. First, verify the relationships between your known ancestors and the new-found ancestors. Then you can move back into the "unknown" once again.

Listen to this conversation between a beginning genealogist and one who has been working in family history a bit longer.

"What do you really know about this person?"

"I was told he was born in Virginia."

"But how did I come to know that information?"

"Oh, I remember, I found that on the 1880 census record."

"Since records are kept on a county level in Virginia, what county was the person living in?"

"I don't know! Wait! Yes, it was written on that 1880 census. It was Franklin County. But this only tells me where he was living in 1880 and that he was born in Virginia. I will need to go back in time starting with 1880 and see if he remains in this same county."

"Correct! So what will your goal be?"

"My goal is to find the birthplace of this person."

"You've got the idea."

"But I really want to find out who this person's parents are, too."

"That is another goal. It goes on a separate planner.

Don't Skip Generations or Sources

In the above example, it would be very tempting to skip the present generation, since you already know a person's name, the year of birth and the location, then just jump back to the parents' names. Resist that temptation. Don't skip generations or sources. By finding the birthplace of the individual, you may also find the parents' names. And you might find even more.

Let's say that you also have the individual's marriage date and place, so you are tempted to skip looking it up because you think you already "know" it. You do not, however, have a *primary source* for the information. You only have hearsay evidence from a published family history, so you must select as another goal to find the marriage record or marriage application.

When you find the original marriage location, you may also find in the marriage application the names of the parents. Had you not sought these primary sources, the information would have been lost to you. Therefore, the reason for your third goal would be to find documentation for the marriage date for the individual you're searching, because it might contain information on the parents.

WITHIN REASON, Get Them All

You need to record all of the individuals of the same surname in the same locality (even the common surnames, such as Smith, if you are searching in a small town or township), the neighbors who may have traveled with them for several generations, and the relatives who appear on one record or another. You obviously wouldn't want to get all the Smiths in New York City, but would want to get all the Smith individuals in the same block or building. You are doing this because, even though your third great-grandfather did not state on his marriage record the names of his parents, his sister, who lived in the same county, might have stated the names of her parents.

Find the Current County Jurisdiction

Look at a current atlas or map and determine where the location would be today. Then make a copy of that area, in case you want to contact genealogy societies, historical societies, or local libraries there to see if they have records or information on the individual for whom you are searching.

Locality Analysis

Next, you must determine the name of the location at the time of the event, since records are cataloged and retained in their original jurisdiction. Use gazetteers of the time period, geographical dictionaries, maps, and books to guide you to the name of the county, and possibly the town which might have existed during the years your relatives lived there. County boundaries during the early years of settlement in the United States were constantly changing, and towns were sprouting like dandelions, only to find themselves absorbed into larger municipalities as the nation grew, or in some cases, dying and blowing away like tumbleweeds in sparsely populated areas.

List All Sources Searched, Both Negative and Positive

Because we must list our negative searches (so we don't repeat them), as well as our positive searches, it is a good idea to put all of this information onto a Research Planner, which we discussed in Chapter 8. That way, we can just note whether we found something or not, and we don't repeat searches.

Determine What Others Have Already Discovered

Avoid the duplication of effort with a preliminary survey. This involves searching major biographical databases, such as *www.FamilySearch.org*, *Ancestry.com's* public trees, the *International Genealogical Index*, the Library of Congress database, *Google.com* and using Google books. Often this information is secondary, but it can help you find locations for primary sources. .

COMMUNICATION

How can you learn more from your relatives? This involves the principle of communication, and there is a game that demonstrates this principle: Pair off two people, and make one the "describer" and the other the "listener." Have them sit back-to-back, with the describer facing the screen for an overhead projector. Show a simple design on the screen, and give the listener a blank piece of paper and a pencil. Have the describer tell the listener exactly what to draw, in order to reproduce the design on the screen. Only verbal instructions can be given, and the players have three minutes to complete the task. The resulting "design" can be quite a surprise, and nothing whatsoever like the original.

If visual communication had been used in addition to verbal, the results would have been much different. This is equally true in family history research. Have you ever had someone try to explain a genealogy problem to you, orally? Do you find yourself wishing it could be on paper in Pedigree Chart fashion, or at least in a list, with one generation succeeding another? This is because we think better when we can use as many of our senses as

YOUR TURN:

List below three new goals you can now set for your family.

1.

2.

3.

possible on complex research problems.

As we listen to problems, it is also important to ponder our commonality as a human family. Such a collective overview will provide us with wider insights about records. This is why we spent several pages in this book on history, since it is the combined story of the lives of individuals. Think of those things we do today that our ancestors also did in the past.

We too are born.
We too are surrounded by the traditions of the day.
We too are involved with the economic, social, political and religious backgrounds of those around us.
We too may marry.
We too may have to fight against others to preserve our way of life.
We too may have children to raise, to be anxious about, to teach, to set out on a path of their own.
And, finally, we too will die.

Terms to Understand

per·spec·tive - A mental view or outlook; the relationship of aspects of a subject to each other and to a whole.

Terms to Understand

cus·tom - A practice followed by people of a particular group or region.

Terms to Understand

ven·er·ate - To regard with respect, reverence, or heartfelt deference.

Terms to Understand

tomb·stone in·scrip·tion - A memorial engraving on a grave marker, which is customarily made of stone. The engraving usually includes the deceased's name and birth and death dates; it may also include information about the deceased's family, or a few words which are meant to characterize the deceased's life.

Each of these events is common to all of mankind, so our commonality provides ideas of where we might have gone if set against the background or environment in which they lived. Because of this, it is vitally important for a good genealogist to know the historical background of his or her ancestors. Did they take part in any of the great struggles of their countries? Out of necessity, were they pilgrims to a new land? How many were forced out as refugees? Can these great struggles provide clues to the types of records available at those terrifying times?

Humans must work for their survival. What did your ancestors do? If someone spent his or her entire life in a particular occupation, it might provide clues to finding and unveiling an individual. A tin miner in Cornwall, England can be found digging coal thousands of miles away in Pennsylvania. A cloth maker in Ireland can be found among the mills of Massachusetts.

Were your ancestor's circumstances such that he or she was left to struggle throughout life? Were his or her children able to move up the social ladder? What correspondence passed between separated family members? This will never be discovered until we communicate with all family members, for each member carries a personal piece of the family puzzle. Therefore, correspondence with others is another principle of research.

Often, we may receive very astute answers to our genealogy problems, either in conversations or in written form, and these may inspire us, encourage us and help us to set other goals. But visually, the Pedigree Chart and Family Group Records keep the problem in focus. In difficult moments, the correct **perspective** can be most valuable. Try to use the forms and charts you have learned about as you communicate with others so that they can better help you, and vice versa.

CUSTOMS

Since all of us must die some day, cemetery searching or probate browsing are other tasks to be undertaken. In different cultures, various **customs** surround death. In China, for example, a deceased individual is **venerated** and given a new name at death. Without this knowledge you could find yourself looking for the wrong name. **Tombstone inscriptions** of a lengthy and descriptive nature became increasingly important in some areas of New England, and this source could be very helpful in your searching. Therefore, knowing the customs can help you to find the correct records.

The same principles apply when searching birth information. If I had been born in Finland, I would have been given a patronymic name, Karen Brunostytar. I would also have received the name of the farm where I was born as my surname. If my brother had been born on a different farm, he would have been given a different surname. This makes it easy to trace localities, but difficult to find people, unless you also know that the Lutheran Church in Finland took a survey each year and grouped the people together in family groups. These records have been microfilmed for the years between 1680 and 1860.

But if I had been born of a certain tribe of Native Americans, my name could have been given to me because of a dream my mother had the night I was born. When I came of age, I would have received another name, and if a favorite relative died, I would have been given his or her name as a remembrance. Without a knowledge of these customs, you might make serious errors in your research; but with a knowledge of this background, your search is more rewarding.

In conclusion, the history of the family as a unit should be considered. What periods of time are involved? What places may be of consequence? Are names of villages or farms important? Are the occupations known? Can a good map or local history be located?

UNDERSTANDING THE WRITTEN WORD

Dialect is the form in which a language develops in a particular locality, and it is usually conspicuous in its peculiarities of vocabulary, pronunciation and usage. When you do not have firsthand knowledge of a locality, dialect can provide some interesting situations, and if you combine dialect with the practice of phonetic spelling, more challenges await you.

Since a uniform method of spelling words is relatively modern, names and places were written down as they sounded to the transcriber—or as he or she thought they should be spelled. For example, the name *Hare* is listed in an English register. Sometimes, the "H" is dropped from the beginning of the word when it should have remained. Sometimes, it is added when it does not belong there. The result is that this same name was later spelled *Aire*, and when the family immigrated to America, it became *Eyre*. Careful attention should be placed on the spelling variations of any surname beginning with a vowel or the aspirate "H."

The same can be true of place names. I have seen the word *Albemarle*, written in the original script on **microform** in the Family History Library. Albemarle is a county in North Carolina, but this was spelled *Arber Marble*. I can almost hear it with a southern accent and a pirate's speech. I have seen the English town Bicester spelled *Bister*, and Barugh Green, Yorkshire, England spelled *Bark Green*, because these spellings reflect local pronunciations.

NAMING CUSTOMS

Naming patterns, **nicknames** or interchangeable names, such as Mary-Polly, Sally-Sarah, Ann-Agness, Ann-Hannah, Peggy-Margaret, Jenny-Jane, and Nancy for Ann, are all part of family history. Children with more than one given name may use the middle name on one census and the first name on another census. Were the names Biblical (such as David, Solomon, Hezekiah), historical (George Washington, Thomas Jefferson, Henry Harrison), royal (Elizabeth, Charles, Henry), or were they in honor of a patron saint (Bernadet, Christopher, etc.)? Was the mother's maiden name used as a given name in subsequent generations? Even though we think of surnames as fixed from generation to generation, it is folly to think that all people with the same surname are related. Surnames are a recent invention in the history of mankind and they came from localities, occupations, hero worship, given names, things in nature, animals, and much more.

There are "superior letters," consisting of omitting a letter or letters from a word and raising some of the letters above the line, resulting in , *wth* for *with* and *wch* for *which*, and *yt* and *ye* representing *that* and *the*, the *y* being a survival of the "**thorn**," a letter found in ancient alphabets and pronounced like *th* yet writ-

Terms to Understand

di·a·lect - A regional variety of a language distinguished by pronunciation, grammar, or vocabulary, especially a variety of speech differing from the standard literary language or speech pattern of the culture in which it exists.

Terms to Understand

nick·name - A descriptive name added to or replacing the actual name of a person, place, or thing; a familiar or shortened form of a proper name.

Terms to Understand

mi·cro·form - An arrangement of images reduced in size, as on microfilm or microfiche.

Terms to Understand

thorn - The runic letter þ originally representing the sound of the Modern English *th*, as in *the* and *thin*, used in Old English and Middle English manuscripts.

Terms to Understand

`til·de` - A diacritical mark (`~`).

Terms to Understand

`con·trac·tion` - A word, as *won't* from *will not*, or phrase, as *o'clock* from *of the clock*, formed by omitting or combining some of the sounds.

Terms to Understand

`sus·pen·sion` - The omission of one or more letters from a word, and replacing them with a period or colon as a form of abbreviation.

Terms to Understand

`mis·sion` - The purpose or specific work of an organization or institution.

ten somewhat like the letter y. Examples also include abbreviated words, such as the name *Jno Richrd* for *John Richard,* or *chamrs* for *chambers,* as well as *His Matie* for *His Majesty. Mr.* and *Mrs.* are a survival of this practice.

There are also special alphabets, legal languages (like Latin), calendar changes, and saints' days to become acquainted with.

Suspensions leave off the final letters of a word and replace them with a period, colon, or various strokes. The oldest form of suspension was the use of the initial letter of a word.Rx, for example, was the abbreviation for recipe, a sign still displayed by druggists at prescriptions centers, as well as *wid.* for *widow,* and *ite.* for *item.* Then there are writing customs. This includes **contractions,** in which letters are left out in the middle of the word, and this process is tagged with a certain stroke or other sign. A "P" with a **tilde** on the top may stand for *per, par, pre,* or *pro,* or sometimes an apostrophe stands in for missing letters, as in *P'fect* or *Edm'nd's.*

In the months to come, you may want to set a goal to learn to read the language of the ancestor you are researching (both the handwriting and non-English words). In addition, you can learn what kind of records are available and where they are available for public use in the area where the ancestor lived.

WHICH REPOSITORY CAN SOLVE THIS PROBLEM?

Once we are organized, we notice what is missing and we try to fill in the gaps. The questioning mind asks "Who would have this information? Where can this information be found if someone knowledgeable is not available?" That leads us to a fundamental need to understand record repositories.

At first, the best repository for you may be the one closest to your home. That's fine! Use what you have, and go from there. But you should be aware that there are differences, commonalities, and unique **missions** for archives, public libraries, and family history centers. Some we have covered in depth, but we can only cover others in a very general manner, because the records found within them need to be studied first. Let's discuss these important differences, commonalities and unique missions for those that contain the records we are currently using.

Archives: The primary mission of archives is to preserve original materials. They often house primary materials in their original medium,for a specific limited to the time period and the localities defined in the mission statement for a particular facility. So far we have learned about the National Archives in Washington, D.C. and its Regional Record services facilities.

Family History Centers: Family History Centers have as their mission to help people trace their families. They may have primary materials in microform and secondary printed materials in book, microform, or electronic format from all over the world. They are limited by the open records of the various countries, the budget of the center, the number of volunteers they have available, and the space allowed. We have learned about the various centers in this book.

Libraries: The mission of a library is to provide reference materials for the public. They often are funded by constituents with specific needs and desires they must address and that may limit their abilities to have genealogical materials. Libraries are good for genealogists, because we use general reference tools as well. A library has secondary materials in book, microform, or electronic format, limited to the particular mission of that library. We learned about a huge library in Salt Lake City. The largest genealogical library in the world. But we have also learned that we can take advantage of local libraries to help us as well.

Commonalities: Each repository provides a part of the puzzle you need to solve your research problem, and each may have materials unavailable in other repositories. Because of their unique missions and space limitations, each is limited to obtaining materials regarding specific time periods, localities and events.

Plan Your Research Process with the Help of a Planner

Do not confuse a *Research Planner* with a *Research Log*. The latter records only what was found. The former records *not* only what was found, but also what was not found when an item was searched, and what records *should* eventually be searched. Using a Research Planner is a very important step in setting goals, as it helps to focus your attention on what you are doing, and it reminds you to apply the other seven basic rules of research.

Goal planning could also include learning more about topics surrounding family history, talking more to relatives, and finding out more about sources that are new to you such as probate records, or bounty land applications.

If you will keep your goals clearly defined, write down your strategy, enlist **allies**, and gather applicable resources, you will be able to visualize your plan, recognize when you're making progress, and note your accomplishments. After all, if you don't know where you're going, how will you know when you've arrived?

CONCLUSION

Goal setting, and the accompanying steps to reaching the goal draw on the sum total of your knowledge, research skills, and organizational abilities. As goals are reached, they must be recorded with sufficient detail to give a clear and accurate picture of what took place. And when you have completed this documentation, you can begin the Research Cycle anew.

An important principle is perseverance. Imagine that I have given you a piece of salt water taffy, and like the taffy, our research also starts out sweetly. Answers come quickly. But the further back in time we go, fewer and fewer records are available. This might mean a thorough, painstaking review of all existing probate or property records, or a page-by-page search of an unindexed census. We have to chew harder now. While we started out with good intentions, the obstacles find their way to us. The words are hard to read, and the film machine may make us dizzy as we roll it on and on. We may become fatigued or rushed, and the pressures cause our resolve to dissolve like the taffy we just ate; it was sweet when we started, but it was soon gone.

Now imagine I've given you a stick of gum. We can prove we are made of tougher ingredients if we will persevere, even though the times are rough and the pressures mount. No matter how many times we apply pressure and chew, the gum still remains. Ultimately, that perseverance will pay off, because even the lack of success in one set of records is one area checked off, never to be repeated. One of the biggest reasons most people hire professional researchers is that they want them to do the jobs they do not like to do themselves. But if you possess the necessary perseverance, you will find great rewards in doing the work on your own.

Understandably, fatigue, weariness and exasperation over a particular problem may occur. We may also find ourselves rushed or pressed, and as a result we may think and write things we would not have done if we were fresh and had time to ponder and remember. This brings me to another principle. The principle of cooperation. By exploring options and sharing examples with friends and associates, we can help to identify the necessary principles involved and discover our own research **deficiencies**. Perceptive questions and logically reasoning with one another produces profound results. This is critical thinking at its best.

This review of all of the elements that contributed to successful research may sound intimidating, but once you've applied these techniques you will find them

Terms to Understand

de·fi·cien·cy - The quality or condition of being incomplete or insufficient.

Terms to Understand

al·lies - Persons in helpful association with others, often working toward a common goal.

empowering and rewarding. While you might achieve results by chance, a systematic, organized, goal-centered research approach is the best way to achieve consistent results.

ASSIGNMENT 15: MAKE PLANS FOR THE FUTURE

1. Select one line to focus on in the intermediate level of study, preferably including those who lived in the U.S. and were born before 1830. Write down which line you have selected.

2. Where did this selected family live? List states and counties.

3. Include all of the information you have on this line as a baseline of knowledge. You may do this in the form of a GEDCOM or print-outs from your genealogy computer program, but be sure to include all your notes as well.

4. What do you want to know about this family? Remember to be specific as you record ALL you currently know about the family and set about recording various goals to achieve a perhaps larger overall objective.

YOUR TURN ANSWERS

Personal preferences are expected on all Chapter 15 responses.

COMPUTER CHECKLIST #15

1. Assume that you know you have entered a note on someone but you don't remember where that note is. How would your program find a note in your general notes field?

2. How do you find and make a list of all of the individuals for whom you made TO DO notes?

WEB SITES

www.acpl.lib.in.us/genealogy/genealogy.html
Scroll down to "where." Click on link.
Allen County Public Library
Allen County, Indiana

www.bpl.org/
This website will take you to the main library page. Then search for genealogy.
Boston Public Library
Boston, Massachusetts

www.dar.org/library/
This link takes you to genealogy areas in the DAR library.
DAR Library
Washington, D.C.

www.loc.gov/library/
Library of Congress
Washington, D.C.

www.archives.gov/genealogy/
National Archives
Washington, D.C.

www.nehgs.org/
New England Historic Genealogical Society Library
Boston, Massachusetts

www.newberry.org/nl/genealogy/genealogyhome.html
Newberry Library
Chicago, Illinois

www.library.ca.gov/collections
Sutro Library
San Francisco, CA

www.lib.byu.edu/dept/uvrfhc/
Utah Valley Regional Family History Center
Brigham Young University, Provo, Utah

BIBLIOGRAPHY

Bowker, R. R. *American Library Directory 1999-2000.* 52nd ed. New Providence, New Jersey: 1999.

Carson, Dina, ed. *Directory of Genealogical and Historical Society Libraries, Archives and Collections in the U.S. & Canada.* Niwot, Colorado: Iron Gate Publishing, 1998.

Clifford, Karen. *The Great Ancestral Hunt* [CD]. Salt lake City, Utah: Genealogy Research Associates, Inc., 1998.

National Historical Publications and Records Commission. *Directory of Archives and Manuscript Repositories in the United States.* Phoenix: ORYX Press, 1988.

The Genealogical Index of the Newberry Library. 4 vols. Boston: G.K. Hall, 1960.

Genealogies in the Library of Congress: A Bibliography. Baltimore: Magna Charta Book Co., 1972.

Greenlaw, William Prescott, comp. *The Greenlaw Index of the New England Historic Genealogical Society.* 2 vols. Boston: G.K. Hall, 1979.

Guide to Genealogical Research in the National Archives. Rev. ed. Washington, D.C.: National Archives Trust Fund Board, 1985.

Guide to the National Archives of the United States. Washington, D.C.: National Archives and Records Administration, 1987.

Grundset, Eric G. and Steven B. Rhodes. *American Genealogical Research at the DAR.* Washington, D.C: DAR, 1997.

Kvasnicka, Robert M., comp. *The Trans-Mississippi West 1804-1912, Part I: A Guide to Records of the Department of State for the Territorial Period.* Washington, D.C.: NARA, 1993.

Schaefer, Christina K. *The Center: A Guide to Genealogical Research in the National Capital Area.* Baltimore: Genealogical Publishing Co., 1996.

Szucs, Loretto Dennis and Sandra Hargreaves Luebking. *The Archives: Guide to the National Archives Field Branches.* Salt Lake City: Ancestry, 1988.

Library Catalog. 3 vols. Washington, D.C.: DAR, 1982.

CHAPTER 16

Sharing Your Family History Research

Sure, I said, heav'n did not mean,
Where I reap thou shouldst but glean,
Lay thy sheaf down and come,
Share my harvest and my home.

—Thomas Hood

The true joy of genealogy lies in sharing your successes and failures with family and friends. Every research experience will add to your knowledge, experience, and understanding. Sharing not just the results of your inquiries, but the insights you've gained along the way will make your learning more meaningful and will help others at the same time. As exciting as family history research is, you cannot expect to become an expert in the discipline overnight.

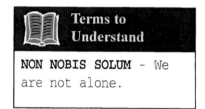

Terms to Understand

NON NOBIS SOLUM - We are not alone.

SHARING

Family history research is intrinsically rewarding. Always share the results of your efforts!! By sharing, you add to the great pool of information from which each of us can benefit. You will also benefit personally as others respond to the data you provided, and you will meet "living, breathing" relatives you did not know existed. At the same time, you will gain a greater understanding of the world in which you live, and you will make lasting friendships.

As the motto of the National Genealogical Society states: *NON NOBIS SOLUM*. We are certainly NOT alone. Genealogy research is most enjoyable and productive when it is a shared activity. There are many ways to share your family history findings such as the following:

1. Share through GEDCOM files certain surnames you've researched with relatives you meet online with similar surnames.
2. Share your entire file with millions of people by submitting a GEDCOM file to *www.familysearch.org* then clicking on the tab SHARE. More on this method below.
3. *World Family Tree™*. No charge for others to find you or for you to search for others on the *http://www.genealogy.com* Internet index,but the person who finds your information will have to pay a subscription fee to read

the information. Cost is about $10 a month.

4. *Kindred Konnections*™. Again, no charge for others to search for your submission or to search for theirs on the Internet site, but there is a minimal fee for obtaining the actual information. See *http://www.mytrees.com*. Other information is available for your subscription fee as well, however.

5. Build and post your own Web page. Web sites are easily built with commercial products such as *Dreamweaver* but you must pay those monthly rental fees for online space and security.

6. Share copies of electronic files, printed files, and published books by placing copies in local libraries or submitting articles to genealogical periodicals.

7. *MyFamily.com*™. No charge for others to find you, but subscriptions are required to actually view source information. This is the parent company for *www.Ancestry.com*.

8. *Family Pursuit*™. Collaborative Genealogy Research Software to help reduce duplicate efforts and accelerate research. Family members can coordinate research activities through tasks and discussions such as sharing

YOUR TURN

1. Turn to the back of this chapter and notice the Web sites listed. Go online and test the ability to search for your own family on each of these powerful sites. Try to select someone who was born prior to 1900. Who did you search for? Where was this person born? When was he or she born? What were the results of your search?

2. Which site was most effective?

3. Which site did you not like? Why did you not like that site?

their research planners so others can avoid duplication. Available at *www.familypursuit.com.* It is an online genealogy service with a focus on coordination and cooperation.

9. *Rootsweb.com* is a non-profit arm of *Ancestry.com.* They require you to register, but the service is free. They accept pedigrees as well.

10. *www.USGenWeb.org* is a non-profit organization that also accepts pedigrees.

What is the Process for Sharing Online

I will use the *FamilySearch*™ Internet site as my example just to illustrate how easy it is to share your information. Once you log on to the site using *www.familysearch.org,* click on the tab SHARE.

You are asked to initially sign in with your name, e-mail address, country, and preferred language. You can provide your mailing address if you want. There is optional church membership registration. Then you select a password and username. Information is then provided on how to submit your genealogy.

First your GEDCOM will be checked for file format errors and you will be informed by mail of any problems. You will have the opportunity to correct and resubmit.

A copy of your GEDCOM will be placed in the Granite Mountain Records Vault for preservation.

A copy of your GEDCOM may be published. Currently they are being published in a CD-ROM format known as *Pedigree Resource File* which may be purchased for a nominal fee, or it may also be available at a local family history cen-

YOUR TURN

1. Return to the same Web sites in the previous "Your Turn" assignment. Locate the place where you can submit information. Which one appears to work easiest?

2. Which one is more difficult?

3. What cautions did you notice?

ter free of charge. Submitted GEDCOM files may later be published on the Internet with other pedigree linked files.

An index of the current *Pedigree Resource File* may be made available for searching on the FamilySearch Website. The full content of the information on the *Pedigree Resource File* is not available online at this time.

Submitting your genealogy is easy. First obtain permission from any living persons mentioned in your genealogy. For privacy reasons you must remove any references to living individuals if you do not have permission to submit it. Make sure your notes do not contain any offensive or inappropriate statements about another person.

Save your genealogy in a GEDCOM format on your home computer. We have covered this information in earlier chapters. A GEDCOM file can be accepted by the *World Family Tree, Kindred Konnections, Ancestry,* and many others.

Submit the GEDCOM file to the FamilySearch Website and agree to the conditions.which you should read giving permission for *FamilySearch*™ to share the information with the world.

Continue Your Research

It is very easy to share with others. It doesn't matter how you share, but it is hoped that you will share. Without the sharing that has been done in the past, none of us would reap the benefits of what is available today. And then continue your research. Use the Research Cycle over and over with each new name or goal you determine to pursue.

Maintain the organization you started with your Family History Notebook filing system. You have acquired some solid foundation skills and you are ready to move on to the next phase of genealogy. This second phase of your education will include the in-depth study of important record sources needed to solve family mysteries prior to the year 1850. New sources will also help you "cross the waters" to your immigrant ancestor's homeland, and this activity will permit you to become involved in another culture. You will also learn how the computer can help *solve* research problems, not merely record the results of your work.

If you are like most researchers, once you have completed this next level, you'll want to publish the results of your adventures! The process of transferring information from a computer database program to a publishing program with narratives, photographs, and even multi-media sound and video is speedily and easily accomplished using today's computer programs. Other specialized reports that meet national standards, such as those set by the National Genealogical Society or the New England Historic Genealogical Society, can also be printed.

THE FUTURE

This book and its successors are dedicated to helping you learn more research techniques, insightful suggestions on sources, fascinating details about your own origins, and ultimately how to publish your own family history in electronic format or by traditional means.

Watch the Web site *http://www.genealogylessons.com* for updated information to this book as it becomes available, for links to on-line genealogy training lessons, updated techniques for working with computer programs and much more. I'm sure your adventures will just continue.

ASSIGNMENT 16: SHARING YOUR FAMILY HISTORY RESEARCH

Of course you are not finished with your family history at this time. That does not mean you should not share what you have in order to obtain more from others working on your same lines. Study your Pedigree Chart. Which family could you share information on now? Do not include living people in your study. They will not be included on what you share because of privacy rights. Which family did you select?

YOUR TURN ANSWERS

Personal preferences apply to these answers.

COMPUTER CHECK LIST

1. Prepare a submission of your family materials for the *Pedigree Resource File*™, a Web site online, the *World Family Tree*™, *MyFamily.com*, *MyTrees.com*, or *FamilyPursuit.com*, and indicate which one you did.

2. Which of all the Web sites did you like the most for sharing your information?

WEB SITES

All these sites accept submissions. This is not a complete list but it is sufficient for beginning students:

www.familysearch.org
You may submit your data to the Pedigree Resource File, or you may send in your genealogy to be preserved in several ways.

www.ancestry.com
You may submit your family for sharing and preservation directly online at their site even if you do not use the FamilyTreeMaker program.

www.kindredkonnections.com
Accepts GEDCOM submissions, which then allows you a free month to search and use their database.

http://www.FamilyPursuit.com
Collaborative genealogy research software, and a sharing website.

BIBLIOGRAPHY

Polk, Timothy W. *How to Outlive Your Lifetime! A Complete Guide to Preserving a Place in Your Family's Heart and History.* Sunnyvale, California: Family Life International, 1994.

Sources Used in this Book for "Terms to Understand"

Bremer, Ronald A. *Compendium of Historical Sources.* Bountiful, Utah: AGLL, Inc., 1997.

Encarta World English Dictionary. New York: St. Martin's Press, 1999.

The American Heritage Dictionary for DOS. Sausalito, California: Writing Tools Group, Inc., 1991.

Webster's New World Dictionary of the American Language. New York: Warner Books, Inc. 1985.

The Internet and Genealogy

One of the most popular uses of the Internet is for Genealogy. As demonstrated throughout this book, there are several types of sites on the Internet that are useful for those who are tracing their relatives—either living or dead.

Users of the Internet should be familiar with the different search engines available to them. Search engines allow the Internet user to enter a string of characters which brings up a "hit list" containing that string of characters in its title or description of contents. Some of the most popular search engines are Yahoo, Alta Vista, and Excite. Others are DogPile, Mamma, Google, Go.com., and Ask.com. All search engines use a little different logic, so the search results may be different and certainly will be displayed on the monitor differently.

The Internet has allowed one aspect of genealogy to fully evolve—finding living relatives. Several of the search engines mentioned above provide the means of finding living individuals with whom the Internet user may have lost touch. One of the most popular locators of living individuals is Yahoo's "People Search." Just enter the name and choose a state or other locality and a list of individuals with addresses and telephone numbers is delivered to your screen.

Finding genealogy sources is another aspect of family history research which has benefitted from the Internet. There are many sites on the Web that will help a genealogist to locate records. This book covers, for example, *familysearch.org*, which allows a genealogist to determine what records are available at the Family History Library in Salt Lake City—hence, what is available to Family History Centers, the local branches of the Family History Library. Several other libraries also have catalogs of their holdings online.

The Library of Congress (*www.lcweb.loc.gov*) has many of their collections either cataloged or imaged and online. The Library of Virginia (*www.lva.lib.va.us*) is also digitally imaging many of their documents and placing them online. Some of the larger genealogy libraries around the country also have Web sites, such as the New York Public Library (*www.nypl.org*), the Allen County Public Library (*www.acpl.lib.in.us*), and the New England Historic Genealogical Society (*www.nehgs.org*).

There are many Web sites that provide indexes and abstracts of genealogical records. USGenWeb is a nationwide project that places information about every county and every state on the Internet. Information being placed on these sites includes compilations of cemetery inscriptions, Bible records, biographies, etc.

Remember that information abstracted from original records is secondary, at best, and can have transcription errors in it. The same can be said for information compiled by individuals and submitted to such programs as Ancestral File and Pedigree Resource File, maintained by The Church of Jesus Christ of Latter-day Saints in Salt Lake City. Information in such files is only as correct and complete as the submitter makes it. Too many beginning genealogists simply download such information without checking its accuracy and completeness. These beginners then add a few new personal pieces of information and resubmit it—errors and all. Hopefully this will not be the method employed by the users of this book.

Other programs available on the Internet which may be helpful to genealogists are the genealogical queries sites, such as GenForum and RootsWeb. There are also chat rooms, where Internet users can have a real-time discussion on a subject of their choosing.

The Internet of today offers many benefits to the genealogist. But remember, it also has much inaccurate information on it. Everything that is found and downloaded from the Internet should be verified for accuracy and documented for future users of that information.

Genealogical Forms

The following section contains:

- U.S. Census Transcription Forms
- Soundex/Miracode Transcription Forms.
- Research Planners
- Guide to the Family History Center

GENEALOGY RESEARCH ASSOCIATES, INC.

1850 United States Federal Census Transcription

Street/route name	Street/route number	Dwelling in order of visit	Family in order of visit	The name of every person whose usual place of abode on the first day of June, 1850, was in this family	Age	Sex	Color	Profession, occupation, or trade of each male person over 15 years of age	Value of real estate owned	Place of birth, naming the state, territory or country	Married within the year	Attended school within yr.	Person over 20 who can't read/write	Deaf, dmb, blind, insane, idiotic, pauper, convict	Estimated birth year

Head of Household _____ State _____ County _____ City/Township _____ Written page number _____

Printed page number _____ Enumeration District _____ Macrofilm roll number _____ Call number _____ Repository _____

GENEALOGY RESEARCH ASSOCIATES, INC.

1860 United States Federal Census Transcription

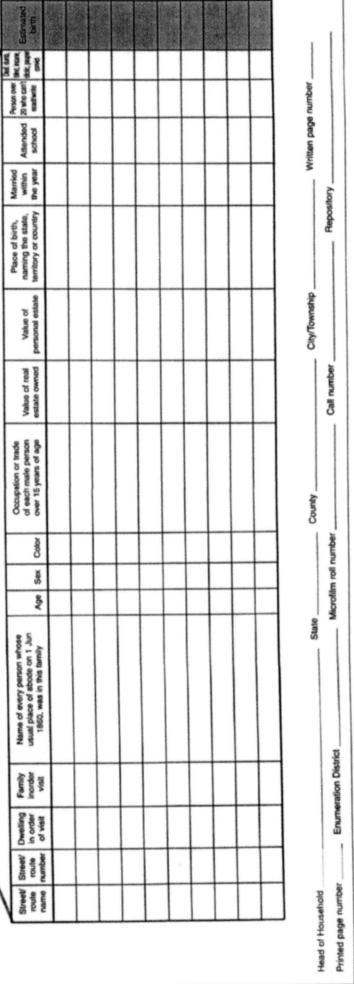

SCHEDULE 1.—Free Inhabitants in _____ in the County of _____ State _____ enumerated by me, on the ___ day of June 1860. _____ Ass't Marshal

of _____ Post Office

Street/ route name	Street/ route number	Dwelling in order of visit	Family in order visit	Name of every person whose usual place of abode on 1 Jun 1860, was in this family	Age	Sex	Color	Occupation or trade of each male person over 15 years of age	Value of real estate owned	Value of personal estate	Place of birth, naming the state, territory or country	Married within the year	Attended school	Person over 20 who cannot read, write	Deaf dumb, blind, insane, idiotic, pauper, convict	Estimated birth

Head of Household _____

Printed page number _____ Enumeration District _____ State _____ County _____ City/Township _____

Microfilm roll number _____ Call number _____ Repository _____ Written page number _____

GENEALOGY RESEARCH ASSOCIATES, INC.
1870 United States Federal Census Transcription

SCHEDULE 1.—Inhabitants in _____, in the County of _____, State _____, enumerated by me on the ___ day of _____, 1870.

Post Office: _____

Street name	Cross street	Dwelling number	Family number	Name of every person whose usual place of abode on 1 Jun 1870, was in this family	Age at last birthday	Sex	Color	Occupation, trade or profession	Value of real estate owned	Value of personal estate owned	Place of birth	Father foreign b.	Mother foreign b.	Month if born within year	Month if married within year	In school within year	Cannot read	Cannot write	Deaf & dumb, etc.	Males of 21 yrs. eligible to vote	Males of 21 yrs. not eligible to vote	Estimated birth year

Head of Household _____ State _____ County _____ City/Township _____

Printed page number _____ Enumeration District _____ Microfilm roll number _____ Call number _____ Repository _____ Written page number _____

© 1997 Genealogy Research Associates, Inc. 4267

GENEALOGY RESEARCH ASSOCIATES, INC.
1880 United States Federal Census Transcription

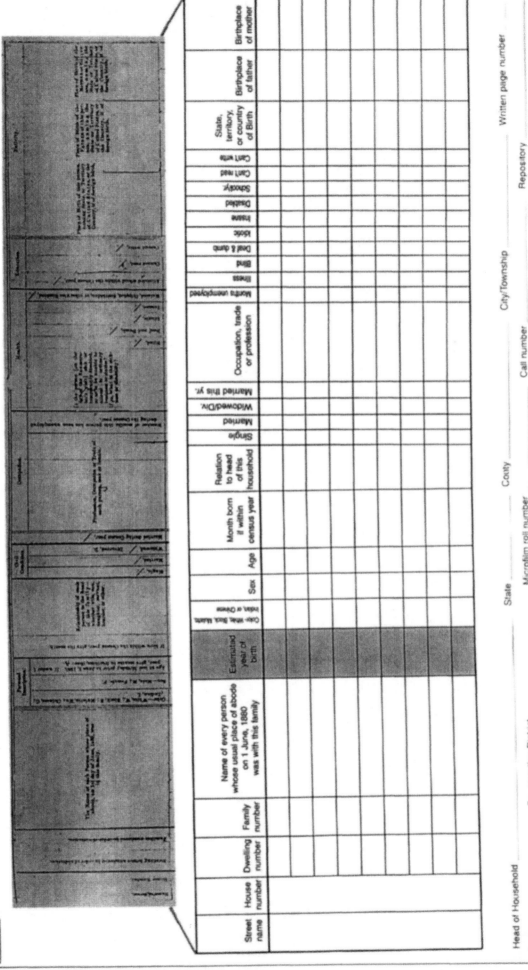

Street name	House number	Dwelling number	Family number	Name of every person whose usual place of abode on 1 June, 1880 was with this family	Estimated year of birth	Oah-west, Black, Mulatto, Indian, or Chinese	Sex	Age	Month born if within census year	Relation to head of this household	Single	Married	Widowed/Div.	Married this yr.	Occupation, trade or profession	Months unemployed	Illness	Blind	Deaf & dumb	Idiotic	Insane	Disabled	School/yr.	Can't read	Can't write	State, territory, or country of Birth	Birthplace of father	Birthplace of mother

Head of Household _____

Printed page number _____ Enumeration District _____

State _____ Cousty _____ City/Township _____

Microfilm roll number _____ Call number _____ Repository _____ Written page number _____

© 1997 Genealogy Research Associates, Inc.

GENEALOGY RESEARCH ASSOCIATES, INC.
1900 United States Federal Census Transcription

SCHEDULE No. 1.—POPULATION.

Supervisor's District No. _____
Enumeration District No. _____

Sheet No. _____

Name of Institution, _____

Ward of city _____

_____ day of June, 1900, _____, Enumerator.

Street name	House number	Dwelling number	Family number	Name of every person whose usual place of abode on 1 June, 1900 was with this family	Relation to head	Color	Sex	Month of birth	Year of birth	Age	Sing., Mar., Wid., or divorced	# of yrs. married	# of children	# of children liv.	Birthplace	Birthplace of father	Birthplace of mother	Year of Immigra.	Years in U.S.	Naturalized?	Occupation, trade or profession	Mo. unemp./yr.	Attended school	Can read	Can write	Can speak english	Own/rent	Free/Mortgage	Farm/House	Farm schedule

Head of Household _____ State _____ County _____ City/Township _____ Written page number _____

Printed page number _____ Enumeration District _____ Microfilm roll number _____ Call number _____ Repository _____

GENEALOGY RESEARCH ASSOCIATES, INC.

1910 United States Federal Census Transcription

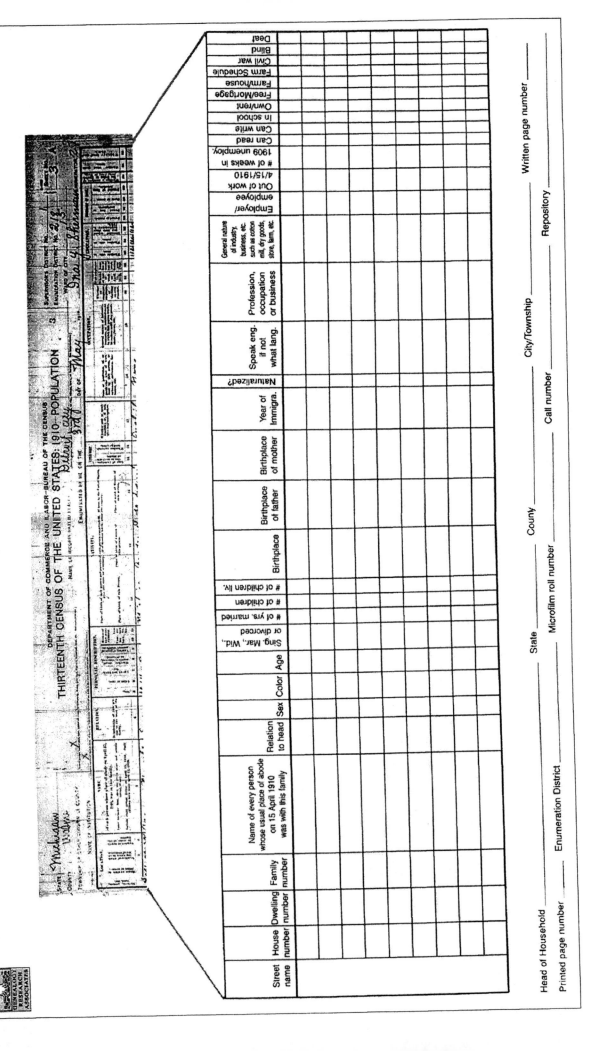

Street name	House number	Dwelling number	Family number	Name of every person whose usual place of abode on 15 April 1910 was with this family	Relation to head	Sex	Color	Age	Sing. Mar., Wid., or divorced	# of yrs. married	# of children	# of children liv.	Birthplace	Birthplace of father	Birthplace of mother	Year of Immigra.	Naturalized?	Speak eng. if not what tang.	Profession, occupation or business	General nature of industry, business, etc. such as cotton mill, dry goods, store, farm, etc.	Employer/ employee	Out of work 4/15/1910	# of weeks in 1909 unemploy.	Can read	Can write	In school	Own/rent	Free/Mortgage	Farmhouse	Farm Schedule	Civil war	Blind	Deaf

Head of Household _____

Printed page number _____   Enumeration District _____

State _____   County _____   City/Township _____

Microfilm roll number _____   Call number _____   Repository _____

Written page number _____

1920 United States Federal Census Transcription

DEPARTMENT OF COMMERCE—BUREAU OF THE CENSUS

FOURTEENTH CENSUS OF THE UNITED STATES: 1920—POPULATION

Street name	House number	Dwelling number	Family visit number	Name of every person whose usual place of abode on 1 January 1920 was with this family	Relation to head	Home owned or rented	Own free or mortgaged	Sex	Color or race	Age	Marital status	Year of Immig. to U.S.	Naturalized or alien	Year of naturalization	Attending sch.	Can read and write	Birthplace	Mother tongue	Birthplace of father	Mother tongue of father	Birthplace of mother	Mother tongue of mother	Can speak eng.	Occupation	General nature of industry, business, etc., such as cotton mill, dry goods store, farm, etc.	Whether an employer, employed, or working on own account	No. of farm schedule

Head of Household _____ State _____ County _____ City/Township _____ Written page number _____

Printed page number _____ Enumeration District _____ Microfilm roll number _____ Call number _____

1880 CENSUS SOUNDEX FORM

SOUNDEX NO: YEAR: STATE:

HEAD OF FAMILY: VOL: ED:

SHEET: LINE:

COLOR: MONTH: AGE: BIRTHPLACE: CITIZENSHIP:

COUNTY: MCD

CITY: STREET: HOUSE #

NAME	RELATION-SHIP	AGE	BIRTHPLACE	CITIZENSHIP

1880 CENSUS SOUNDEX FORM

SOUNDEX NO: YEAR: STATE:

HEAD OF FAMILY: VOL: ED:

SHEET: LINE:

COLOR: MONTH: AGE: BIRTHPLACE: CITIZENSHIP:

COUNTY: MCD

CITY: STREET: HOUSE #

NAME	RELATION-SHIP	AGE	BIRTHPLACE	CITIZENSHIP

1900 CENSUS SOUNDEX FORM

SOUNDEX NO:			YEAR:		STATE:				
HEAD OF FAMILY:							VOL: SHEET:	ED: LINE:	
COLOR:	MONTH:	AGE:	BIRTHPLACE:		CITIZENSHIP:				
COUNTY:					MCD				
CITY:		STREET:				HOUSE #			

NAME	RELA-TION-SHIP	BIRTH MONTH	BIRTH YEAR	AGE	BIRTHPLACE	CITIZENSHIP

1900 CENSUS SOUNDEX FORM

SOUNDEX NO:			YEAR:		STATE:				
HEAD OF FAMILY:							VOL: SHEET:	ED: LINE:	
COLOR:	MONTH:	AGE:	BIRTHPLACE:		CITIZENSHIP:				
COUNTY:					MCD				
CITY:		STREET:				HOUSE #			

NAME	RELA-TION-SHIP	BIRTH MONTH	BIRTH YEAR	AGE	BIRTHPLACE	CITIZENSHIP

1910 CENSUS SOUNDEX FORM

CODE	HEAD OF FAMILY OR INDIVIDUAL NAME		ED	SHEET
COLOR	AGE	BIRTHPLACE	VOL.	
COUNTY	CITY		STATE	
ENUMERATED WITH:				

NAME	RELATIONSHIP	AGE	BIRTHPLACE

1910 CENSUS SOUNDEX FORM

CODE	HEAD OF FAMILY OR INDIVIDUAL NAME		ED	SHEET
COLOR	AGE	BIRTHPLACE	VOL.	
COUNTY	CITY		STATE	
ENUMERATED WITH:				

NAME	RELATIONSHIP	AGE	BIRTHPLACE

1910 MIRACODE

COUNTY	CITY	VOLUME	ED #	VISITATION	
CODE SURNAME	GIVEN NAME	RELATIONSHIP	RACE /AGE	BIRTH PLACE	RESIDENCE

SURNAME	GIVEN NAME	RELATIONSHIP	RACE/AGE	BIRTH PLACE

1910 MIRACODE

COUNTY	CITY	VOLUME	ED #	VISITATION	
CODE SURNAME	GIVEN NAME	RELATIONSHIP	RACE /AGE	BIRTH PLACE	RESIDENCE

SURNAME	GIVEN NAME	RELATIONSHIP	RACE/AGE	BIRTH PLACE

1920 CENSUS SOUNDEX FORM

CODE	HEAD OF FAMILY OR INDIVIDUAL NAME		ED	SHEET
COLOR	AGE	BIRTHPLACE	VOL.	
COUNTY	CITY		STATE	
STREET			HOUSE NO.	
ENUMERATED WITH:				

NAME	RELATIONSHIP	AGE	BIRTHPLACE	CITIZEN.

1920 CENSUS SOUNDEX FORM

CODE	HEAD OF FAMILY OR INDIVIDUAL NAME		ED	SHEET
COLOR	AGE	BIRTHPLACE	VOL.	
COUNTY	CITY		STATE	
STREET			HOUSE NO.	
ENUMERATED WITH:				

NAME	RELATIONSHIP	AGE	BIRTHPLACE	CITIZEN.

GENEALOGY
RESEARCH
ASSOCIATES

Research Planner

Remember to have only one goal per Research Planner.

Goal _____

_____

Surname/Subject _____ Researcher _____

Area _____ Client _____

Source Location		Description of Source	Object	Time	Remarks		
Date source searched	Library or repository & call #	(State, county, type of record, and time period of record)	(Person's name or what is sought)	(Person's age or date of event)	Comment or ID # of family	Index	File

GENEALOGY
RESEARCH
ASSOCIATES

Research Planner

Remember to have only one goal per Research Planner.

Goal _____

_____

Surname/Subject _____ Researcher _____

Area _____ Client _____

Source Location		Description of Source	Object	Time	Remarks		
Date source searched	Library or repository & call #	(State, county, type of record, and time period of record)	(Person's name or what is sought)	(Person's age or date of event)	Comment or ID # of family	Index	File

GENEALOGY RESEARCH ASSOCIATES

Research Planner

Remember to have only one goal per Research Planner.

Goal _____

_____

Surname/Subject _____   Researcher _____

Area _____   Client _____

Source Location		Description of Source	Object	Time	Remarks		
Date source searched	Library or repository & call #	(State, county, type of record, and time period of record)	(Person's name or what is sought)	(Person's age or date of event)	Comment or ID # of family	Index	File

Research Planner

Remember to have only one goal per Research Planner.

GENEALOGY RESEARCH ASSOCIATES

Goal _____

_____

Surname/Subject _____   Researcher _____

Area _____   Client _____

Source Location		Description of Source	Object	Time	Remarks		
Date source searched	Library or repository & call #	(State, county, type of record, and time period of record)	(Person's name or what is sought)	(Person's age or date of event)	Comment or ID # of family	Index	File

GUIDE TO THE FAMILY HISTORY CENTER

Surname or locality you are searching _____

Today's Date _____ GOAL_____

The family you are searching is thought to have lived in these counties or states: *(Records are recorded by county name...locate the county if you know the city or town by using a gazetteer)* _____

_____   _____   _____

CHECK OFF WHEN ACCOMPLISHED

 1. I have organized family information onto a pedigree chart _____
 2. I have organized family information onto family group records _____

PRELIMINARY SURVEY BY...

 3. Searching the *Ancestral File* ( )
 4. Searching the *FHLC Surname File* on computer *(FamilySearch* ( )
    Program)
 5. Searching a Surname Index to Periodicals if any ( )
 6. Searching printed Family Histories at the center ( )
 7. Searching the IGI by county, state, surname *(FamilySearch* ( )
    Program)
 8. Searching any other local library source lists if any ( )
 9. Searching the Library of Congress Published Surname Histories ( )
10. Searching the Patron Locality Surname File ( )

ORIGINAL RESEARCH...

11. The federal census records of the county already available ( )
    at the FHC
12. The AIS: census indexes 1600-1850/60 by surname on microfiche ( )
13. Census films from FHL, AGLL or record numbers for local ( )
    archives visit
14. The Locality file of the FHLC for Vital Records ( )
15. The Locality file of any other major repository catalog ( )
    available there
16. The Locality file FHC Card Catalog containing their holdings ( )
17. Area Research Guides for specific help on localities/subjects ( )
18. THE HANDY BOOK FOR GENEALOGISTS for localities, or other ( )
    basic books
19. MAP GUIDE TO THE U.S. FEDERAL CENSUSES 1790-1920 ( )
20. Research Papers by the experts in genealogy worldwide ( )
21. WORLD CONFERENCE ON RECORDS ( )
22. Category/Surname/Title References in the FHC Card Catalog ( )
23. Loose Files for maps, miscellaneous information, pedigree ( )
    charts
24. Jacobus, PERSI, and other periodical indexes ( )

 OTHER WAYS THEY HELP YOU...

25. Information on computerizing your genealogy through the PAF ( )
    program
26. Seminars and workshops on your personal area of interest ( )
27. Loan Books of a general genealogical nature ( )
28. Forms, charts, photocopies of books, ( )
29. Social Security Death Index (abt. 1937-1989 by surname ( )
    FamilySearch)
30. Local CDs applying to your area of research ( )
31. Film Register Books ( )
32. Information on creating a GEDCOM to submit family data to ( )
    FHL

GUIDE TO THE FAMILY HISTORY CENTER

Surname or locality you are searching _____

Today's Date _____ GOAL_____

The family you are searching is thought to have lived in these counties
or states: *(Records are recorded by county name...locate the county if
you know the city or town by using a gazetteer)* _____

_____ _____ _____

CHECK OFF WHEN ACCOMPLISHED

  1. I have organized family information onto a pedigree chart   _____

  2. I have organized family information onto family group records _____

PRELIMINARY SURVEY BY...

  3. Searching the *Ancestral File*   ( )

  4. Searching the *FHLC Surname File* on computer *(FamilySearch* ( )
     Program)

  5. Searching a Surname Index to Periodicals if any   ( )

  6. Searching printed Family Histories at the center   ( )

  7. Searching the IGI by county, state, surname *(FamilySearch* ( )
     Program)

  8. Searching any other local library source lists if any   ( )

  9. Searching the Library of Congress Published Surname Histories ( )

10. Searching the Patron Locality Surname File   ( )

ORIGINAL RESEARCH...

11. The federal census records of the county already available ( )
    at the FHC

12. The AIS: census indexes 1600-1850/60 by surname on microfiche ( )

13. Census films from FHL, AGLL or record numbers for local ( )
    archives visit

14. The Locality file of the FHLC for Vital Records ( )

15. The Locality file of any other major repository catalog ( )
    available there

16. The Locality file FHC Card Catalog containing their holdings ( )

17. Area Research Guides for specific help on localities/subjects ( )

18. THE HANDY BOOK FOR GENEALOGISTS for localities, or other ( )
    basic books

19. MAP GUIDE TO THE U.S. FEDERAL CENSUSES 1790-1920 ( )

20. Research Papers by the experts in genealogy worldwide ( )

21. WORLD CONFERENCE ON RECORDS ( )

22. Category/Surname/Title References in the FHC Card Catalog ( )

23. Loose Files for maps, miscellaneous information, pedigree ( )
    charts

24. Jacobus, PERSI, and other periodical indexes ( )

  OTHER WAYS THEY HELP YOU...

25. Information on computerizing your genealogy through the PAF ( )
    program

26. Seminars and workshops on your personal area of interest ( )

27. Loan Books of a general genealogical nature ( )

28. Forms, charts, photocopies of books, ( )

29. Social Security Death Index (abt. 1937-1989 by surname ( )
    FamilySearch)

30. Local CDs applying to your area of research ( )

31. Film Register Books ( )

32. Information on creating a GEDCOM to submit family data to ( )
    FHL

GUIDE TO THE FAMILY HISTORY CENTER

Surname or locality you are searching _____

Today's Date _____ GOAL_____

The family you are searching is thought to have lived in these counties or states: *(Records are recorded by county name...locate the county if you know the city or town by using a gazetteer)* _____

_____ _____ _____

CHECK OFF WHEN ACCOMPLISHED

1. I have organized family information onto a pedigree chart _____
2. I have organized family information onto family group records _____

PRELIMINARY SURVEY BY...

3. Searching the *Ancestral File*   ( )
4. Searching the *FHLC Surname File* on computer *(FamilySearch*   ( )
   Program)
5. Searching a Surname Index to Periodicals if any   ( )
6. Searching printed Family Histories at the center   ( )
7. Searching the IGI by county, state, surname *(FamilySearch*   ( )
   Program)
8. Searching any other local library source lists if any   ( )
9. Searching the Library of Congress Published Surname Histories   ( )
10. Searching the Patron Locality Surname File   ( )

ORIGINAL RESEARCH...

11. The federal census records of the county already available   ( )
    at the FHC
12. The AIS: census indexes 1600-1850/60 by surname on microfiche   ( )
13. Census films from FHL, AGLL or record numbers for local   ( )
    archives visit
14. The Locality file of the FHLC for Vital Records   ( )
15. The Locality file of any other major repository catalog   ( )
    available there
16. The Locality file FHC Card Catalog containing their holdings   ( )
17. Area Research Guides for specific help on localities/subjects   ( )
18. THE HANDY BOOK FOR GENEALOGISTS for localities, or other   ( )
    basic books
19. MAP GUIDE TO THE U.S. FEDERAL CENSUSES 1790-1920   ( )
20. Research Papers by the experts in genealogy worldwide   ( )
21. WORLD CONFERENCE ON RECORDS   ( )
22. Category/Surname/Title References in the FHC Card Catalog   ( )
23. Loose Files for maps, miscellaneous information, pedigree   ( )
    charts
24. Jacobus, PERSI, and other periodical indexes   ( )

   OTHER WAYS THEY HELP YOU...

25. Information on computerizing your genealogy through the PAF   ( )
    program
26. Seminars and workshops on your personal area of interest   ( )
27. Loan Books of a general genealogical nature   ( )
28. Forms, charts, photocopies of books,   ( )
29. Social Security Death Index (abt. 1937-1989 by surname   ( )
    FamilySearch)
30. Local CDs applying to your area of research   ( )
31. Film Register Books   ( )
32. Information on creating a GEDCOM to submit family data to   ( )
    FHL

GUIDE TO THE FAMILY HISTORY CENTER

Surname or locality you are searching _____

Today's Date _____ GOAL_____

The family you are searching is thought to have lived in these counties
or states: *(Records are recorded by county name...locate the county if
you know the city or town by using a gazetteer)* _____
_____   _____   _____

CHECK OFF WHEN ACCOMPLISHED

1. I have organized family information onto a pedigree chart _____
2. I have organized family information onto family group records _____

PRELIMINARY SURVEY BY...

3. Searching the *Ancestral File*   ( )
4. Searching the *FHLC Surname File* on computer *(FamilySearch*   ( )
   Program)
5. Searching a Surname Index to Periodicals if any   ( )
6. Searching printed Family Histories at the center   ( )
7. Searching the IGI by county, state, surname *(FamilySearch*   ( )
   Program)
8. Searching any other local library source lists if any   ( )
9. Searching the Library of Congress Published Surname Histories   ( )
10. Searching the Patron Locality Surname File   ( )

ORIGINAL RESEARCH...

11. The federal census records of the county already available   ( )
    at the FHC
12. The AIS: census indexes 1600-1850/60 by surname on microfiche   ( )
13. Census films from FHL, AGLL or record numbers for local   ( )
    archives visit
14. The Locality file of the FHLC for Vital Records   ( )
15. The Locality file of any other major repository catalog   ( )
    available there
16. The Locality file FHC Card Catalog containing their holdings   ( )
17. Area Research Guides for specific help on localities/subjects   ( )
18. THE HANDY BOOK FOR GENEALOGISTS for localities, or other   ( )
    basic books
19. MAP GUIDE TO THE U.S. FEDERAL CENSUSES 1790-1920   ( )
20. Research Papers by the experts in genealogy worldwide   ( )
21. WORLD CONFERENCE ON RECORDS   ( )
22. Category/Surname/Title References in the FHC Card Catalog   ( )
23. Loose Files for maps, miscellaneous information, pedigree   ( )
    charts
24. Jacobus, PERSI, and other periodical indexes   ( )

   OTHER WAYS THEY HELP YOU...

25. Information on computerizing your genealogy through the PAF   ( )
    program
26. Seminars and workshops on your personal area of interest   ( )
27. Loan Books of a general genealogical nature   ( )
28. Forms, charts, photocopies of books,   ( )
29. Social Security Death Index (abt. 1937-1989 by surname   ( )
    FamilySearch)
30. Local CDs applying to your area of research   ( )
31. Film Register Books   ( )
32. Information on creating a GEDCOM to submit family data to   ( )
    FHL

Index

W

Z